Songs *of the* Reconstructing South

Recent Titles in
Contributions to the Study of American Literature

Songs *of the* Reconstructing South

Building Literary Louisiana, 1865–1945

Edited by Suzanne Disheroon-Green
and Lisa Abney

Foreword by Robin Miller

Contributions to the Study of American Literature, Number 11

Greenwood Press
Westport, Connecticut • London

Library of Congress Cataloging-in-Publication Data

Songs of the Reconstructing South : building literary Louisiana, 1865–1945 / edited by
Suzanne Disheroon-Green and Lisa Abney ; foreword by Robin Miller.
    p. cm.—(Contributions to the study of American literature, ISSN 1092–6356 : no. 11)
    Includes bibliographical references and index.
    ISBN 0–313–32046–2 (alk. paper)
    1. American literature—Louisiana—History and criticism. 2. African Americans in
literature. 3. Louisiana—Intellectual life. 4. Reconstruction—Louisiana.
5. Louisiana—In literature. 6. Race in literature. I. Disheroon-Green, Suzanne, 1963–
II. Abney, Lisa, 1964– III. Series.
PS266.L8 S67 2002
810.9′9763′09031—dc21   2001058629

British Library Cataloguing in Publication Data is available.

Library of Congress Catalog Card Number: 2001058629

ISBN: 0–313–32046–2
ISSN: 1092–6356

First published in 2002

Greenwood Press, 88 Post Road West, Westport, CT 06881
An imprint of Greenwood Publishing Group, Inc.
www.greenwood.com

Printed in the United States of America

The paper used in this book complies with the
Permanent Paper Standard issued by the National
Information Standards Organization (Z39.48–1984).

10 9 8 7 6 5 4 3 2 1

Copyright Acknowledgments

The editors and publisher gratefully acknowledge permission for use of the following material:

Extracts from "A Summer Tragedy" (copyright 1933) and GOD SENDS SUNDAY (copyright
1931) by Arna Bontemps. Reprinted by permission of Harold Ober Associated Incorporated.

From ABSALOM, ABSALOM! by William Faulkner, copyright © 1936 by William Faulkner
and renewed 1964 by Estelle Faulkner and Jill Faulkner Summers. Used by permission of Random House, Inc.

From *Fabulous New Orleans* by Lyle Saxon. © 1989 used by permission of the licenser, Pelican
Publishing Company, Inc.

To the victims of the 11 September 2001 tragedy:
May the lessons of history grant us the wisdom to persevere.

Contents

DEPICTIONS OF RACE AND CLASS, 1865–1945

LOUISIANA DURING THE MODERNIST PERIOD,
1919–1945

Foreword: The Artful and Crafty Ones of the French Quarter

Robin Miller

Rain drizzles steadily in these narrow streets; the chill of the wind stings the face and hands. The sun will set in a few hours. Though winter has not officially set in on this November day, the conditions here are right, except for the wind.

Nowhere is there mention of rain on that night when the French Opera House burned in New Orleans's French Quarter. But there is mention of death—the death of something rich in culture and history. Author Lyle Saxon would eulogize this loss in *The New Orleans Times-Picayune* later that night, saying, "The heart of the old French Quarter has stopped beating" (1).

That is where this particular story really begins, not walking through the French Quarter on a November day in the year 2000, but on the night of 4 December 1919. Still, a walk through the small streets of what continues to be the heart of New Orleans does have a way of bringing to life this long–ago scene. Again, no mention of rain appears in any passages written about that 1919 December night, but conditions were similar—south Louisiana humidity, no doubt mixed with a chill. Then late in the evening, a fire bell rang, prompting French Quarter residents to rise from their beds. Saxon was among them.

Flames rose from the French Opera House on the corner of Bourbon and Toulouse Streets. Saxon watched from the curb as flames destroyed not only the building, but also the beauty, elegance, and tradition that it represented. Not only operas but grand Mardi Gras balls were played out in this hall. The French Opera House was one of the few places that continued to attract uptown New Orleanians to the Vieux Carré. It was believed that the opera's demise would surely bring about the neighborhood's. In *The Romantic New Orleanians,* author Robert Tallant writes "for this New Orleanians grieved, for despite the neighborhood they had kept going to the opera when there was anything to see, and to those people who had wanted the French Quarter saved that night in December, 1919, seemed the last blow" (308). Which is why Saxon mourned while sitting on the curb; he feared that this event marked the beginning of the end of his beloved French Quarter. Sitting next to him was his friend, painter Alberta Kinsey. Tallant writes, "They both wept, quite openly" (311).

Standing now on that same curb, it is difficult to imagine a magnificent structure having once been here. Shops and bars have taken its place. A small, tarnished bronze plaque on one building's side is the only commemoration of the French Opera House's existence, but the Quarter still stands, and its heart has never stopped beating. In fact, its beating became stronger that night, as it transferred itself from one vessel to another, from the opera house to Saxon. Or perhaps the true spirit of the French Quarter was in Saxon's heart all along.

Saxon's heart not only beat stronger but louder. The opera house may have attracted New Orleanians to the neighborhood, but Saxon's presence prompted them to stay. The opera house stood as a monument. Saxon preserved the past while inspiring the Quarter's renewal through literature and art, or, as William Faulkner would later refer to the people who followed Saxon's lead, "the Artful and Crafty Ones of the French Quarter" ("Dedication," n.p.).

So the scene is set. The French Opera House no longer stands, but Saxon's homes at 612 and later 536 Royal Street do. Even the house that he owned at his death in 1946 at 534 Madison Street stands just around the corner from the St. Louis Cathedral.

Back in 1919, Saxon was living in the house at 612 when the opera house caught fire. His friends thought him foolish, because the Vieux Carré was not considered a safe place to visit and was a much less desirable place to live. Uptowners referred to it not as the French Quarter but Frenchtown, as if saying it left a bad taste in their mouths. Frenchtown, they believed, was a place of filth and danger. They were right. Tallant confirms these assertions:

What went on down there, besides the constant incidents of violent crime and a great deal of other human destruction by poverty, hunger, drink and narcotics, were many cheap, sordid and depraved things. There was much filth. Courtyards were filled with refuse and garbage. There was little plumbing and inadequate sewage. Patios, once beautiful Creole gardens, were trash heaps and breeding places for mosquitoes and germs. (308)

The French Quarter had become a slum. The Mafia used it as a base for some activities, and Tallant writes of rampant prostitution, especially along Bienville, Conti, and Dauphine Streets. Author Christine Wiltz writes of this part of the neighborhood—known as the Tango Belt—in her book *The Last Madam*, a biography of noted New Orleans madam Norma Wallace. The Tango Belt was named for the dance, an international craze by 1913. Wiltz writes, "The area was thick with dance halls and cabarets, restaurants and cafes where women could wear their 'tango bustles' and couples could indulge their obsession with the stylish, sensual dance—vulgar and immoral to many—twenty-four hours a day" (18). The French Quarter as presented in Wiltz's book was alive, reveling in Tango Belt activity. She shows that Uptowners were preoccupied with money and tradition, and the writers' and artists' idea of revitalization was naive compared to the ongoing party in the Tango Belt: "In fact, they didn't seem to have any idea what was going on there; it was rarely written about, and it certainly wasn't the romantic French Quarter scene most artists were painting" (19). The story is different today. A walk along streets that composed the Tango Belt produces a hollow silence within a city of constant activity. In days past, life filled this part of the Quarter occupied by Saxon and his friends. Clubs and shops occupy a great part of this area, but historic sites have been preserved, and property values are high. Yet in Saxon's time, living in the Quarter was economical, another factor that attracted the artful and crafty.

Saxon's friends advised against his move in the beginning. He was a young reporter for *The Times-Picayune* at the time and had yet to write the books that would win him fame—*Gumbo Ya-Ya*, *Fabulous New Orleans*, *Lafitte the Pirate*, and *Children of Strangers* among them. His obituary for the French Opera House, in fact, was the first piece to win him notice as a writer. And there he was, living in the most dangerous part of the city. In fact, most of Saxon's friends tried to discourage him. He would be murdered, they said. But from boyhood visits to New Orleans from his birthplace in Baton Rouge, Saxon had been in love with New Orleans, especially with the French Quarter. He was determined to live there. He furnished his house with family heirlooms, purchased antiques, and opened a salon that he intended to maintain, wherever he lived, for the remainder of his life. Saxon, however, had not yet begun to write books.

Tallant writes that Saxon invited friends to visit and talked some into staying: "Then there began an influx of painters and writers, most of them poseurs and fakers, but some genuine workers" (311). Among the genuine was Alberta Kinsey, the painter who wept alongside Saxon for the opera house's demise. Tallant's story presents Kinsey as an Ohio schoolteacher who had taken a vacation to paint in New Orleans. Saxon talked her into staying and found her a room in the French Quarter. But this account is not totally true. She was indeed an Ohio schoolteacher but had moved to New Orleans to attend Newcomb College. Kinsey would later recount to *The Tensas Gazette*, "I came to New Orleans to go to the art school at Sophie Newcomb, but never went there a single day. It's individuality that counts. If a person has individuality, it will come out." Kinsey found that individuality in the French Quarter. She fell in love with the old buildings in their states of decay. Soon she found herself in a circle of writers and painters that included not only Saxon but authors William Faulkner and Sherwood Anderson, literary critic and poet John McClure, painter Edith Fairfax Davenport and author Roark Bradford, who also wrote for *The Times-Picayune*.

These names offer only a sampling. The list continues. The circle included Pulitzer Prize–winning author Oliver LaFarge, playwright Flo Field, and author James Feibleman, who would later in his autobiography, *The Way of a Man*, refer to New Orleans in the decades between the two world wars as "something of a literary center" (271). The list continues with Richard Kirk, who wrote several volumes of epigrammatic verse. Then there were those writers associated with the literary magazine *The Double Dealer*, including Louis Gilmore, Basil Thompson, Julius Friend, Lillian Friend Marcus, Paul Godchaux Jr., Hamilton Basso, and Albert Goldstein. Feibleman, Field, McClure, and Kirk were associated with the magazine, too, as were Anderson and Faulkner.

The Double Dealer also offered works by Robert Penn Warren, Jean Toomer, and Thornton Wilder. Author Ernest Hemingway's first published piece appeared in the magazine. The Double Dealer published its forty-eight issues at 204 Baronne Street from January 1921 until May 1926. As described by the New Orleans City Guide, The Double Dealer was formed by "a group of young intellectuals, who decided it was time that the city break with the old literary traditions and become acquainted with the new" (116). The Double Dealer was a "cosmopolitan, anti-puritanical, and liberal magazine with decidedly modern tendencies" (New Orleans City Guide 257). It had taken its name from William Congreve's play, boldly proclaiming, "To myopics we desire to indicate the hills; to visionaries, the unwashed dishes . . . We mean to double deal, to show the other side, to throw open the back windows stuck in their sills from misuse, smutted over long since against even a dim beam's penetration" (New Orleans City Guide 116). These were strange words to a city's readers accustomed to a romantic tradition of literature. Still, these words, along with the magazine's published works to follow, won The Double Dealer national acclaim.

The Double Dealer was also a sign of divisiveness among the artful and crafty ones. Now the building at 407 comes into sight on this rainy walk along Royal Street. This building was once the Pelican Bookshop, where The Double Dealer crowd would gather. Yet Saxon, who worked to attract writers to the French Quarter, was excluded from these gatherings, perhaps because he chose instead to devote his time and work to the better-paying crowd at The Times-Picayune. It is difficult to imagine a literary gathering of The Double Dealer group on this day, a Saturday afternoon as tourists crowd Royal Street, even in inclement weather.

Feibleman tries to dispel what has been written about the writers' circle in the Vieux Carré. He writes in his autobiography: "In perspective of time, attention has centered on the French Quarter as though it had been a sort of organized literary colony. Nothing could have been less true. Some writers knew each other, a few were friends; many, however, were comparative strangers" (271). Yet his friend Basso describes it as a "Creole version of the Left Bank" and writes, "If I never much hankered after Paris in the 1920s it was because . . . I had Paris in my own backyard" (Harvey 71). Whatever the opinion, the fact remains that writers met here at 470 Royal Street. Saxon knew them but did not join them. John W. Thomas suggests in his biography of Saxon that the writer simply may not have been interested in writing for the magazine since his writing was generating good money from The Times-Picayune. Saxon was still a salaried reporter at the time, and his pieces in the Sunday editions were well read. He "may not have been enthusiastic to publish in an organ that had not paid its contributors since 1922" (44). Thomas is also quick to point out that speculating about Saxon's intentions is vain:

If Saxon shunned this famous publishing venture of the Quarter because he thought it inferior to the Sunday literature of The Times-Picayune, his taste today looks especially and unfortunately shortsighted. To the newspaperman, it should be remembered, however, the difference between a story or sketch for The Times-Picayune and for The Double Dealer in the 1920s could have simply been the difference between twenty-five dollars and nothing. (44)

Thomas, however, continues by saying that Saxon was not excluded from William Spratling's and William Faulkner's *Sherwood Anderson and Other Famous Creoles*. This is the book in which Faulkner classified his circle as artful and crafty. By the book's 1926 publication, the artful and crafty ones were thick in the Quarter. Painters staked out street corners, and writers tapped away at typewriters in second story apartments. Spratling was a young professor of architecture at Tulane University at the time. He was also a member of the Arts and Crafts Club, located at 712 Royal Street and organized in 1922, a year after the creation of *The Double Dealer*. Along with Spratling, Alberta Kinsey and Edith Davenport, artists within the Quarter included Xavier Gonzales, Paul Ninas, Caroline Durieux, Boyd Cruise, Knute Heldner, Colette Heldner, Charles Reinike, Clarence Millet, Conrad Albrizio, Weeks Hall and John McCrady, who incidentally, was brother-in-law to Hamilton Basso. Sculptors Enrique Alvarez, Albert Rieker and Angela Gregory also mingled in this crowd.

Another footnote to the Quarter's writer-artist connection would be Saxon's help in securing Gonzales a commission to paint a mural for Dixie's Bar of Music. Though located on St. Charles Avenue, the bar was a favorite hangout for some of the Quarter circle. Saxon suggested that owner Dixie Fasnacht commission Gonzales for the painting known as "Jazz Mural" at Dixie's Bar of Music. The mural is now in the Louisiana State Museum's art collection.

Saxon, meantime, wrote about Dixie's Bar in his posthumously published book, *The Friends of Joe Gilmore*. He also dedicated a chapter to his friend Alberta Kinsey. So it is not unusual to open *Sherwood Anderson and Other Famous Creoles* and find caricatures of Kinsey and Saxon on facing pages. Spratling drew these caricatures, as well as others in this book, and Faulkner wrote the introduction and commentaries below the caricatures. The two men roomed together at the time at 625 Orleans Alley, overlooking St. Anthony's Garden behind the St. Louis Cathedral. A short turn right on Royal Street into that alley that runs between the cathedral and the Presbytere brings the vicinity of their residence into view. Sherwood Anderson and wife Elizabeth arranged for Faulkner's stay with Spratling. The two would become friends and eventually publish the small book that would read like a who's who of the artful and crafty ones in the French Quarter.

Spratling and Faulkner meant the book to be a parody of sorts. As Spratling would explain it in a later edition of the book:

In 1926, Faulkner and I, as a sort of private joke, published a book called *Sherwood Anderson and Other Famous Creoles*. The title was a parody on Miguel Covarrubia's *The Prince of Wales and Other Famous Americans*, which had just appeared. The thing consisted of a group of my caricatures of various people who were then engaged (no matter how remotely) with the arts in New Orleans. Faulkner did the editing and we paid old man Pfaff to print us four hundred copies, which we then proceeded to unload on our friends at a dollar and a half a copy. (12)

Booksellers now offer those editions for no less than $2,500. The parody in the title, of course, is the fact that Anderson was not of Creole descent, much less a New Orleans native. The caricature, which, incidentally, he did not find funny, appears first. He is followed by many already mentioned in this story of the French Quarter, along with those not yet mentioned, including: Nathaniel C. Curtis, Tulane architecture professor who would later write books about New Orleans's buildings; anthropologist Frans Blom; photographer Pops Whitesell; *Le Petit Theatre du Vieux Carré* founder referred to in books only as Mrs. James Oscar Nixon; and artist, Charles Bien.

Some of these people would find fame after leaving the French Quarter; others would live out their lives in this small part of the city, their work receiving little to no recognition until after their deaths. Still, at one time they were all together in the French Quarter, not so much as Feibleman would portray them but as does Faulkner in his foreword to *Sherwood Anderson and Other Famous Creoles*:

First, let me tell you something about our Quarter, the Vieux Carré. Do you know our quarter, with its narrow streets, its old wrought-iron balconies and its southern European atmosphere? An atmosphere of richness and soft laughter, you know. It has a kind of ease, a kind of awareness of the unimportance of things that outlanders like myself—I am not a native—were taught to believe important. So it is no wonder that as one walks about the quarter one sees artists here and there on the shady side of the street corners, sketching houses and balconies. I have counted as many as forty in a single afternoon, and though I did not know their names nor the value of their paintings, they were my brothers. And in this fellowship where no badges are worn and no sign of greeting is required, I passed them as they bent over their canvasses, and as I walked onward I mused on the richness of our American life that permits forty people to spend day after day painting pictures in a single area comprised of six blocks.[1]

The six blocks to which Faulkner refers are the same six blocks that were falling into ruins, proclaimed a dangerous slum at the beginning of this story. They were the same place Saxon declared a residence and set out to form into an artists' colony. The French Quarter became just that, and though Saxon eventually left it for New York, he could not stay away. He would return and expand this colony into Natchitoches Parish, introducing the artful and crafty ones of the Quarter to Cammie Garrett Henry of Melrose Plantation. There they would stay, writing and painting, then gather around the dining room table in the evening and discuss their work. Author Ross Phares, the only surviving member of the Melrose artists' colony, remembers those conversations as rich. "There never has been nor will ever be conversation as rich as heard at that table," he says in an interview that I conducted in June 1999. But Melrose Plantation is another place, one that deserves its own story.

This story stops here in the rain, continuing through Orleans Alley, where lived Spratling and Faulkner, then turning left onto Chartres Street and making another quick into Madison Street. Madison is a short street just past the St. Louis Cathedral. It is here in front of the house at the 534 address that this story ends.

Oh, the tour could have continued down Royal to the house at 823, where Kinsey lived and kept her studio, but it is better to stop here at Madison, better to look at this structure that was the last house owned by Saxon. He never actually lived here, nor was it ever his desire. Yet the house has some history. John Steinbeck and his wife were married here, and Saxon entertained numerous friends in the arched courtyard somewhere behind the locked doors. But today the house stands quietly, probably as quietly as it stood at Saxon's death in 1946.

The artful and crafty ones still inhabited the Quarter. The colony was strongest in the 1920s and 1930s. Preservation was already under way; the Quarter was being restored. Faulkner had already gone and would win the Pulitzer and Nobel Prizes for Literature. Spratling would make his way to Taxco, Mexico, where he would design sterling silver art and jewelry. *The Double Dealer* would fold, and Anderson would go to bigger things. But most of the artists would live and work in the Quarter until their deaths.

Though Saxon never lived in this house, it was his way of keeping a presence in the Quarter. But he is not here now. Gone, too, are the artful and crafty ones that he led here. Tourists pass by, without notice. The rain keeps drizzling on this cold day as if weeping not for the demise of an opera house but for a bygone spirit.

NOTE

1. *Sherwood Anderson and Other Famous Creoles* was self-published by William Faulkner and William Spratling in 1926 through the Pelican Book Shop in New Orleans. The book was compiled as a combination tribute and gag on the people to whom Faulkner refers as the "artful and crafty ones in the Quarter." Only a few copies of the book were published, and the authors apparently thought page numbers to be unnecessary. University of Texas Press reprinted a facsimile edition of the book in 1966.

REFERENCES

Case, Harold M. "Melrose 'Mecca of the Muse'—'Jewel of the Cane River.'" *The Tensas Gazette* 1933. Northwestern State University of Louisiana, Watson Memorial Library, Cammie G. Henry Research Center, Melrose Collection, Scrapbook 257.

The Double Dealer. Ed. Julius Friend and Basil Thompson. New Orleans, Louisiana. 1921-26.

Federal Writers Project. *New Orleans City Guide*. Boston: Houghton Mifflin, 1938.

Feibleman, James K. *The Way of a Man*. New York: Horizon P, 1969.

Harvey, Cathy Chance. *Lyle Saxon: A Portrait in Letters, 1917–1945*. Diss. Tulane U, 1980.

Phares, Ross. Personal interview. June 1999.

Saxon, Lyle. "Fire Leaves Home of Lyric Opera Heap of Ruins." *The New Orleans Times-Picayune* 5 Dec. 1919: 10.

Spratling, William and William Faulkner. "Dedication." *Sherwood Anderson and Other Famous Creoles*. Austin: U of Texas P, 1966.

Tallant, Robert. *The Romantic New Orleanians*. New York: E.P. Dutton, 1950.

Thomas, John W. *Lyle Saxon: A Critical Biography*. Birmingham, AL: Summa, 1991.

Wiltz, Christine. *The Last Madam*. New York: Faber and Faber, 2000.

Acknowledgments

A collection such as this one does not come together without the assistance and tolerance of a large number of people, and this project is no exception. We would like to take this opportunity to express our gratitude to a sizeable list of people who have offered their support to this undertaking.

We first wish to thank our families, who have exhibited tremendous patience with our late nights and crazy schedules, as well as mountains of manuscript pages cluttering every square inch of our houses while we worked on editing this project. We are also grateful for their understanding when we went underground for days at a time when deadlines were looming. We especially want to thank Douglas Hollingsworth and Charles L. Green, as well as Kathryn Green and J. Alex Green, for filling in the voids in all other areas of our lives while we were consumed by this book. They vacuumed floors, washed clothes and dishes, and spent a lot of evenings entertaining themselves while we lived at the office. To them we owe the greatest debt. We are also thankful for the support of our parents: Paula and Joe Abney, Fred Disheroon and Diane Donley, Tommy and Betty Hollingsworth, and Richard and Elaine Green. Their constant encouragement has been a blessing for which we are very grateful.

Sharon Sweeters, the tireless and tolerant secretary of the Louisiana Folklife Center, has dealt with a barrage of tasks ranging from paperwork management to crisis management. Her unflagging cheerfulness and efficiency have helped this project come to fruition. Many thanks go to our editorial assistant, Jeffery Guin. His diligence and attention to detail, along with his pleasant demeanor made work on this project much more enjoyable. Our team of graduate assistants, Jodie L. Blair, Jamie C. Brazzell, and Kris Hailey, also aided and abetted in the production of this manuscript. Susie Scifres Kuilan, who has now moved on to her doctoral work, was also instrumental in completing the manuscript. We are thankful for her assistance, which was donated out of the goodness of her heart. We also appreciate the assistance of the Department of Language and Communication at Northwestern State University, with J. Rocky Colavito as head, for providing us with this assistance. The departmental secretaries, Bobbie Jackson and Bessie Jones, have also lent a great deal of support, even coming up to the office on weekends to let us use the copier and printer. We are grateful for the assistance of each of these individuals.

We also wish to express thanks to our weekly research group: Helaine Razovsky, Helen Sugarman, and Shelisa Theus. Their insights and feedback have been timely and much appreciated. We also acknowledge the assistance of Fleming Thomas and the other research librarians at the Watson Library at Northwestern State University for their help with interlibrary loan materials and other research services.

We wish to thank the contributors to this volume. Many of our contributors went above and beyond in order to get revisions back to us quickly and were exceptionally pleasant in the process. We value their contributions and their collegiality. Finally, we appreciate the able assistance of George Butler, Tod Myerscough, and Nina Duprey at Greenwood Publishing. They have provided a wealth of information and have made this process far easier than it might have been. We are truly grateful for the support and assistance of the people mentioned here, as well as others who we may have inadvertently neglected to mention.

Introduction: Building Literary Louisiana, 1865-1945

Suzanne Disheroon-Green and Lisa Abney

People who are unfamiliar with the American South envision the region in terms of the political cliché of the "Solid South." They often view this diverse region as if it were a monolithic entity, easily described by a handful of catch phrases. Non-Southerners tend to imagine the Mason-Dixon line—though few could identify precisely where it is—as an invisible boundary beyond which lies a colorful, but mysterious place. This apocryphal South is defined in terms of stereotypes, and its voice is a montage of Hollywood clichés: the fat sheriff with his mirrored sunglasses; the Southern belle, now a faded middle-aged debutante with big hair, sheltered from reality by a stream of never-ending social obligations; the half-drunk Bubba, tossing beer cans into the kudzu as he races his pick-up down a back road to a dilapidated trailer occupied by an indeterminate number of dirty children, big dogs, and a long suffering wife, once pretty, but aged beyond her years. Throw in a crooked politician wearing a white suit and a Bible-thumping evangelist, and we have, what is for many non-Southerners, a stereotypical, small Southern town. What we do not have is a vision of the South as it is, or ever was.

The South is not monolithic, and perhaps the best example of the heterogeneity inherent in the Southern region can be found in the state of Louisiana. Despite its numerous similarities with the South at large, Louisiana is a region possessing a unique cultural identity. The colonial impulses of France and Spain, the importance of religion, and the dramatic shift in racial politics which ensued with the purchase of the Louisiana territory from France in 1803 shaped the historical, cultural, and legal systems of the state, and by extension, its literary heritage. We see these influences, most especially, in the expectations placed on women and people of color, in the narrative and folk traditions, in the effects of Reconstruction, and in the ways in which Modernism was negotiated during the pre-Civil Rights era.

The essays in this volume explore the influences at work on Louisiana writers and those writing about Louisiana in the era beginning with Reconstruction and ending with World War II. Authors such as Alice Dunbar-Nelson, Lyle Saxon, and George Washington Cable characterize the racial caste system, pointing out the flaws in its construction and its effects on community and interpersonal relationships. Ruth McEnery Stuart, Kate Chopin, and Sallie Rhett Roman depict the lives of women in Louisiana and their struggle when assuming non-traditional roles. Writers such as William Faulkner and Arna Bontemps draw upon the region's rich narrative and folk traditions—elements which provide the foundation for their works and reflect the complicated social fabric of the region. Before discussing the specific literary selections addressed in this volume; however, some background regarding Louisiana's history, politics, and culture may prove useful in contextualizing the literary works under consideration in this volume.

LOUISIANA'S UNIQUE LANDSCAPE: HISTORY, POLITICS, AND ECONOMICS

Louisiana writers of the post-bellum era could not help but be influenced by the rich cultural and historical heritage that had, from the French colonial period, affected the development of the region. The French influence, together with those of the Spanish, American, African, and indigenous peoples of the state, blended to form the gumbo that is Louisiana culture. The discussion that follows explores some of the elements that shaped the development of post-bellum Louisiana history, politics, and economics.

Louisiana's History and Politics

The colonial period in Louisiana was paralleled in the British colonies in what became the eastern seaboard and the southern United States by a movement toward the formation of a lasting government for the newly emerging republic. In the colonies, the growth and development of local autonomy had inevitably led to conflict with Great Britain and, ultimately, to the American Revolution. While conflict raged in the British colonies, Louisiana flourished under French dominion, and the French influence continues even today. Francophone languages are the most widely spoken after English in Louisiana. Additionally, Catholicism, which was supported by both French and Spanish governments, established one of its strongest American footholds in south Louisiana as early as the mid-1600s and is still widely practiced throughout the state. As important as they are to the identity of the state, these differences merely scratch the surface of Louisiana's cultural milieu.

The history of Louisiana, prior to its becoming a territory of the United States, is a complicated one. The region was inhabited by indigenous peoples long before European imperialists arrived seeking land and riches, as archaeological research on the mounds at Poverty Point in West Carroll Parish has demonstrated. The indigenous culture represented by these mounds is estimated to have arisen around 2000 B.C.E., reaching its height around 1000 B.C.E. The expeditions of Hernando de Soto, who explored what is now the American Southeast for the Spanish, marked the first European interaction with the indigenous peoples (Wilds, Dufour, and Cowen 1). Serious colonization did not begin in Louisiana until the early 1700s, at which time an estimated "13,000 to 15,000 Indians, in groups speaking at least twenty-two distinct languages" populated the region (Wilds, Dufour, and Cowen 2). The Native American populations suffered greatly upon the arrival of European explorers, settlers, and missionaries, as these individuals carried diseases to which the Native Americans had little natural immunity. Further, war between the Native Americans and Europeans was a constant threat.

During this time, several explorers, including de Soto's second-in-command, Luis de Moscoso de Alvarado, may have traveled through Louisiana by way of the Mississippi River in their efforts to explore Mexico. More than a century after de Soto's first forays into Louisiana, the territory was claimed for the French king, Louis XIV, by Robert Cavelier, sieur de La Salle. The youthful owner of a substantial tract of land in Canada, La Salle dreamed of following the Mississippi River to its mouth, while "claiming the lands for France—and not coincidentally, fur-trapping monopolies for himself" (Wilds, Dufour, and Cowen 6). La Salle's plan was finally permitted by the French king, and La Salle launched his expedition four years later, in 1678. With La Salle's expedition, Louisiana began a sustained period of French governance that ended with the cession of Louisiana to the Spanish in 1762.

The transfer of Louisiana, and especially New Orleans, to Spanish control in the 1760s was initially met with consternation by the residents of the region. In fact, the sale was kept secret for two years, until 1764. When the transfer of power became public knowledge, a demonstration was staged during which the participants decided to write to the French king, imploring him to buy Louisiana back from Spain. Despite the colonists' fears, life under Spanish rule did not change a great deal. Only after the Louisiana territory became a part of the United States in 1803, after being returned to French control long enough to be sold, did the colonists' day-to-day existence changed dramatically. Thomas Jefferson arranged to purchase the entire Louisiana territory from Napoleon Bonaparte for fifteen million dollars. As General Horatio Gates remarked to the President, "Let the Land rejoice, for you have bought Louisiana for a Song" ("American Originals").

During the postcolonial period, Louisiana became as an American territory, functioning in many ways as it had during its colonial days; however, the influx of new residents from other parts of the American South exerted a substantial influence upon the racial tolerance of its populations. Prior to the Louisiana Purchase, the wealthy landowners in the territory had benefitted from the slave economy, but it did so under more strict governmental guidelines than were enforced in the American states. By the time the Civil War broke out, Louisiana had adopted an identity more American than colonial, and for the most part, its residents fought on the side of the South during the War. During the Civil War era, Louisiana suffered much of the same devastation as the rest of the region, especially after the removal of the capital of the Confederacy from Richmond to New Orleans, and finally to Shreveport shortly before the demise of the Confederate States.

By the end of the Civil War, Louisiana's regiments had suffered great losses

(Wall 183), and because of the high numbers of men who left their farms and plantations to fight, agricultural production also declined dramatically. Women and children were left to tend the crops, and their efforts proved far less successful than those of their husbands and slaves. Because of the Union blockades during the war years, cotton could not be transported to market, and hence, became a profitless crop. Additionally, the South relied upon the North for the manufacture of its raw goods, but the inability to transport goods northward dealt a death-blow to the cotton economy. To make matters worse, sugar crops failed, and the loss of slaves as a source of both capital and labor meant the end to many planters' occupations (Moore 57-61). Farms, cotton gins, sugar houses, and many other agricultural processing sites were destroyed; high numbers of livestock had been confiscated or killed by either Union or Confederate troops. Levees and flood–control dams were neglected during the war and had been weakened by the ravages of nature, yet Louisiana had almost no capital to begin repair of these important flood prevention devices. The levees remained largely unattended until the Army Corps of Engineers took control of the levee system after the flood of 1927 (Wall 185). By the end of the war, Louisiana lay in a state of ruin, and even the simple task of providing enough food for a family was a great challenge.

While Louisiana's landscape suffered the effects of the devastation of the Civil War, its people, too, faced many difficulties—particularly its African–American population. Because of Louisiana's political structure and disenfranchised status within the Union, the rights of African Americans were difficult to enforce. During Reconstruction, Union troops occupied New Orleans and assisted in the implementation of Lincoln's plan to re-incorporate the Southern states into the Union. Unfortunately, this plan was ill-formed and unenforceable, and after his re–election in 1865, Governor James Madison Wells, along with Louisiana's legislators, tried with all their might to re–establish control similar to that of the antebellum era. Since slavery was no longer a viable option, and the economy was still in need of a cheap source of labor, Louisiana's legislators set to work passing the convict-lease system which was similar to the antebellum slave codes in its treatment of the workers (Shugg 212-214; Wall 186). Convicts were leased by farmers to perform work that had previously been the duty of slaves, and often this work was arduous and dangerous. This system wrecked the lives of many of the convicts, while Samuel L. James, the architect of the convict-lease system—which was well ensconced by the late 1870s——grew extremely wealthy. James held the exclusive contract with the government to lease convicts for five thousand dollars per year. While he leased the convicts from the state for this meager amount, his profits as lease agent made him a multimillionaire. Legislators tried numerous times to limit his power and to renegotiate his lease, but they failed to make any real impact on his way of doing business. The James Gang, headed by Samuel James, derived its name from the famous criminals, Frank and Jesse James, and the activities of those in the Louisiana version of the James Gang were as almost illegal and unscrupulous as their more famous namesakes.

Aware that these new laws and systems resembled previous patterns of oppression, the African Americans and Union sympathizers banded together to form the Republican Party of Louisiana. Additionally, the federal government understood that little could be done to maintain the rights of African Americans without military intervention, which the government knew would be too costly to enforce. In an effort to maintain African-American rights, Congress passed the Reconstruction Act of 1867, which divided the South into five distinct military districts, placing a general in command of each district. Each general was charged with conducting voter registration drives with the aim of increasing African-American participation in the voting process, while simultaneously limiting the voting power of white males, who were required to take an oath which stated that they had never aided the Confederacy. The Reconstruction Act disenfranchised the majority of white males in Louisiana, for few could or would swear such an oath. This act, coupled with the onslaught of Northern opportunists—carpetbaggers and Republicans who saw the South as ripe for the picking—worked to integrate schools, theaters, and restaurants while capitalizing on the South's weakened economy (Tunnell 149). Squeezed out of their state government, white males retaliated by forming several groups whose focus was to stop African Americans and other Republicans from voting. Groups modeled upon the Ku Klux Klan, such as the Knights of the White Camelia, rapidly spread throughout the state (Ficklen 205). By 1868, the Knights and other groups had effectively crippled Republican voting.

The Republicans, however, refused to be stymied by the actions of the Knights, and they formed a Returning Board, which held final authority regarding vote tabulation and validity (Hair 6-8). The Returning Board was created to stop the Democrats from winning elections; accordingly, they could disallow any vote which they viewed as being garnered through illegal or fraudulent means (McGinty 65-67). The board hindered Democratic progress and aided Republican efforts to win elections. After the Returning Board was formed, white Democrats ceased to register to vote, and Republican candidates reigned. By 1868, African Americans comprised the majority of the population in the state and hailed Reconstruction government as a glorious reform which empowered them.

Once federal troops left the South in the late 1870s, the Reconstruction government quickly disintegrated, allowing Louisiana Democrats to regain (Wall 196). These post-Reconstruction Democrats, often called "Bourbon Democrats" (Wall 205), were politically conservative whites who were determined to return Louisiana to the ways of the antebellum period. These Democrats had survived the Civil War and the turbulent time of Reconstruction. They lay in wait for the opportunity to regain power; their chance arose as soon as federal troops left Louisiana (Lonn 400-415). The Bourbon governor, Francis T. Nicholls, faced much controversy and conflict, as many of the Bourbon Democrats had fallen under the spell of the Lottery–Ring, a left-over corporation from Reconstruction days (Hair 130-135). The Lottery–Ring was a corrupt business which took in huge sums of money, paying only a small amount in prizes. Nicholls and the northern Louisiana Protestants had little use for the Lottery–Ring, yet attempts to minimize the organization ended Nicholls's term prematurely, for the Lottery–Ring had many friends in high places. The Lottery–Ring and the James Gang became legendary for their corrupt and money hungry practices during this era.

During the 1880s, Samuel D. McEnery, was one of Louisiana's most corrupt governors. The corruption of McEnery's administration was so rampant that even his fellow Bourbons turned against him. The Bourbons then appealed to former governor, Francis T. Nicholls, to reassume the role of governor. During his second term, Nicholls renewed his fight against the Lottery–Ring and the James Gang, yet the two entities defeated Nicholls' reform efforts. The election of Murphy Foster, from the Anti-Lottery Democrat faction, finally led to the dissolution of the Lottery–Ring.

During the Democrats' reign over Louisiana politics, many citizens of North Louisiana grew weary of political corruption and began supporting the newly emerging Populist Party. The Populists gained grass roots support in Winn Parish and expanded the party's membership to a few of the neighboring parishes. The Populist Party formed an odd alliance of white farmers and disenfranchised African Americans, who shared the desire for fair elections and equal justice. Poor whites and blacks had been treated badly or ignored by the Bourbon Democrats, and the pro-business, low-tariff stance of Murphy Foster did little to assist the poor. The 1890 legislature instituted Jim Crow railroad laws for Louisiana which called for separate but equal treatment of African Americans in transportation and led to the landmark *Plessy vs. Ferguson* case—Louisiana's most famous lawsuit (Wall 222). The ascendency of the pro-Jim Crow attitudes led many African Americans to become interested in the platforms of the Populist Party. The Populist Party's life, however, was short because of the corrupt politics of the Democrats, who strong–armed African Americans into voting for their party.

After the ordeal with the Populist movement, the Democrats began to realize that they could not always count on intimidation and doctored election results in order to win elections; hence, they modified voting rights as a way of protecting their interests. The Democrats called a Constitutional Convention in 1889 to accomplish the goal of maintaining control of elections. The laws passed during this Convention effectively froze out the poor and illiterate residents of Louisiana. Voters were forced to prove their literacy, to pay one dollar a year for poll tax, and to produce proof of land ownership. The Democrats succeeded in their plan to limit the number of voters. Voter rolls dropped dramatically among poor whites and African Americans, and for the most part, voting remained a wealthy, white man's privilege.

From 1908 to 1928, upland cotton planters and a powerful group of New Orleans Democrats, called The Choctaw Club of Louisiana or the Old Regulars, controlled the Louisiana political scene. The Choctaw Club was reminiscent of its predecessor, the Lottery–Ring, but it did not have the cloak of legitimacy offered initially by the lottery. This New Orleans–based clique amassed a great deal of power; its members lobbied for the appointment of their supporters to state jobs, thus ensuring a good living for their supporters and bureaucratic power for the faction. As a result, few reforms occurred during this time, despite the attempts of Governors W.W. Heard and Newton C. Blanchard to improve living conditions for the disenfranchised, poverty–stricken residents of Louisiana. In 1920, John A.

Parker, a former Progressive Party member turned Democrat, ran for governor and became the governor who provided a bridge between the old–style Democrats such as McEnery and the neopopulism of Huey Long. Parker was resented by the average citizens of Louisiana because of his elitist and dismissive attitude. He alienated a high percentage of the electorate, leading voters to embrace the neopopulism of Huey Long. Parker's aloof manner, coupled with the post–World War I crash of cotton prices, led Louisiana's farmers to rebel. They began to exert their rights, demanding paved farm to market roads, agricultural aid, improved educational systems, and less corrupt industry and public utilities officials. By 1924, the message of Huey Long had reached the populace, and Long almost forced a run-off election. In 1928, he ran again, and this time he won.

Huey P. Long was governor from 1928 to 1932 and served as a United States Senator from 1932 to 1935. Long is a Louisiana legend because of his promise to attack corruption. His life is the subject of many documentaries and fictional works, such as Robert Penn Warren's *All the King's Men* and Adria Locke Langley's *A Lion is in the Streets*. Each depicts Long's life with thinly veiled fictional characters in their novels. Long moved Louisiana away from its established political system and redistributed power within the state. Political control by the Old Regulars had already lessened, and Long's rise to power sent the machine into a more rapid decline. Long's tenure as governor led to many important changes within the state, but he drew fire from the wealthy for his plans of income redistribution and social reform. His radical initiatives account for a substantial measure of his success among poorer voters, despite the criticism from his detractors. He saw the need for increased health care for the impoverished public, so he worked to increase funding for charity hospitals. Long lobbied for the founding of Louisiana State University's Medical School. Indeed, Long's paradigm for reform became the prototype for many later reform initiatives at the federal level, such as Franklin D. Roosevelt's "New Deal," John F. Kennedy's "New Frontier," and Lyndon Johnson's "Great Society" (Wall 245).

Long, unlike many Southern politicians, relied upon African Americans and poor whites to stay in office. The governor's quick wit and keen intellect allowed him to verbally best his detractors; to them, however, he was no gentleman. They viewed him as uncouth, loud, verbose, and unfit to govern (Kane 80-82). He quarreled with both his enemies and his allies, forcing many of his appointees to sign undated resignation letters upon assuming office, lest he need to rid himself of them later. Long's style of politics often illustrated his unscrupulous behavior and showed the ways in which America was changing. Franklin D. Roosevelt, the president under whom Long served, called him one of the two most dangerous men in America—the other most dangerous man was Douglas MacArthur. Despite the fact that Long entered politics because he wished to help the disenfranchised and the poor, he became blatantly power hungry and cared little for the subtleties of politics or polite society, and ultimately, this behavior led to his downfall.

After winning his Senate seat, Long connived to keep his Lieutenant Governor, Paul Cyr, out of the Governor's position (Martin 87). He succeeded, and Long's childhood friend, Oscar K. (O.K.) Allen, took office instead (Leibling 11). Huey

Long continued to run the state from Washington, with O.K. Allen acting as a political pawn for his boyhood friend (Kane 93), acquiescing to all of Long's suggestions concerning the governing of the state. After becoming Senator—and still keeping his grip on Louisiana's politics—Long commanded O.K. Allen to call a special session of the Legislature in order to gerrymander the district of Benjamin Pavy, an anti-Longite. On 8 September 1935, the morning of the first day of the special session, Pavy's son-in-law, Dr. Carl Weiss, shot Huey P. Long. Long died two days after the shooting from internal bleeding. While the public mourned Long's death, his enemies heaved a sigh of relief.

The Long legacy in Louisiana includes school reform, free textbooks for students, property tax reductions, farm subsidies, road and bridge construction, poll tax repeal, and poverty relief for the elderly. Under Long's direction, the construction of the thirty–four–story Louisiana state capitol began. No longer intimidated by the old–style politicians, the people of the northern parishes became invigorated and began to stand up for their beliefs. To many Louisiana residents, Long was a savior, looking out for their interests and providing them with the services that they had long been awaiting.

For a short time after Huey Long's death, the Long machine fragmented as his top men scrambled for position. O.K. Allen died in office in 1935, and James A. Noe finished Allen's term as acting governor. Many thought that Noe would prevail as gubernatorial candidate, but instead, the party selected as their candidate a virtual unknown, Richard Leche. Leche, a judge from New Orleans, was paired with Huey's brother, Earl K. Long. The pair won, and Leche, despite the scandal that riddled his term, enhanced Louisiana's public works tremendously. Because he had no history with Roosevelt, Leche teamed with powerful Senator Allen Ellender and Earl K. Long to bargain with Roosevelt's forces to bring many Works Progress Administration projects to Louisiana. For example, Lyle Saxon's tenure as the director of the Louisiana arm of the Federal Writer's Project was funded under the auspices of the Works Progress Administration.

Despite his success in expanding many of Huey Long's projects, such as enhancing public schools and medical access for Louisiana residents, Leche resigned under a cloud of shame in 1939. The corruption in his administration was extreme, even by Louisiana standards. Earl K. Long then ran for governor after serving as acting governor following Leche's resignation. Long fought a hard race, yet the people of Louisiana, who were experiencing economic downturns because of the Great Depression, chose Sam Houston Jones, a little–known attorney from Lake Charles, to lead them. Jones gave the citizens reform; he abolished the deduct system[1], instituted new anti–nepotism rules, prevented the holding of two state jobs at one time, and opened voter registration rolls to the public for scrutiny. He also re-organized the Louisiana State University Board of Supervisors and other state agencies and implemented new accountability measures. The new governor instituted the Civil Service program in Louisiana government, taking care to institute the system in a way that allowed him to purge the system of Longites and to replace them with his allies. Jones restored a desperately needed system of checks and balances in Louisiana. Following Jones's term, Louisiana's singing governor, Jimmie Davis, easily won against Longite Lewis Morgan, for the voters of Louisiana had bitter memories of the Leche debacle. Davis, famous for writing and performing the hit song, "You Are My Sunshine," was governor from 1944 to 1948, and is best remembered for his success in balancing Louisiana's budget and for increasing allocations for higher education. Many of his contemporaries viewed him as a do-nothing governor, yet Davis's administration was conducted without scandal.

In spite of numerous efforts to improve education and other public programs, Louisiana still had the highest level of illiteracy in the United States as late as the 1890s. Its people were relegated, for the most part, to blue–collar and agricultural occupations, and not surprisingly, Louisiana has suffered high levels of poverty until well into the twentieth century. The Democrats dominated Louisiana politics until late in the twentieth century, when ironically the Republicans began gaining the votes of the conservative Southern whites. Throughout Louisiana's sordid political history, true reform from either party was slow in coming and has yet to be fully achieved.

The Rise of Industry in Louisiana

Louisiana has long been an agricultural center; cotton, rice, sugar, and later, peanuts were important crops, and livestock has played an equally significant role over the past two centuries. Agriculture, however, has not been the sole industry in the state. The timber, petrochemical, and military industries have played important roles in the development of the history and culture of Louisiana as well as in the state's literary traditions.

The timber industry in Louisiana dates back to the 1700s, when early colonists logged cypress trees and marketed them in the French West Indies (Brown and Montz 30). By the 1820s, domestic demand for the trees had increased, corresponding with decreased foreign demand. The demand for cypress, and similarly, for pine remained steady well into the early years of the twentieth century.

In turn-of-the-century Louisiana, clear cutting of the virgin cypress and pine timber stands became commonplace. An integral part of the Louisiana economy, cypress cutting proved to be a difficult task, and workers earned little, but their pay was generally consistent. As most Louisiana residents lived by hunting, fishing, and subsistence farming, logging was one of the few industries which yielded steady pay. The rise of the timber industry was not only attractive to the loggers and their families but also fueled Louisiana's economy and spurred the construction of railroad systems and urban development (Moore 87).

The growth of the timber industry was made possible by the increased availability of rural railroads. During the mid-nineteenth century, the age of the railroad dawned in Louisiana, and railroad tracks began to cover the state, connecting backwater towns to sawmill towns. An overhead railroad log skidder— a system for transporting logs using cables and rail cars was invented, and thus, the process of transporting logs eased. Overland accessibility remained limited in some cases, however, and, even after rail expansion occurred, both marine and land transport methods co–existed for many years, for there was enough timber business to bring profits to every participant.

While cypress logging was indeed dangerous because of the swamps and wetlands in which the trees grew, the virgin pine stands, found predominantly in northwestern and western Louisiana, held their own set of challenges. Louisiana's western pine district spanned a triangular zone which extended north from Alexandria to Many and then, south to Lake Charles. These longleaf pines, rarer today than in the past, towered above the ground to over 100 feet and generally had a diameter of three feet or larger. The foliage canopy of virgin longleaf pines blocked the sunlight from reaching the ground (Stokes 3). For many, the task of clearing farm land was daunting, as they had no heavy equipment to push down the trees. When loggers approached farmers about buying timber, the small farmers of the region quickly took the opportunity to earn a good sum of money and to have someone else clear away the trees. For many in the region, timber was "found money" and rapidly became a resource which could be handily exploited, yet like cypress, it was not carefully managed.

Timber supplies in some states had been depleted prior to the war due to clear cutting, and thus Louisiana found itself in a prime position for the timber industry to blossom. Foreign investors and Northerners brought large sums of money into the economy of the state, and a new, wealthy Louisianian emerged, the timber baron. Kate Chopin modeled her protagonist in *At Fault*, David Hosmer, upon the timber barons of her time. Hosmer, like many of his time, traveled the United States harvesting the virgin timber. While the timber boom brought huge profits to investors, sawmill owners, loggers, and landowners, the spoils, however, were relatively short–lived. By 1913, cypress milling peaked when Louisiana produced more than one billion board feet (Brown and Montz 37). Less than a decade later, the large-scale timber industry had done its job so well that it no longer had any timber to harvest. All the large stands of cypress had been ravaged (Brown and Montz 36).

The petrochemical industry, which developed as the timber industry began to decline, came into being after Spindletop, the notable oil strike in Beaumont, Texas. Spindletop was less than thirty miles from southwestern Louisiana, and intelligent Louisianians capitalized upon the idea that there might be oil in Louisiana, too. These early drillers proved correct, and the first commercial oil field was founded at Jennings in 1901. After this oil strike, several oil and drilling companies expanded throughout the state, seizing the opportunity to profit from black gold. The demand for oil products increased as automobile and internal combustion engine production grew, and by 1922, Louisiana oil production comprised eight percent of the total produced in the United States annually. Almost all of the oil came from Louisiana's northwestern parishes—Caddo, Claiborne, and DeSoto.

While oil formed a significant portion of the Louisiana economy, natural gas also came to be an important Louisiana export. For many years, drillers who hit natural gas pockets viewed the substance as a waste of their time and money, for no one had realized that the gas could be put to use. Gas storage was impractical since it could not be stored in tanks like oil, and pipeline technologies, which later came into use, had yet not been invented. When drillers hit these natural gas pockets, they often let them spew out in hope that oil would emerge after the vapor release, leading to the release of over 200 million cubic feet of natural gas by 1912 (Wall 277). The best example of wasted resources comes from Monroe's Carbon Black plants. Carbon Black was an integral element to printer's ink, paint, and dyes, and one way which it was produced was to burn off natural gas. Unfortunately, its production wasted ninety-seven percent of the gas used in the manufacture of Carbon Black. As a result, the pollution in Ouachita Parish was abominable during the years when Carbon Black was produced using this method. Today, Louisiana still holds substantial natural gas reserves, despite the excessive waste of the early twentieth century.

As timber, oil, and gas emerged as important industrial pursuits, so, too, did sulfur and salt. New sulfur mining technologies allowed sulfur to be infused with pressurized hot water and forced to the earth's surface, where it could be pumped and collected. Currently, Louisiana ranks only behind Texas in sulfur production and is the national leader in salt production (Wall 279). Louisiana's industrial development has not always had a smooth path, for many governors of the state varied in their treatment of big business, and a discernible plan for bringing industry to Louisiana was not in place until the late twentieth century.

While the agriculture, timber, and petrochemical industries grew in Louisiana, the state also enjoyed a growing economy due to a rapidly emerging military complex. Between the start of World War I and the end of World War II, Louisiana housed major military installations such as Camp Beauregard, Fort Polk, Camp Livingston, Esler Field, Barksdale Air Force Base, Chennault Air Force Base, and numerous other military sites. Many industrial and military entities grew during the war years, such as Higgins Industries of New Orleans (Calcote). Louisiana's economy was changing dramatically, and Huey P. Long's influence in these changes cannot be ignored, for he laid the groundwork for Leche's and his successors' later expansion efforts.

Despite the development of both peace-time and war industries, Louisiana's residents still maintained a low standard of living. The 1940s and 1950s brought good economic times for some, but for most of the population, agriculture was their occupation, and their incomes reflected this struggle. Even with Roosevelt's farm assistance programs, Louisiana's dirt farmers were often left far below the poverty line, and many had to leave their farms permanently in order to seek jobs in industry or to join the Civilian Conservation Corps (CCC), a branch of Roosevelt's New Deal. Despite the burgeoning industrialization of Louisiana, however, the years before and after the rise of mechanized agriculture in Louisiana were hard on poor whites and African Americans who had barely survived under the sharecropping system.

Urbanization and Statewide Settlement Patterns

New Orleans has been the largest urban center in the state dating back to the colonial era; however, from 1880 to 1900, Shreveport, Alexandria, Monroe, Lafayette, Lake Charles, and Baton Rouge grew rapidly because of the timber and petrochemical industries and the relocation of state government. Alexandria and Shreveport, because of their proximity to the Red River, maintained fairly consistent growth levels and developed trade via the river. Even though these cities were emerging population centers, most of Louisiana's land remained rural until well past 1900.

As industry in Louisiana expanded, people began to depart their small towns and move to the more urbanized areas. After Reconstruction, farmers and planters sought labor for agricultural work; for the most part, former slaves continued to work in these occupations. As industry and commerce began to grow, shipyards and railroad companies needed labor to survive; hence, high numbers of Italian and Chinese immigrants were encouraged to come to Louisiana to work, as the Irish had been beginning in the 1840s. Immigrants living in America in the late nineteenth and early twentieth centuries found greater opportunities than those available in the homeland on one hand, but on the other, immigrant status often meant relegation to the lower socioeconomic classes.

The influx of immigrants resulted in a substantial portion of Louisiana's residents remaining bilingual, and the use of two languages and knowledge of two cultures obviously shapes the manner in which these speakers tell their stories. Today, educators recognize the value of knowing two or more languages; in the past, educators embraced a different view; English–only movements abounded. Teachers often chastised children for speaking their native Creole French, Cajun French, Spanish, or Native American languages in school. Italian and Chinese immigrants were ridiculed, persecuted, and forced to assimilate, as had been their Irish and African predecessors. While at school, children were not allowed to speak any language other than English. This strict control of language stigmatized these cultures and their languages and served to keep their speakers in a state of subservience. For this reason, many native speakers of languages other than English often did their best to eschew all things ethnic and to assimilate into mainstream American culture. The documentation of these languages, narrative structures, and folk practices in fiction often gives linguists, rhetoricians, and folklorists a better picture of cultural elements which have been intentionally hidden or extinguished. The push toward assimilation caused many to abandon traditional ways; however, others maintained their traditions by practicing them privately within their own communities or families. Some Louisiana residents had the good fortune and a work ethic that allowed them to maintain themselves apart from larger society. They stayed out of the fray and lived as they pleased, and fortunately, a few of these communities still exist in Louisiana, as is the case with Isle Brevelle on the Cane River and several French-speaking Cajun communities in South Louisiana.

WOMEN, WORK, AND CULTURE IN RECONSTRUCTION LOUISIANA

Women's roles in Louisiana culture were restrictively coded and transcended barriers of race and class. The status of women in Louisiana was determined primarily by the paternalistic teachings of the Catholic Church, which designated men as the heads of households. By the time of the Louisiana Purchase, the governorship of the territory had begun implementing the Civil Code, more commonly known as the Napoleonic Code, which further restricted the rights of women under the law.

The Napoleonic Code was hailed as a breakthrough over the British Common Law model in several regards. Common Law, the system of governance from which most American laws outside of Louisiana derive, allowed the judicial branch of government to interpret the law, to set precedents, and through these authorities, to at least partially fulfill the role of lawmaker. The Napoleonic Code, or Civil Code, attempted instead to inscribe a comprehensive set of standards which were derived from the customs of the culture—in this case, the French culture and earlier Roman law. Under this system, the "duty of the judge is to *apply* the law as enacted. Judicial interpretation is limited to interpreting ambiguous provisions of the law" (deKeyzer 3). Similar issues of the Code were cross-referenced so that judges would not be in the position of having to interpret the law, but rather of allowing the law to speak for itself.

Much of the early Napoleonic Code concerned family and property matters, since most of the "2,281 articles in the Civil Code dealt with the right of property," which was defined as "the right to enjoy and dispose of one's property in the most absolute fashion" (DeLaine, "Code Napoleon" 2). In addition, the Code defined the rights which men held over their wives and children. For example, the Civil Code was explicit about making husbands legally superior to their wives. A husband owed "protection" to his wife, but she owed him "obedience." Married women could not enter into contracts, nor could they conduct business, and although in the case of a divorce, recognition was given to community property, the husband controlled all property during the marriage, even property that had belonged to the wife before the marriage took place (DeLaine, "Code Napoleon" 2). Divorce, although uncommon in any event during the colonial period, was much harder to obtain for women than for men. While a wife could be divorced for a single act of adultery, a husband could be divorced on the same grounds only if he "committed the act within the family home" (DeLaine, "Code Napoleon" 2). The Napoleonic Code did little to protect the rights of women.

The status of women in Louisiana culture is a recurring theme in the literary tradition that grew out of this manner of thinking. Many women had first-hand experience with the inherently discriminatory nature of the Napoleonic Code. For example, Kate Chopin, upon the death of her husband, had to petition the Louisiana courts in order to be appointed the legal guardian of her biological children, despite the fact that she and her husband had been happily married at the time of his death. Because of the Civil Code, legal custody of the minor children devolved to Oscar Chopin's nearest living male relative, his brother, Lamy Chopin. Only after a protracted struggle in the Louisiana courts was Kate Chopin named the "Tutrix" of her children, and even this ruling carried the stipulation that her brother-in-law serve as "under tutor" so that he might keep an eye on her (Toth 161). These types of social restrictions on the lives and decisions of women are addressed by writers of the era, such as Kate Chopin, George Washington Cable, Lyle Saxon, and Ruth

McEnery Stuart. Each of these authors portrays women stepping outside conventional roles in order to secure a living, to care for children, or to seek self-fulfillment.

DEPICTIONS OF RACE IN POST-CIVIL WAR LOUISIANA

One of the primary differences between Louisiana, which derived from French rule, and other parts of the South may be seen in perceptions of racial categories. From the beginning of the colonial era, the French settlers operated outside of the binary racial system favored by Americans, which sought to disenfranchise people of color. During the French colonial period, slavery became a *de facto* way of life, slaveholders were required to meet minimum standards for the care and spiritual education of their slaves, and failure to meet these standards could result in slaves being confiscated by the government. In the interest of discouraging owners from abusing their slaves with impunity, the French government devised the *Code Noir* or Black Codes. These laws guaranteed certain basic rights to those held in enforced servitude. For example, the *Code Noir* cautioned slaveholders against denying their slaves religious instruction in the Catholic faith and against forcing their slaves to work on Church-sanctioned holy days; additionally, the Code allowed slaves the right to speak against their owners if they were unjustly treated. Another major difference between slave conditions in colonial Louisiana as compared to the rest of the American South regards slave marriages. The *Code Noir* expressly forbade slaves to be forced into marriages and disallowed owners from compelling slaves to live together without being married:

The ceremonies and forms prescribed by the ordinance of Blois, and by the edict of 1639, for marriages, shall be observed both with regard to free persons and to slaves. . . . We also forbid all our white subjects, and even the manumitted or free-born blacks, to live in a state of concubinage with slaves. . . . we also forbid all masters to force their slaves into any marriage against their will. (Gayarré 531-32)

Further, slaves could, in some instances, earn or purchase their freedom, and the result of this public policy was the growth of a large population of *gens de couleur libre*[2], or free people of color.

While the remainder of the Southern region viewed race as a binary proposition—an individual was either white and free or black and enslaved—because of its colonial legacy, Louisiana's racial system had developed differently. A middle racial caste, consisting of these *gens de couleur libre,* sometimes grew wealthy, purchasing substantial parcels of land which they developed into lucrative plantations. In northwestern Louisiana, for example, a colony of *gens de couleur libre* grew and gained influence in the region as a result of the manumission of Marie Thérèze Coincoin. Coincoin was originally a slave owned by the St. Denis family of Natchitoches Parish, who was granted her freedom as a result of her faithful service and her hand in saving her mistress's life. When western medical techniques had failed to cure Mme. St. Denis of a terminal illness, Coincoin reportedly begged for the opportunity to try herbal remedies and methods of folk healing. Mme. St. Denis made a full recovery, and Coincoin was not only set free, but the St. Denis family assisted her in purchasing the initial parcel of land which formed the foundation for the Isle Brevelle colony, where Melrose Plantation now stands. With the help of two slaves, Coincoin started her plantation, which grew tremendously over the next several years. As Mills has reported, Coincoin "had worked hard as a slave and she continued to do so as a free woman. . . . She was the first in the area to recognize the suitability of Natchitoches soil for the cultivation of the lucrative indigo. Only this dye, it was said, produced the desired depth of blue for the uniforms of European armies" (xxvii). Through the toil and foresight of Coincoin, the colony grew and prospered.

Coincoin devoted much of her energy in the first years to gaining the freedom of her children, eventually purchasing all of her offspring who were enslaved. Several of her children were born out of her relationship with the wealthy landowner Claude Thomas Pierre Metoyer. Before her death, she divided her extensive land holdings among these children, and "for almost half a century following her death, the Metoyers of Cane River enjoyed a wealth and prestige that few whites of their era could match" (Mills xxviii). These children, too, married and had families of their own, often intermarrying with "*gens de couleur libre* from Haiti and New Orleans. . . whose background[s] passed inspection" (Mills xxviii). As a result, the population of free people of color grew exponentially during the era leading up to the American purchase of the Louisiana territory and the Civil War.

One of the results of the intermarriage of this financially independent population of free people of color was the solidification of the tripartite racial system. Despite their mixed racial heritage, "the men of the family were accepted and accorded equality in many ways by the white planters. It was not uncommon to find prominent white men at dinner in Metoyer homes, and the hospitality was returned" (Mills xxviii). Clearly, this third, middle caste resulted in a more racially sophisticated society than that found throughout the rest of the Southern region. For example, as late as the 1850s, free people of color were voting, albeit illegally, in elections in Rapides Parish (Genovese 401). Further, as Charles Barthelemy Roussève has argued, "French and Spanish colonists of Louisiana were more considerate of their mixed-blood children than were settlers in other parts of America . . . [they] accepted them as members of their families, freed them, and educated them. Eventually, the descendants of many were totally absorbed into the white Creole group" (25). This "process of acculturation took place throughout lower Louisiana during the eighteenth century" (Hall 239), and caused incidents of passing to become common and to a large extent tacitly approved. Hence, when American law began to be enforced in the Louisiana territory, it is not surprising that the free people of color were devastated at the prospect of seeing the tripartite caste system collapse into a binary distinction whereby they became members of a group that they had traditionally considered beneath them, the African-American slaves.

French culture had not placed the kind of intense restrictions on people of color that were commonplace in the United States. People of color, especially those of African descent, were presumed to be enslaved in the United States; whereas, the presumption in Louisiana had traditionally been that a person of color was free unless compelling evidence was offered to support the claim of that individual's enslavement. Because of this presumption of freedom and because of the concentrated population of *gens de couleur libre* in places such as Isle Brevelle on the Cane River, a three-tiered racial hierarchy—consisting of enslaved African-Americans, free people of color, and whites of European descent—had evolved.[3] This racial caste system had worked well for decades in Louisiana because members of all castes followed its implicit guidelines. As Gary Mills has pointed out, "preservation of this third racial class in Louisiana society was contingent upon strict adherence to the caste system by its members" (xiv). This system began to break down when America assumed control of the Louisiana territory, and over the next fifty years, the *gens de couleur libre* saw their freedoms rapidly fall away. By the time the Civil War began, most white Louisianians shared the racial views of the American South, and the restrictions upon people of color came to be more harshly enforced in Louisiana than anywhere else in the country because of the influx of white, slaveholding Americans from other parts of the United States. The conditions for slaves in Louisiana became so bad, in fact, that being sold down the river or sold south to a Louisiana plantation, particularly a sugar plantation, was tantamount to a death sentence.

The postcolonial era in Louisiana led to a variety of changes throughout the region, especially with regard to racial attitudes and the legal status of all people of color, both those who were enslaved and those who were free. The breakdown of the tripartite caste system led to suffering for many, perhaps for none more than the *gens de couleur libre*, many of whom had built affluent lives for themselves during the more tolerant colonial era.

Reconstruction government ultimately helped few except for wealthy government officials and Northern opportunists despite the fact that it initially created better educational opportunities and allowed for the formation of churches in the African-American community. Most African Americans remained relegated to manual labor or agricultural occupations as the sharecropper system replaced slavery. The sharecropper and crop-lien systems kept workers impoverished, serving as a *de facto* system of enslavement and oppression since many poor whites and African Americans were inescapably bound to the system. Sharecroppers' incomes in any growing season were rarely enough to cover the credit which was extended to them by landowners and commissaries, thus causing many to become caught in the endless cycle of poverty and debt. Sugar cane workers, however, fared the worst of all agricultural laborers because the crop-lien and sharecropper systems were not suited to the kind of work that the sugar crop entailed. Generally, sugar workers toiled not only when cane was growing but also during cane grinding. By the 1880s, many sugar plantations had been sold to large corporations who grew the sugar, and these companies had no interest in renting shares to poor whites or African Americans. While the companies offered crude housing, they paid little to the worker, who often made less than a dollar a day.

Frustrated by the endless cycle of poverty in the 1880s, the sugar workers unionized, seeking fair wages and decent living conditions. These efforts led to the

Thibodaux Massacre of 1887. The workers, led by their advocates, the Knights of Labor, fought for increased wages since the workers had recently suffered a pay decrease because of a bad crop in 1886 and the likelihood of another in 1887. On 22 November 1887, a fight broke out between planters and strikers. Over thirty workers were killed, and many others were injured. As a result, no other significant labor movements occurred in the sugar fields until the 1950s. While cotton and sugar crops maintained steady growth, but perpetuated poverty for their workers, rice became another important crop which stimulated the economy of the Lafayette and Lake Charles area when many midwestern farmers moved to the region to start rice farms (Wall 230).

In addition to the grinding poverty created by the sharecropping system, African Americans suffered discrimination when the Louisiana legislature passed additional restrictions upon them in 1894. Interracial marriages were expressly outlawed, and by 1908, strong cohabitation statutes were passed which forbade blacks and whites from living together—to do so invited a felony conviction. Racial segregation laws were strengthened, and by 1920, Native Americans and African Americans could not cohabitate. Lynchings increased during the period from 1882 to 1952, and racial violence became a way of life for many in Louisiana.

Not surprisingly, this complicated racial history has exerted a substantial influence over the works of Louisiana writers. Some, such as Kate Chopin, George Washington Cable, Grace King, and Ruth McEnery Stuart, have at times been classified as local color writers because their work exhibited a regional flavor. However, the work of these writers transcends the merely "local," in part because they deal with universal issues such as the role of women in society and the ways in which members of society negotiate constructions of race. Lyle Saxon, Alice Dunbar-Nelson, and George Washington Cable present characters from all levels of society and from diverse ethnic backgrounds. The work of these and other Louisiana writers has helped both their contemporaries and ours toward a better understanding of the Louisiana cultural milieu.

LOUISIANA DURING THE MODERNIST PERIOD, 1919-1945

Modernism exerted its influence on American literary artists between 1914 and 1965. World War I, the Great Depression, and World War II influenced the writing of many authors of the period both in Britain and in America. The changes which these events wrought upon Europe made their way into the writing of expatriate authors such as Ernest Hemingway, Gertrude Stein, F. Scott Fitzgerald, and T. S. Eliot. Back in the United States, writers such as William Faulkner and Tennessee Williams felt the constraints of provincial, Southern society and bristled against them. The Modernist movement marked a departure, particularly in American literature, from the work of the Romantics, the Realists, and the Naturalists. Modernist texts differed in form and content from their predecessors. They reflected feelings of disenfranchisement, hopelessness, alienation, loss of community, a skewed vision of love, and the inhumanity of humans to one another; their literary forms evolved and changed incorporating experimental narrative techniques and structures never before seen in English language literature.[3]

Additionally, their content often shocked average American readers, for graphic sexual scenes, violence, and extreme cruelty generally appeared in these writings.

While the general public was sometimes taken aback by these new kinds of writing, average citizens, like these writers, grappled with many societal problems during the time spanning from the advent of World War I to the end of World War II. World War I coupled with the great influenza epidemic of 1918 led many Americans began to feel as if their worlds were unraveling. While the Roaring Twenties were an exciting time for some people, for veterans who were returning from World War I, as well as for their families, life was many times far from rosy. Many of these veterans had seen their friends die and had barely survived themselves, never completely recovering from what they had seen. High rates of alcoholism coupled with battle fatigue and exposure to damaging chemical weapons, such as mustard gas, severely reduced the quality of life and longevity of veterans.

Further, the horrors of war had led many to question why such tragedies occur. Agnosticism and atheism increased as people became disenchanted with religious doctrine and its explanations for the cruelty and devastation taking place in the world. In America, many citizens who had lived as farmers realized that the economy of the Great Depression would no longer allow them to stay on the farm, and these families, who were ill-equipped for urban life, were often forced to move to cities in hope of better opportunities. On the farm, they could raise food; in the city, they were forced to pay for all their food, and their wages generally did not cover the cost of city living. As people moved from rural communities, they began to lead a fragmented existence. Without their communities, many became isolated and often succumbed to alcohol or drugs to numb the intense pain of this isolation and its resulting sense of hopelessness. Some, instead of falling prey to alcoholism or drugs, exhibited depression and hopelessness. From 1914 to 1945, self-preservation was the rule of the day, for resources were scarce in urban areas. In rural areas, communities may have been stronger, but resources remained limited.

The hopelessness of the era was pervasive, and the literature reflected this lack of hope. In Bontemps's novel, *God Sends Sunday*, the main character, Augie, lives his life as a displaced person. His relationships with women are numerous and transient, and he continually feels disenfranchised, wandering hopeless and unfulfilled. When he stays with his family, he still remains isolated and feels little connection or happiness. A side-effect of this hopelessness was the decline in traditional values. While Louisiana's government had long been ridiculed for its crooked politics, the Long and Leche administrations illustrated political corruption at the state's highest level. Adria Locke Langley's thinly veiled portrait of Huey Long in her fictional character, Hank "Big Lion" Martin, illustrates this new morality, which in effect, allows its practitioners to run roughshod over anyone or anything that gets in their way. Many of Faulkner's characters similarly represent this new morality. Jason of Faulkner's *The Sound and the Fury* provides another example of the lack of ethics and changed morality which increased during this period.

Showing the seedier side of life had been the goal of Realists and Naturalists such as Frank Norris, Sinclair Lewis, Edward Bellamy, and Theodore Dreiser, yet lurid, sexual details had never been depicted in the ways that the Modernists would come to illustrate. These affairs and romantic entanglements often showed a skewed vision of love, which Modernist writers typically chose as a central theme or motifs for their works. William Faulkner depicts graphic images of incest which would have scandalized readers from earlier periods of time. Even the work of Arna Bontemps, an author whose writing is conservative—especially when compared to the works of writers such as Faulkner—reflects the Modernist side of Louisiana. In *God Sends Sunday*, Bontemps illustrates the lives of street hustlers and women of questionable moral virtue. While Modernist writers demonstrate graphic sexuality, they also address issues such as suicide, as can be seen in "A Summer Tragedy." The elderly Pattons face suicide because they live in a fragmented community; they have no living children, no friends, no caregivers. They love one another deeply, yet their love does not allow them to overcome their physical challenges. Their loss of hope for recovery from strokes and blindness leads them to drive themselves into the Red River, for they feel that they have no other option. These qualities typify modernist characters.

Bontemps's work, though set in the Modernist period, lacks the experimental narrative style that writers such as William Faulkner, James Joyce, and T.S. Eliot employ in their works. Linear narrative constructions rarely appear in Faulkner's novels, and his style illustrates new variations in storytelling which do not make use of traditional, linear western narratives. His work employs shifting narrators and varying perspectives on the same event, and this innovative style, termed "stream of consciousness narrative" by contemporary critics (Mahaffey 514), became one of the hallmarks of Modernist writing.

By the time that some of the expatriate writers returned to America in the late 1920s and 1930s, the Modernist movement had made its impact upon them, and their works drew upon elements which critics today ascribe to the Modernists. Those writing about Louisiana, such as William Faulkner and Adria Locke Langley—as well as writers from Louisiana including Arna Bontemps, Kate Chopin, and Lyle Saxon—depict characters who illustrate many of the aforementioned elements and show Louisiana's own Modernist influences.

OVERVIEW OF ESSAYS

This collection is organized thematically, focusing upon three of the major influences exerted on writers during the post-Civil War era: women, work, and culture; race and class; and Louisiana Modernism. The first section of this collection addresses various aspects of women, work, and culture prior to World War I. Nancy Dixon's essay focuses on the works of Sallie Rhett Roman of *The New Orleans Times-Democrat*, illustrating Roman's views of race, class, and gender and the construction of reality in two of Roman's novellas: *Tonie* and *Folette of Timbalier Island*. Roman's work, like that of many of her contemporaries, went virtually unnoticed and was out of print for decades; now, however, due largely to Dixon's research, Roman's work has re-emerged. Richard Collins's essay, "Under Reconstruction: Lafcadio Hearn in New Orleans (1877–

1887)," addresses Hearn's writings from his New Orleans years. Collins discusses the manner in which Hearn uses the term Reconstruction in his analysis of Hearn's novel, *Chita: A Memory of Last Island*. Tiffany Duet's essay, "'Do You Not Know That Women Can Make Money?': Women and Labor in Louisiana Literature," focuses upon the works of Chopin, Cable, and King to illustrate the difficulties faced by women who were forced to become self-supporting during the late 1800s and early 1900s. Joan Wylie Hall's "Living 'Amid Romance': Ethnic Cultures in Ruth McEnery Stuart's New Orleans Stories" examines the ways that the immigrant groups of New Orleans influenced the development of the city's culture. Stuart's work, like that of Roman, has been rediscovered in recent years and gives readers another opportunity to view the culture of Louisiana during the Reconstruction era.

The second section of the collection highlights the issues of race and class in Louisiana from 1865-1945. Pamela Glenn Menke's essay, "Behind 'The White Veil': Alice Dunbar-Nelson, Creole Color, and *The Goodness of St. Rocque*," focuses upon the depictions of race through the eyes of a bi-racial writer. Larry D. Griffin's essay, "Masking and Racial Passing at Mardi Gras in Lyle Saxon's 'Have a Good Time While You Can,'" examines some of Saxon's lesser-known fiction and analyzes the use of the masking motif as part of the larger folk tradition of Mardi Gras and the more constrained tradition of racial passing. Susie Scifres Kuilan writes about Grace King's *Balcony Stories*, assessing King's treatment of race and gender as represented by her use of blindness imagery. Suzanne Disheroon-Green focuses upon social class and women's choices in her analysis of Lyle Saxon's *Children of Strangers* and Zora Neale Hurston's *Their Eyes Were Watching God*. Both female protagonists choose paths which society condemns, yet they find ways to deal with the consequences of their actions. R. Allen Alexander examines Cable's depiction of race in *The Grandissimes*. Alexander argues that the African-American characters in Cable's work are multidimensional, rather than ones who are easily reduced to the flat, one-sided characters that those of his contemporaries sometimes appear to be.

The final segment of the collection examines the work of Louisiana writers during the Modernist period. Lisa Abney's essay, "Cakewalks, Cauls, and Conjure: Folk Traditions in Arna Bontemps's *God Sends Sunday* and 'Summer Tragedy,'" examines the folk traditions which appear in Bontemps's writing. While Bontemps's works were written in the Modernist period, they do not exhibit the modernist methods of experimental narrative that appear in Faulkner's work. Bontemps's work provides a realistic depiction of African-American communities during the 1920s—both urban and rural. In "William Faulkner's Two-Basket Stories," Jo LeCoeur takes a new approach to Faulkner's work by comparing its narrative structure to that employed by Louisiana and Mississippi Choctaws. This essay examines the narrative styles in *The Sound and the Fury* and *Absalom, Absalom!* Erin E. Campbell examines racial passing as embodied by a modernist text in her essay, "'The nigger that's going to sleep with your sister': Charles Bon as Cultural Shibboleth in *Absalom, Absalom!*," demonstrating the results of attempting to pass for white as depicted in Faulkner's novel. Philip Dubuisson

Castille's essay deals with the Adria Locke Langley novel *A Lion Is in the Streets*. This relatively unknown novel, overshadowed by Robert Penn Warren's *All the King's Men*, chronicles the life of a Huey Long–style politician through his rise to power. Castille's essay examines both the text and the film versions of the novel. The final essay of this collection is Suzanne Disheroon-Green's "Mr. Pontellier's Cigar and Robert's Cigarettes: Opening the Closet of Homosexuality and Phallic Power in *The Awakening*."

The writings of Louisiana authors are both regional and universal in their appeal. These writers, in their day, addressed issues that continue to effect both Southern and mainstream American culture today. The essays contained in this collection offer insight into the motivations and influences on an important group of writers who lived through a difficult era in United States history and creatively depicted this time in their works.

NOTES

1. The deduct system was a program initiated by Long and continued by Leche which automatically donated a ten percent of all state worker's salaries to the Longite campaign treasury (Wall 287-88).

2. The term *gens de couleur libre* or free person of color includes both monoracial African Americans and bi-racial individuals. For a further discussion of this issue, see Gary Mills, Virginia Domínguez, and Sybil Kein.

3. For further discussions of Modernism, see entries in Hugh Holman, Northrop Frye, and Vicki Mahaffey.

REFERENCES

Brown, Claire A. and Glen N. Montz. *Baldcypress: The Tree Unique, the Wood Eternal.* Baton Rouge: Claitor's P, 1986.

Calcote, Sharon. Unpublished memo to Barbara Roy, Ira Babin, and Phillip Jones. 12 Dec 2000.

deKeyzer, Gregory R. Olivier. *The Civil Law in Louisiana.* 2001. 1 March 2001. http://www.lna.org/l_espirit/civillaw.htm

DeLaine, Thomas. "The Civil Code." *Code Napoleon: The Civil Code.* 2001. 1 March 2001. http://frenchculture.about.com/culture/frenchculture/library.

Domínguez, Virginia. *White by Definition: Social Classification in Creole Louisiana.* New Brunswick, NJ: Rutgers UP, 1986.

Ficklen, John Rose. *History of Reconstruction in Louisiana Through 1868.* Baltimore: John Hopkins UP, 1910.

Frye, Northrop, Sheridan Baker, and George Perkins. *The Harper Handbook to Literature.* NY: Harper, 1985.

Gayarré, Charles. *History of Louisiana: The French Domination.* 3rd ed. Vol 1. (4 vols.) New Orleans: Armand Hawkins, 1885. 531-540.

Genovese, Eugene D. *Roll, Jordan, Roll: The World the Slaves Made.* New York: Vintage, 1976.

Hair, William Ivy. *Bourbonism and Agrarian Protest: Louisiana Politics, 1877-1900.* Baton Rouge: Louisiana State UP, 1969.

Hall, Gwendolyn Midlo. *Africans in Colonial Louisiana: The Development of Afro-Creole Culture in the Eighteenth Century.* Baton Rouge: Louisiana State UP, 1992.

Holman, C. Hugh and William Harmon. *A Handbook to Literature.* 6th ed. New York:

Macmillan, 1992.

Kane, Harnett T. *Louisiana Hayride: The American Rehearsal for Dictatorship, 1928-1940.* New York: William Morrow, 1941.

Kein, Sybil, ed. "Introduction." *Creole: The History and Legacy of Louisiana's Free People of Color.* Baton Rouge: Louisiana State UP, 2000.

Liebling, A. J. *The Earl of Louisiana.* New York: Simon & Schuster, 1961.

Lonn, Ella. *Reconstruction in Louisiana After 1868.* New York: Russell & Russell, 1918.

Mahaffey, Vicki. "Modernist Theory and Criticism." *The Johns Hopkins Guide to Literary Theory and Criticism.* Ed. Michael Groden and Marin Kreiswirth. Baltimore: Johns Hopkins UP, 1994.

Martin, Thomas. *Dynasty: The Longs of Louisiana.* New York: Putnam's Sons, 1960.

McGinty, Garnie W. *Louisiana Redeemed: The Overthrow of Carpet-bag Rule, 1876-1880.* New Orleans: Pelican, 1941.

Mills, Gary B. *The Forgotten People: Cane River's Creoles of Color.* Baton Rouge: Louisiana State UP, 1977.

Moore, J.H. *Andrew Brown and Cypress Lumbering in the Old Southwest.* Baton Rouge: Louisiana State UP, 1967. 87.

National Archives and Records Administration. "American Originals: Exhibit: The Louisiana Purchase." March 1996. 1 March 2001. http://www.nara.gov/exhall/originals/loupurch.html.

Rousséve, Charles Barthelemy. *The Negro in Louisiana: Aspects of His History and His Literature.* New Orleans: Xavier UP, 1937.

Shugg, Roger W. *Origin of Class Struggle in Louisiana: A Social History of White Farmers and Laborers During Slavery and After, 1840-1875.* Baton Rouge: Louisiana State UP, 1939.

Stokes, George. "The Day the Whistle Didn't Blow: Folklife Resources in the Louisiana Timber Industry." *Louisiana Folklife,* 6.2 (1981): 1-16.

Toth, Emily. *Kate Chopin: A Life of the Author of the Awakening.* New York: Morrow, 1990.

Tunnell, Ted. *Crucible of Reconstruction: War, Radicalism and Race in Louisiana, 1862-1877.* Baton Rouge: Louisiana State UP, 1984.

Wall, Bennett H., Light Townsend Cummins, Judith Kelleher Schafer, Edward F. Haas, and Michael L. Kurtz. *Louisiana: A History.* 3rd ed. Wheeling, IL: Harlan Davidson, 1990.

Wilds, John, Charles L. Dufour, and Walter G. Cowan. *Louisiana Yesterday and Today: A Historical Guide to the State.* Baton Rouge: Louisiana State UP, 1996.

Wells, Carol, ed. *War, Reconstruction and Redemption on Red River: The Memoirs of Dosia Williams Moore.* Ruston, LA: McGinty, 1990.

WOMEN, WORK, AND CULTURE IN RECONSTRUCTION LOUISIANA

Sallie Rhett Roman of the New Orleans *Times-Democrat*: Race, Women, and Southern Aristocracy in the Novellas, *Tonie* (1900) and *Folette of Timbalier Island* (1900)

Nancy Dixon

A relatively unknown, but nonetheless vital, addition to the canon of post-bellum Louisiana writers is Sallie Rhett Roman, a turn-of-the-century writer for the *New Orleans Times-Democrat*. In her writing, Sallie Roman addresses many of the same issues as her Louisiana contemporaries Lafcadio Hearn, Grace King, Kate Chopin, and Ruth McEnery Stuart. Bloodlines and ancestry, women's roles, artistic outlets for women, social conventions, marriage, and women's independence, as well as Christianity and spirituality all play important roles in Roman's work. Unlike her more liberal, and by today's standards, enlightened contemporaries, however, Roman also championed such causes as white supremacy, male superiority, and the Southern aristocracy. She first raises these issues in her political editorials, but her interest in them spans her entire writing career, and we can learn more about her as a turn-of-the-century, Southern, woman writer by examining the role that these issues play in her later fiction, particularly in her two novellas, *Tonie* and *Folette of Timbalier Island*.

Roman was born Sarah Taylor Rhett in 1844 to Elizabeth Burnet and Robert Barnwell Rhett, a firebrand secessionist from Charleston, South Carolina. In 1863, Sallie married Judge Alfred Roman, son of the first Creole governor of Louisiana, André Bienvenu Roman, of Vacherie, Louisiana. Although the couple's marriage seemed by all accounts to be a happy one, their fathers may have arranged it to some degree, as they were political acquaintances at the very least. After the Civil War, as the political climate of New Orleans shifted, and Alfred Roman lost his appointed judgeship, Much of the family sugar plantation, upriver in Vacherie, had been claimed by the Mississippi River and lacked the irreplaceable free workers that slavery provided. Consequently, Sallie Roman entered the workforce in 1889 to help provide for her large family of eleven children, many of whom later entered the workforce as well.[1]

Writing for the New Orleans newspaper seemed a natural line of work for

Sallie Rhett Roman, for the Rhett family had owned the pro-secessionist *Charleston Mercury* for many years leading up to and during the Civil War. Her husband also was associated with several Louisiana newspapers, including the French *L'Autochtone* and *L'Abeille*. Although it seems unlikely for a woman of Sallie Roman's social standing to begin a career as a political editorialist, by 1892, unlike in the rest of the nation, over half of the newspapers in Louisiana had women writers and even distinguished editors, such as Pearl Rivers[2] (*Biographical and Historical Memoirs* 170). Roman's career as a political editorialist lasted only two years before she turned to writing short fiction for the newspaper. During those two years, Roman signed her articles simply S. R. Although anonymity among editorialists was a common practice of the time, women working in such a capacity was not. Robert Bush, Grace King's biographer, claims that King signed her first article to appear in the *Times-Democrat* P. G. because using a pseudonym "was entirely proper for a young woman of New Orleans, where the achievement of newspaper publicity was frowned upon" (52).[3] Besides, a woman of Roman's social standing could hardly broadcast the fact that she was now the family breadwinner. However, after her husband's death, and once she began contributing fiction to the newspaper, she began signing her pieces, using the gender neutral S. Rhett Roman. During Roman's short career as a political editorialist with *The New Orleans Times-Democrat*, from 1889 to 1891, she championed conservative views that would carry over into her fiction. She undoubtedly got the job as a political editorialist, in part, because of her husband's political connections with the newspaper's owner, "Major" E. A. Burke, a Bourbon-Lottery-Ring politician like Roman's husband, Alfred.[4] Sallie Roman, like the conservative Bourbon-Lottery-Ring faction, believed in home rule in the South, conservative taxation, and white supremacy. Of those three basic tenets, white supremacy is the one subject that Roman continued to address after her transition from political editorialist to weekly fiction writer, and she did so either by omitting African-American characters from her fiction altogether or by assigning them the traditional, inferior position of servant to rich, white characters.

Historians have discovered that the very conservative views held by women of Roman's social standing were the rule, not the exception. Indeed, most aristocratic, white women in Louisiana would have sided with Roman, and perhaps that, in part, accounts for her popularity as a writer. She often received fan mail and continued to submit weekly pieces to the *Times-Democrat* for over twenty years.

Most of Roman's early fiction pieces are short local color sketches, but as she grew as a writer, her works became less moralistic and cautionary. She concentrated on the Gothic spectacle in her early fiction, which often included a damsel in distress caught in a horrific scene, only to be rescued by a daring, young hero. In her later and longer works, her female heroes, although still often saved by a dashing, young hero, were much more capable and independent. Surely, Roman's own independence as the family's primary provider had to influence her shift from the helpless and hapless hero to the clever and competent characters that her later protagonists became.

One of the most interesting aspects of Roman's writing is often what she chooses to omit from her stories, particularly concerning the subject of race. An analysis of her fiction establishes a clearer picture of her as an enigmatic artist keenly aware of her audience and also offers a closer examination of the historical, cultural, and literary climate of Louisiana at the turn of the century. Roman, for the most part, ignored blacks in her writing, thereby contributing to the concern that Toni Morrison addresses in her monograph, *Playing in the Dark: Whiteness and the Literary Imagination*, that "traditional . . . American literature is free of, uninformed, and unshaped by the four-hundred-year-old presence of, first, Africans and then African-Americans in the United States" (5). Roman first practices complete omission of blacks from her writing in her editorial, "Immigration," published in *The Times-Democrat* on 3 May 1891.

In "Immigration," Roman observes that post-Civil War Louisiana lacks a slave workforce to provide "free" labor for bolstering the economy and capitalizing on the state's natural resources. Roman recommends immigration as a solution, not the employment of the native black population. Specifically, Roman desires only the "good population from the Northwest and from Europe," meaning white immigrants, preferably Nordic, not those of color. In fact, blacks are one of the few races that Roman refuses even to acknowledge. However, few others escape her censure, as she refers to "those criminal Italians," and calls the Chinese "a race infected with ineradicable vices." Jews she terms "a tenacious, energetic and money-making people" (Roman, "Immigration" 12). Her overt racism, though startling to readers today, is in keeping with the politics that she and the newspaper embraced. Her disregard for blacks and Italians crosses over into her fiction, particularly into her novellas, *Tonie* and *Folette of Timbalier Island*.

Roman's strength as a writer lies in her longer serialized fiction, which appeared in 1900, approximately midway through her career. A critical analysis of two of her novellas, *Tonie* and *Follette of Timbalier Island*, reveals just how much Roman draws on the writing fashionable in Louisiana at the turn of the century, such as local color and the *roman-feuilleton*, serialized, sentimental fiction popular in French newspapers of the time. We can also see that she pays tribute to the *bildungsroman* and formulaic women's fiction so widely read earlier in the nineteenth century. In *Tonie* and *Folette*, the influence of such popular Louisiana fiction as Grace King's *Monsieur Motte* (1888), Lafcadio Hearn's *Chita* (1888), and Ruth McEnery Stuart's *The Story of Babette* (1894) is also undeniable. All these works involve the struggles of a young, beautiful orphan and the questions of her true ancestry. As in much of the popular women's fiction of the time, Roman's heroines do indeed triumph and are rewarded in the end with marriage to a handsome, wealthy, aristocratic hero. Tonie's and Folette's husbands are both lawyers, probably a tribute to her husband, Alfred Roman. However, as much as Roman is concerned with bloodlines in her fiction, she conspicuously avoids the question of race and miscegenation.

In *Tonie* and *Folette of Timbalier Island* both protagonists are in search of their true ancestry, but unlike Grace King's *Monsieur Motte* and Kate Chopin's "Désirée's Baby," there is no question of miscegenation, a subject that Roman never addresses in any of her writing. Roman is concerned only with classism, not racism. Her heroines are undoubtedly white; they simply cannot be married off to rich love interests until it is discovered that they are from aristocratic lineage.

Tonie opens with a young New Orleans lawyer, Jack Hamilton, lost in the marsh on a duck hunting expedition. The young, beautiful Tonie, who lives in this all but deserted marsh with her father, Pierre Drouhet, and their black maidservant, Suzette, rescues him and takes him to meet her father. Jack, very predictably, falls in love with Tonie, but they are separated when Tonie and her father must return to France in order for him to reclaim his rightful inheritance and title which his evil and conniving brother has stripped from him.

Tonie was serialized in the newspaper over a ten-week period, and Jack is brought to the Drouhet cottage to meet Tonie's father, but not the black Suzette, in the first installment.[5] Suzette does not even appear until the third installment, even though she helped rear Tonie and serves as the "black mammy" figure ever-present in the plantation literature of the South. Grace Elizabeth Hale writes in *Making Whiteness: The Culture of Segregation in the South, 1890–1940*: "The mammy figure revealed . . . a desperate symbolic as well as physical dependence on the very people whose full humanity white Southerners [including Roman] denied " (112). Whereas other white, Southern writers, such as Sherwood Bonner, Joel Chandler Harris, and Thomas Nelson Page, included the "black mammy" figure in their fiction, usually for humorous or poignant effect, Roman's portrayal of the black nursemaid is downright dismissive, as is Tonie's attitude when she finally introduces Suzette to Jack: "That's Suzette, our cook. My old nurse" ("Pierre Drouhet's" 6). Roman's attitude toward the black nursemaid coincides with that of her character, Tonie, who treats Suzette with "a sweet imperiousness," ever aware of their dominant–subservient relationship ("Pierre Drouhet's" 6). Roman assigns Suzette only four short lines in the entire novella, and after the sixth installment, her character disappears completely.

Suzette's role as the homemaker and mother figure in a household of only three must be much more significant than Roman is willing to admit. Tonie's and her father's lives would have been significantly altered without Suzette, yet Roman's indifference toward her black characters—and perhaps her racism—seems to keep her from allowing characters such as Suzette to have any real substance. In fact, Roman's attitude toward her characters seems rather cavalier in that she allows a single white man and a single black woman to live together with absolutely no threat of sexual contact, especially given the very real history of white man's sexual exploitation of black women observed by other Louisiana writers.

Suzette's male counterpart, Ambroise, receives similar treatment from Roman. He is a cook at the hunting lodge in English Lookout, where Jack initially sets out to go duck hunting. In the first installment, Jack and his hunting partners discuss the different exotic meals that Ambroise will prepare, but Ambroise does not appear until the second installment, and then he utters a mere three words, "All right, sir," when acknowledging Jack's commands. Roman never bothers to make Ambroise's role in the novella very clear. We only know that he lives alone, forsaken in the desolate marsh, where he remains only to serve and cook for the various wealthy, white hunters, such as Jack Hamilton, who deign to stop by for a few days of sport. Yet, like Suzette, he is a faithful servant, for Roman writes that "Ambroise always expected him [Jack]" ("Counter Currents" 6). Nonetheless, Ambroise is a more fully realized character than Suzette, perhaps because he is male, as Roman espoused male superiority in much of her writing. Both characters speak French, but Suzette musters only a few exclamations now and then, whereas Ambroise speaks in complete sentences at least three times. Ambroise is also accomplished at the art of French cooking, and his character is not abandoned during the course of the story. In fact, most of his dialogue—all two sentences—appears in the last installment of the novella. Still, his role is vague, and as with the role of Suzette, it furthers the plot in no way. The two are simply stock characters.

Nevertheless, the characters Suzette and Ambroise seem almost complex in light of two of the other black servants who appear in the novella, Johnson and Ann. Roman never does identify these servants as being black, but nineteenth-century readers would have rightly assumed, as we do, that they are indeed African American. In the second installment, as Jack is fed up with the hustle and bustle of city life and longs to see Tonie again, he orders his butler/valet, Johnson, to pack his valise. We never see nor hear about this character again in the course of the novella, and we are offered no introduction or explanation for his existence. Given that he is Jack's butler/valet, it seems odd that he is not at least in the background every time Jack enters the scene. Does Roman find blacks so insignificant or unpalatable that she is able to ignore the invaluable roles that they played in white life, or has she simply forgotten their importance in her own life because she no longer has slaves or can afford extensive help? Perhaps both are close to the truth.

Afterward, Tonie and her father mysteriously disappear from the marsh, leaving Suzette behind to tell Jack, who then turns to his New Orleans society friends, Maude Sefton and her sister, Julie Catesby, for solace. The Seftons' African-American maid, Ann, appears in the second installment, with no introduction, and Ann is neither identified nor mentioned again until the seventh installment which appeared some five weeks later. After that, Ann is completely abandoned after never having uttered one line of dialogue. Like other black characters in Roman's fiction, Ann and Johnson are talked *about*, ordered around, but seldom or never speak.

As Toni Morrison goes on to explain, black characters in fiction by white American writers have historically served "as the objects of an occasional bout of jungle fever" or "to provide local color or to lend some touch of verisimilitude or to supply a needed moral gesture, humor, or bit of pathos" (15). In Roman's case, these characters are so shapeless and dim, in every sense of the word, that they add nothing to the text. In fact, we learn more about Roman and her racist values through her minimal use of African-American characters than we do about the characters themselves or their effect on the white characters in Roman's works.

Roman's racism is not aimed only at African-American characters in her fiction, as is seen in her portrayal of the swarthy, Italian fisherman, Jo Benachi in *Folette of Timbalier Island*. Roman was not alone in her scathing characterization of Italians in Louisiana fiction. Ruth McEnery Stuart, in her novel *The Story of Babette*, also sets forth an unflattering portrayal of the Italian family that kidnaps her hero. Roman's novella also owes much to Lafcadio Hearn's *Chita*, which appeared in the *Times-Democrat* twelve years earlier. Both works involve heroines who are thrown alone into the world by a devastating tempest. Both Roman and Hearn also criticized the writing of Émile Zola as too pessimistic, and, according to Arlin Turner, Hearn sought a style that was "romantic and idealistic," a style to which Roman also aspired (xxxiii).

Folette, like Tonie, is motherless and lives on the deserted yet Edenic Louisiana Gulf Coast island of Timbalier, where she was orphaned when her father's Danish merchant vessel shipwrecked during a violent storm.[6] Initially, Roman describes Folette as even more plucky than Tonie, with "exuberant spirits, reckless daring, and all that surplus energy which led her so often into difficulties of various kinds and degrees, but through which she emerged usually triumphant" ("Folette" 2:6). Roman's description of Folette foreshadows that Folette, even more so than Tonie, must endure the "trials and triumph" of which Nina Baym writes in *Woman's Fiction: A Guide to Novels by and about Women in America, 1820-1870*. According to Baym, "a heroine . . . beset with hardships, finds within herself the qualities of intelligence, will, resourcefulness, and courage sufficient to overcome them" (22). Whereas Tonie simply has to overcome the question of her ancestry, Folette must wield a dagger to escape her kidnapper, Jo Benachi. Just as Tonie learns how to manage a pirogue and is therefore able to rescue Jack Hamilton, Folette learns how to swim, sail, fish, and use a knife. These practical lessons provide Folette, like Tonie, with "dauntless courage and self-reliance" (Roman, "Folette" 2:6). Both heroines are fortified by the stark Acadian landscape, but in *Folette of Timbalier Island* Roman writes, "how vastly superior Folette was, how different in race and nature from the sturdy brown-visaged Acadian, Sicilian and half-Spanish children . . . of that queer isolated little island" (2:6). It is no accident that Folette's father, it is later discovered, was a wealthy Danish merchant named Thurge Petersen. In *Folette*, Roman does not hide her disdain for people of color or her high regard for Nordic races any more than she does in her editorials.

No matter how derisively Roman's handles her non-white characters in *Folette of Timbalier Island*, the characters at least further the plot and are more fully realized than the forgotten black characters in *Tonie*—probably because they are not black. In fact, Roman first introduces Benachi rather favorably as the "most prosperous fisherman of the island . . . half Greek, half Italian, his black eyes and straight features recalled the old Roman race, and gay, reckless and daring, Benachi made more money, and spent more, than all the others" ("Folette" 2:6). Ruth McEnery Stuart likewise describes the Italian family that kidnaps Babette as fundamentally good, but in both works, these Italians end up being villains. Helen Taylor writes in *Gender, Race, and Region in the Writings of Grace King, Ruth McEnery Stuart, and Kate Chopin* that Stuart's "unsympathetic portrayal of the Italian community can be seen to voice the deep hostility of the city's bourgeois whites toward the New Orleans 'dagos' during the 1880s and later . . . creating for northern editors and readers a sense of the dangers, excitement, and evils of what they already saw to be an exotic multiracial city" (107–8). Roman's audience would have held the same hostility toward Italians as Stuart's audience. That hostility, at least in part, accounts for Benachi's complete transformation from hardworking fisherman to kidnapper and potential rapist.

Folette's passage into womanhood is a struggle which is typical of a *bildungsroman*. As her surrogate parent, Valsin, an old Acadian fisherman, notices her budding sexuality and sees that Jo Benachi is not blind to it either, he rushes Folette off the island to the shelter of the New Orleans convent, where many of Roman's heroines complete their rites of passage. During the three years that Folette spends in the convent, she changes her name to Joris, a name that she found painted on a piece of her father's dismantled ship years earlier. This change is significant. Folette, which means little wild one, no longer uses the French diminutive ending, opting instead for the strong and foreign Joris. However, she has changed more than just her name and can no longer return to the Edenic Timbalier Island as the little girl who bounced on the knees of the local fishermen. Roman clearly presents the options available to young, unmarried women of the time, other than marriage. In New Orleans, Folette is a "caged bird," and her singing is the pride of the convent, but she cannot go on stage, where she will be tempted by "wrong ambitions." However, if she returns to the island to take up teaching, as Tonie finally does in Roman's earlier novella, Folette will be "cut from all human intercourse." Folette does return to the island "prison," where she has no recourse except to marry well or to recover her hidden family fortune (Roman, "The Taming" 2:5). Predictably for Roman, she does both, but not until she overcomes the dastardly Benachi.

Initially, Benachi takes on a brotherly role in the novella, and Folette can recall the "gay dances she had had on the beach with Jo and the boys and girls of the village . . . and they would all dance and sing." But after Folette transforms into the mature woman Joris, she remembers only "how rough he was sometimes, and [that] he had a hateful look." When thinking of him she has a "slight shudder" and asks "was it repulsion?" (Roman, "The Taming" 2:5) Folette's changed attitude toward Benachi is understandable in light of her own passage into womanhood, but Benachi's changed attitude toward her, that of sexual predator and kidnapper, is harder to swallow. According to Roman, his motivation and villainous actions stem only from his inherently evil, Italian nature. Besides, Folette must end up with the wealthy American lawyer, Guy Fulton, who washed up on the shore of Timbalier Island just before she left for the convent. Her aristocratic lineage would demand as much.

Once Folette reaches puberty, Valsin hastens her off the island and away from her dark–skinned playmates, but most of all away from Jo Benachi. Although Roman considers the Sicilian Benachi a sexual threat to Folette, he is still white. Roman would never place her white heroines in a similar situation with a black villain because then she would be forced to address the issue of miscegenation, which she refuses to do in any of her writing. Her black characters remain in positions of subservience, never posing a sexual threat to any of her white characters.

Roman remains conscious not only race, but also of class in her writing. In the end, Folette and Tonie are permitted to re-enter the privileged society which had shunned them for so long, but only because they belong there. Through no fault of their own, they are temporarily excluded from that society, and each must fight her way back to where she belongs. Tonie suffers the sins of her father, who is duped into thinking that he murdered his brother some twenty years earlier. But when the truth is discovered that Tonie is actually the Duchess de Morillac, she is embraced by Jack Hamilton and all of the New Orleans elite. Likewise, after Folette outwits Benachi, and she and Guy Fulton discover her true Danish, aristocratic lineage, the New Orleans upper crust welcomes her as one of their own. Her heroines are not only members of the upper class; they have the financial security that goes along with that membership, something that evaded Roman for most of her adult life.

Roman's father and husband preceded her in death, yet neither of them left her in any way financially secure. So, ironically, Roman spent her last years struggling financially and not as one of the wealthy aristocrats of her fiction. She submitted fiction to the *Times-Democrat* until 1910, three years after moving from New Orleans with her sons, Charles and Alfred, to Asheville, North Carolina, where she remained for three years. In 1914, she moved to Columbia, South Carolina, where she died in 1921. Roman continued to write articles that were never published, many of which resemble her early political editorials, including such titles as "The Menace of the Boll Weevil" and "Commercial Importance of Improved Municipal Works."[7] But for the last two years of her life, she fought the United States government for her son Rhett's military pension, which she finally did receive. Even after supporting herself and her family with her writing, to some degree, she still tried to depend, usually unsuccessfully, on the men in her family for financial support. Nonetheless, Roman espoused a certain amount of independence among women in her fiction. She is not the only Louisiana writer whose life and work often seem to contradict one another; such is also the case with Kate Chopin and Grace King.

In 1874, the White League was formed, a paramilitary group fighting to restore white supremacy and Democratic rule to Louisiana. In New Orleans, a bloody battle was fought at the foot of Canal Street in September of 1874, between the Metropolitan Police and the White League over the ousting of Republican Governor Kellogg (Wall 204). Roman's husband was a prominent member of the White League, as was Kate Chopin's husband, Oscar. Grace King's brother was a sergeant in the White League, and all three men fought at the Battle of Liberty Place (Taylor 6). All three women apparently supported the racist efforts of the men in their families, even the seemingly more enlightened Grace King and Kate Chopin. Even though King and Chopin did address racial injustice and miscegenation in their fiction, Roman's racist approach to her fiction is more in keeping with the issues that she and her husband championed throughout their lives. In fact, three months before her death in 1921, Roman returned to New Orleans for the dedication ceremony of the statue commemorating the Battle of Liberty Place.

Including Roman in the canon of post-bellum Louisiana writers allows us to gain more insight to the lives of women writers and their readers in turn-of-the-century New Orleans and the issues that concerned them. Although Roman has not received the acclaim that her perhaps more deserving peers have, she nonetheless had great appeal and was read by a wider audience than they for over twenty years.

We might not agree with Roman's views on such issues as race, class, women's suffrage, marriage, and male superiority, but her longevity with the newspaper indicates that many of her readers did indeed support her conservative views on these issues.

NOTES

1. For more information on Roman's life and writing see Nancy Dixon's *Fortune and Misery*.

2. Pearl Rivers is the pen name of poet and newspaperwoman Eliza Jane Poitevent Holbrook Nicholson (1849-1896). She was the first woman owner-manager of a major newspaper, *The New Orleans Daily Picayune*, from 1876 until her death in 1896.

3. P. G. stands for Pan Gnostics, a New Orleans literary society of which King was a member, according to Robert Bush.

4. The Louisiana Bourbon politicians were so named after the European Bourbon families that were restored to the throne after the fall of Napoleon. Burke, the state treasurer, was allied with the infamous Louisiana Lottery and the New Orleans political faction, "the Ring." For more on Bourbon-Lottery-Ring politics, see Bennett Wall.

5. The ten installments of *Tonie* appeared in serialized form in the *Times-Democrat* as follows: "Tonie" (3 June 1900), "The Drifting Mists of the Marshes" (10 June), "Pierre Drouhet's Cottage on the Knoll" (17 June), "Wanderings" (24 June), "Counter Currents: Whither?" (1 July), "Fauvette" (8 July), "The Village on the Lake Shore" (15 July), "Rocks and Precipices" (22 July), "Homeward" (29 July), and "The Drifting Mists of the Marshes" (5 August). For purposes of ease and clarity, I will refer to them collectively as *Tonie*.

6. *Folette of Timbalier Island* also appeared in serialized form in the *Times-Democrat* over seven weeks: "Folette of Timbalier Island" (9 September 1900), "Folette of Timbalier" (16 September), "Folette of Timbalier" (23 September), "The Taming of the See Gull" (30 September), "The Falcon" (7 October), "Southward" (14 October), and "Back to Timbalier Island" (21 October). I will refer to them collectively as *Folette of Timbalier Island*.

7. These unpublished articles are in the possession of her grandson, Charles Roman of Columbia, South Carolina.

REFERENCES

Baym, Nina. *Woman's Fiction: A Guide to Novels by and about Women in America, 1820–1870*. Ithaca, NY: Cornell UP, 1981.

Biographical and Historical Memoirs of Louisiana. Vol. 2. Chicago: Goodspeed, 1892.

Bush, Robert. *Grace King: A Southern Destiny*. Baton Rouge: Louisiana State UP, 1983.

Chopin, Kate. "Désirée's Baby." *The Complete Works of Kate Chopin*. Ed. Per Seyersted. Baton Rouge: Louisiana State UP, 1969. 240–245.

Dixon, Nancy. *Fortune and Misery: Sallie Rhett Roman of New Orleans, a Biographical Portrait and Selected Fiction, 1891–1920*. Baton Rouge: Louisiana State UP, 1999.

Hale, Grace Elizabeth. *Making Whiteness: The Culture of Segregation in the South, 1890–1940*. New York: Pantheon, 1998.

King, Grace. *Monsieur Motte*. New York: Armstrong, 1888.

Morrison, Toni. *Playing in the Dark: Whiteness and the Literary Imagination*. New York: Vintage Books, 1993.

Roman, Sallie Rhett. "Counter Currents; Whither?" New Orleans *Times-Democrat*, 1 July 1900, 6.

—. "Folette of Timbalier Island." *The New Orleans Times-Democrat*, 9 September 1900, 2: 6.

—. "Immigration." *The New Orleans Times-Democrat*, 3 May 1891, 12.

—. "Pierre Drouhet's Cottage on the Knoll." *The New Orleans Times-Democrat,* 17 June 1900, 6.

—. "The Taming of the Sea Gull." *The New Orleans Times-Democrat*, 30 September 1900, 2: 5.

Taylor, Helen. *Gender, Race, and Region in the Writings of Grace King, Ruth McEnery Stuart, and Kate Chopin.* Baton Rouge: Lousianan State UP, 1989.

Turner, Arlin. "Introduction." *Chita* by Lafcadio Hearn. Chapel Hill: U of North Carolina P, 1969.

Wall, Bennett, ed. *Louisiana: A History.* Arlington Heights, IL: Forum P, 1984.

Under Reconstruction: Lafcadio Hearn in New Orleans (1877–1887)

Richard Collins

Like the word revolution in the decades following World War II, the term reconstruction became, in the decades following the Civil War, a word charged with contradictory connotations, either benign or dangerous, depending on one's beliefs and background. The stated purpose of Reconstruction was to restore the political rights of the seceding states, but to a traditional Southerner nostalgic for antebellum life if not for the Confederacy, Reconstruction meant, at worst, the destruction of a way of life, and at best, the imposition of an experiment in social engineering that, in practice, encouraged corruption in the name of worthy political ends and social ideals. Once tainted in this way, the word lost its denotation as the rebuilding of some tangible structure or of some idea in the mind. It took an outsider like Lafcadio Hearn, neither Northerner nor Southerner, but a Greek-Irish wanderer who was to become an honored Japanese citizen, to use the word without prejudice, to restore its subtleties, and indeed to reconstruct Reconstruction.

Personally uprooted, politically unaffiliated, and culturally divided, Lafcadio Hearn was familiar with the complexities of identity politics and the problems associated with the constructed realities of self, social systems, and cultural artifacts. When he arrived in New Orleans in 1877 at the end of Reconstruction, Hearn was ripe to resolve these issues, not only in terms of his own identity but also in his relations with the worlds of politics and culture. The word, Reconstruction, thus, becomes a semantic nexus through which we can see Hearn rebuilding his identity on three levels: his personal identity as a Greek-Irish orphan of Latin temperament, European education, and Far Eastern sympathies; his political identity as a progressive thinker who was inclined toward egalitarian ideals; and his professional identity as a man of letters whose interests lay in the work of scholarly archaeological reconstruction and whose talents lay in the translation and interpretation of dead or dying cultures.

Lafcadio Hearn's ten years in New Orleans were pivotal in his life and career.

Arriving from Cincinnati, where his notoriety as a sensationalist reporter was enhanced by the personal scandal of having married a former slave, Hearn was impressed with New Orleans as a good place for a dreamer with literary aspirations to reconstruct himself, leaving behind his identity as Paddy Hearn, police reporter, to become Lafcadio Hearn, *litterateur* (Murray 17). Given free reign by the local newspapers, *The Item* and *The New Orleans Times-Democrat,* to write what he wanted, Hearn immersed himself in Creole culture, turning out impressionistic sketches of life in the Crescent City, in addition to book columns, translations and fiction. Unlike George Washington Cable, who was criticized for being condescending toward Creole culture, Hearn appreciated the resistance to progress and the sensuous appreciation for life that he found north of Canal Street in the French Quarter. By 1887, however, Hearn had become disenchanted with the city's sad beauty of physical decay and moral corruption and was ready to explore other cultures, traveling first to the West Indies before settling in Japan. In New Orleans, however, he developed his prose style in significant ways (not all salutary, perhaps) on a variety of topics that revealed his interest in preserving ways of life that were in danger of being lost.

Before leaving New Orleans for New York and Martinique in 1887, Hearn had published five books of translation and cultural interpretation and had written a sixth, a work of fiction, *Chita*, which was published in 1888, a year after his departure. In each of these works, he proved himself not only a creative translator of French literature—his first book was a translation of Théophile Gautier's *One of Cleopatra's Nights and Other Fantastic Romances* (1882)—but also, as Beongcheon Yu and Hephzibah Roskelly have each noted, an astute "cultural translator" in his two collections of retold tales from world literature, *Stray Leaves from Strange Literature* (1884) and *Some Chinese Ghosts* (1887). His appreciation for Creole culture is reflected in the two volumes collecting Creole culture that remain historically and linguistically significant: *La Cuisine Créole: A Collection of Culinary Receipts* and *Gombo Zhèbes: Little Dictionary of Creole Proverbs, Selected from Six Creole Dialects*, both published by W. H. Coleman in 1885 to take advantage of the World International Exhibition of 1884 in New Orleans. He also appreciated the even more exotic ethnic and linguistic mixtures to be found in the swamps and wetlands south of New Orleans, as shown in his impressionistic masterpiece, *Chita: A Memory of Last Island*, published first in *Harper's Magazine* in 1888 and in book form by Harper's in 1889.

His New Orleans career began when Colonel John W. Fairfax employed Hearn as an assistant or "literary" editor in June 1878 when he was most in need of employment. Hearn had been in the city for seven months, living a hand-to-mouth existence, and had just recovered from dengue, or breakbone fever, a mild form of the yellow fever that killed over 4,000 people in the city that summer. *The Item*, which Fairfax began with Mark F. Bigney as a cooperative paper run by journalists and printers, was "a little two-page paper, too insignificant at that time to be preserved even in the city archives or in the public libraries" (Hutson 201). In this paper Hearn published most of his impressionistic sketches of New Orleans, which he called "fantastics"—meditations or prose poems on love and death— that as

Charles Woodward Hutson notes:

were in full accord with the sombre atmosphere of the trebly stricken city to which he had come—city with a glorious and joyous past, but just then ruined by three horrors:—recent war, misrule under the carpet-baggers, and oft-recurring pestilence. He had come expecting much from a semi-tropical environment. He found sorrow and trouble and a wasted land; and his mood was soon in unison with the disastrous elements around him. (199)

Hearn had experienced firsthand the oft-recurring pestilence, having spent the war years in Ireland and the Reconstruction years in Cincinnati, yet he could see the "wasted land" and the "disastrous" (Hutson 199) after-effects of Reconstruction for himself.

Hearn's temperament and his status as a foreigner caused him to remain apolitical, or as apolitical as a journalist might be in post-Reconstruction New Orleans. Like other writers who had come from the North, Hearn tended to take his cue on local politics from the natives, in his case, from George Washington Cable. While it is true that Hearn was "openly sympathetic with regional demands for self-rule and for an end to reconstruction measures imposed from outside" (Skaggs 106), Hearn held few if any deep convictions about Southern politics, and his home-rule sympathies derived from general principles rather than from the peculiar predicament faced by the South. As Yu points out, Hearn really wanted to leave his identity as a political reporter behind in Ohio, his last two pieces on Louisiana politics for the *Commercial* being written under the pseudonym Ozias Midwinter (from Wilkie Collins's 1866 novel *Armadale*) and "only under a virtual ultimatum from Cincinnati" (Yu 85). In "A Romance of Bitterness" (Hearne, *Commercial*, 14 January 1878), Hearn describes the career and grave site of the first "carpet-bag Governor" of Louisiana, W. C. C. Claiborne, but proceeds primarily through quotation of other sources (Hearn, *Occidental* 1: 246). His "New Orleans Letter" of the same period (*Commercial*, 5 January 1878) describes the city not merely as moribund after the period of the Civil War and the measures taken during Reconstruction, but dead: "This period of decay seems to me the close of the romantic era of Southern history" (*Occidental* 1: 244). Later in his literary career, Hearn speaks of the reconstruction of the lost Southern heritage. In one of his first impressions of the city, he speaks repeatedly of resurrection.

While Hearn was liable to idealize the romantic aura of the antebellum South, as discussed by Anne Rowe and Michael Kreyling, he could also on occasion rise to make a moral point when it came to racial inequities. More often, however, Hearn was the bemused observer whose work in *The Item* and *The Times-Democrat*—which consisted of columns, editorials, book reviews, translations, cartoons and poetic sketches—tended to attempt to strike a timeless note. Whether he invoked the ghosts of the past or he predicted the politics and scientific discoveries of the future, his work added literary or philosophical spice to an otherwise topical news day full of political and parochial gossip.

Hearn's apolitical bent did not, however, prevent him from turning his pen to the occasional political satire. "A Visit to New Orleans" (*Item*, 10 May 1879), for example, is a satirical piece that, changing a few topical details, could have been published in a New Orleans newspaper today. The title's visitor turns out to be the Devil, who finds that he has no work to do in "the great City of Pleasure" because everyone in it is going just where the Devil himself is going—to Hell: "The Devil had not been in New Orleans since the period of Reconstruction—a period at which, our readers may remember, it was proverbially said that New Orleans was 'going to the Devil'" (Hearn, *Writings* 1: 124). Hearing that radicalism has been overthrown and that there is a "rumor of reform in politics in Louisiana," the Devil decides to see these changes for himself; during his visit, however, he discovers that, except for the *Picayune*, the newspapers are too virtuous for his taste, but at least the police stations are sufficiently corrupt, as is the auditor's office, which is "almost as good as Radicalism" (*Writings* 1: 125). Indeed, all the public institutions please him because they can

do my work better than I can do it myself, and the people seem to be just fools enough to let them do it. Instead of honest poverty, I find vicious poverty; instead of reform, demoralization; instead of law, I find lawyers; instead of justice, oppression. What Carnival King ever found a city so well prepared for him? I guess I shall leave at once; for I have no work to do as yet in Louisiana. (*Writings* 1: 126)

In a final parting shot, the Devil perches atop the State House and discovers that he may as well leave a "subaltern" to do his job for him, since things are going his way already in Louisiana: "They have an embargo on reform here, it seems to me—just as they have on commerce. After all, New Orleans in 1879 is not very much holier than New Orleans in 1866. I guess I'll adjourn" (*Writings* 1: 126-7). Such damning approval by the Devil suggests that Reconstruction has been a complete failure.

Hearn is far more likely to use the word reconstruction in an aesthetic sense. In "*Les Coulisses*" (*Item*, 6 December 1879), written a few months after the article describing the Devil's visit, Hearn recounts a night at the opera. In this impressionistic fantasy, the theater provides the pretext for Hearn to revisit one of his favorite themes, the Buddhist perception that this life with its deceptive scene-changes is only an illusion, here depicted by the tearing down and building anew of the stage machinery. The entrance of the stage hands breaks the pleasant operatic illusion: "The spell is broken for a moment by Beings garbed in the everyday attire of the nineteenth century, who have devoted themselves to the work of destruction and reconstruction—to whom dreamers are an abomination and idlers behind the scenes a vexation of spirit. "*Va t'en, inseq' de bois de lit!*" (Scat, bedbug!) (*Writings* 2: 233–34). Hearn is speaking not only of the pleasant illusion of the stage, but of the Vieux Carré, Louisiana, and the Old South as colorful stage sets which have been invaded by those who would try to change the setting, reform the infrastructure, and destroy the picturesque atmosphere to reconstruct a new post-bellum society. Hearn himself would, of course, identify with those "idlers behind the scenes" who will have nothing to do with the practical work of either destroying or rebuilding the New South but would rather observe and comment on the process. The final joke is at his own expense, as the Creole stage hands say to the lie-a-bed dreamer, "*Va t'en, inseq' de bois de lit!*", although the Creole idler might well say the same to the industrious carpetbaggers who had come out of the woodwork.

For Hearn, life itself is opera, an illusion more or less pleasant depending on how the stage effects are managed. Since politicians are the stage hands of the public arena, politics is therefore, like all practicalities, a necessary evil, but one should keep in mind that they neither write the score nor sing the libretto:

The music of the many-toned Opera of Life envelops and absorbs the soul of the stranger—teaching him that the acting behind the Curtain is not all a mimicry of the Real, but in truth a melodrama of the visible, tangible, sentient life, which must endure through many thousand scenes until that Shadow, who is stronger than Love, shall put out the lights, and ring down the vast and sable Curtain. (*Writings* 2: 236)

The politicians who enact the sham of the visible world are hardly worth notice in the great scheme of things, and Reconstruction is but one phase in a recurrent shifting of the cosmic landscape.

Reconstruction as an aesthetic concept is carried over into Hearn's reading of other New Orleans writers, especially those concerned with capturing the ephemeral local color. In his review of *The Grandissimes* (1880), Hearn expressed his doubt that George Washington Cable's controversial novel would ever "become a favorite with residents of the Creole city;—its spirit has already been severely criticized by a contemporary;—its paintings are not always flattering to native eyes;—its evocation of dead memories will not be found pleasing" (*Writings* 1: 168–69). In citing Cable's "evocation of dead memories" by setting his novel in 1803, the date of the Louisiana Purchase, Hearn is considering the historical romance as an artistic reconstruction used to offset the dreary reality of the contemporary political Reconstruction. Hearn calls Cable's novel "a genre study of inimitable verisimilitude" (*Writings* 1: 168) but is careful to point out its topicality, bearing "a terrible resemblance to terrible realities" (*Writings* 1: 166) in the political arena of 1880.

Cable himself plays upon the two senses of Reconstruction, the aesthetic and the political, when Honoré Grandissime says to Joseph Frowenfeld: "There are but two steps to civilization, the first easy, the second difficult; to construct—to reconstruct—ah! there it is! the tearing down!" (349). What Honoré identifies as the easy step is the original construction of the Grandissime mythology, the constructed reality of a cultural tradition which his kinsman Agricola Fusilier prefers to the competing structure of history. In the Reconstruction debate between sectionalism and nationalism—that is between the adherents of the rights of states and regions versus those of federal unity—Agricola and Frowenfeld would have to square off against one another, with Frowenfeld coming out the victor. What Honoré realizes, and Agricola cannot, is that the tenure of the old construction of reality (as a tradition locally determined) has come to an end. Such was the feudal, heroic, or epic construction of the Grandissime myth, which parallels *avant la lettre* the Confederacy itself.

What Honoré calls reconstruction, or "the tearing down" necessary for any rebuilding project, is to Agricola, the exemplar of the mythic tradition of the antebellum South, destruction pure and simple. Honoré's grasp of the matter is more complex and, like Frowenfeld's, more forward-looking, since reconstruction is to him what we now might call "deconstruction": an unmasking of the constructed nature of moral and social values, such as Agricola's, that have been taken for granted as essential truths or "reality." Such a progressive interpretation of reconstruction is embodied in the revaluation of Honoré Grandissime's name, which he shares with his bi-racial half-brother, Honoré, free man of color, (f.m.c.). First, the very existence of a double whose difference must be indicated by a legally required suffix, f.m.c., begs the question of a stable identity; second, the Americanization of Creole culture is voiced in a linguistic shift that is mirrored in the narrative, which ends with Honoré (the French accent characterizing him as the "honored" scion of the family) adapting to, and surviving in, the new American political paradigm, while Honoré, f.m.c., emigrates to France, where he dies. To survive, in other words, Honoré must act according to the code of honor (now a noun, without the French accent) promoted by Frowenfeld as he adapts to the new American political and social reality. This personal reconstruction of the environment would have appealed to Hearn because it is entirely in keeping with Darwinian and especially Spencerian ideas of adaptive evolution.

For each of these characters, then, reconstruction implies a destruction of one way of life caused by an examination of the premises that have held up the entire social system, a system which remained unreconstructed until it was brought down by its own inequities (slavery, but also the gradual disenfranchisement of the free people of color of Louisiana in the years leading up to the Civil War). Agricola represents both the strengths and weaknesses of the inherited value system, complete with its clan loyalty and selfish prejudices. Honoré, on the other hand, tries not only to preserve the best of the tradition but also to demonstrate that the strengths of the tradition itself can foster flexibility and fairness through a devotion to honor, not as a sectional (or familial) value, but as a universal (or absolute) value. Honoré's taking on his namesake, Honoré, f.m.c., as a business partner to create *Grandissimes Frères* deprives the Northerner (in this case, Frowenfeld) of the monopoly on progressive values and assures both Honorés (and honor itself) of survival in the new system. Agricola, on the contrary, clings to his inflexible mythology, struggles to preserve the master–slave relationship, and perishes at the hand of Honoré's dark double. Reconstruction, Cable seems to argue, is more an ideological and ethical inner resource than a political vicissitude.

Cable's play upon the various meanings of reconstruction is more overtly political than Hearn's aesthetic sense of the term. This may be due to Cable's very different sense of history. After all, Cable grew up in New Orleans before the war, went through the war as a soldier, and understood the construction-destruction-reconstruction sequence *as* a real historical sequence. Hearn, on the other hand, tends to view the historical sequence as illusory, a simultaneous and haunted layering of era upon era. This difference may account for Cable's being the better writer of narrative, while Hearn's talents lay in interpretation, translation, and criticism. For Cable, construction meant the active building of a culture, destruction being only the necessary transition or inevitable working out of the destiny of a culture flawed at its root, in the South's case flawed by the fundamental inequity of slavery, and in Louisiana's case, by the inequity of the caste system;

Reconstruction was the painful purging of outmoded values, accompanied by the judicious preservation of that which did not hinder the progressive agenda.

Always the artist, and already interested in the Buddhist view of history as illusion, Hearn seems to have seen Reconstruction almost entirely in literary terms. And why not? As a historical period, Reconstruction was officially over with the Compromise of 1877, the same year that Hearn arrived in the South. As Hearn wrote in his "explanatory" note to *Stray Leaves from Strange Literature*, "these fables, legends, parables, etc., are simply reconstructions of what impressed me as most fantastically beautiful in the most exotic literature which I was able to obtain" (*Writings* 2: xvii). In a sense, everything that Hearn wrote was similarly a reconstruction, whether it was the impression of a moment or a review of a book in which he tried, in the fashion of Walter Pater, to tell not "what it is" but only "the peculiar impression which, as a work of art, it produces on the reader" (*Writings* 1: 170). Like most of Hearn's other collections, *Stray Leaves* attempted to capture the essence of stories, legends, myths, and folklore to preserve those fragments of a dying culture that had already passed or was in the process of swiftly passing away.

What Yu calls the "imaginative reconstructions" of *Stray Leaves* became the prototype of Hearn's work in other genres, each a sort of translation, whether condensation, interpretation, variation, or alloy of Oriental and Occidental motifs. These "alloyed" genres and "twice-told or even thrice-told tales" all occupy a mediating position, whether between past and present, between East and West, between North and South, or between literary forms. The central theme of *Stray Leaves*, "the perennial human dichotomy between passion and wisdom" (Yu 49), is also the central theme of much of American literature of the time, both Southern and Northern, that portrays the caricatures of the Cavalier South and the Yankee North. Fond of the Salmacis and Hermaphroditus myth—Hearn's favorite legend, according to Yu (21, 60, 274)—Hearn is less interested in balancing opposing views than in discovering the essential contradiction, the hidden antithesis within the visible thesis in Western terms, or the *yin* within the *yang* in Eastern terms. Sometimes this requires seeing the woman within the man, the black man within the white, the American in the Creole, or the Yankee in the Southerner. In each case, it requires a form of reconstruction in the deconstructive sense.

The last book that Hearn published while living in New Orleans was *Some Chinese Ghosts*, another "alloy," but with this book Hearn was able "to unify the manifold passions" (Yu 55). Instead of apologizing for the reconstructions, as he had in the preface to *Stray Leaves* (even the title of the earlier work is self-effacing), Hearn felt confident in his more focused scholarship and in his own ability to capture the aesthetic truth of the Chinese tales, specifically their "weird beauty" (*Writings* 1: 213). The sense of focus upon, even specialization in, a recognizable *fin de siècle* literary niche seems to have given Hearn heart and to have allowed him to feel that he had completed his own period of personal reconstruction, tearing down the journalist to rebuild a man of letters.

Isolation and loss were lifelong preoccupations for Hearn, who saw himself as a lover of islands and a wandering ghost. An abandoned child, he had difficulty sustaining personal or professional relationships and tended to burn his bridges behind him. On his journey from the Greek island of his birth (Santa Maura or Leucadia, after which he was named) to the island nation of Japan, which adopted him and made his name, New Orleans was a crucial station. Hearn saw the city as an island of Latin repose in a sea of American industry, offering him a place of isolation and stasis where he could examine how the past haunted the present in peaceful coexistence, as though here were a place where the ruins of the past—both cultural and personal—could be preserved.

Hearn's preservationist tendency is most evident in *Chita: A Memory of Last Island*, his first long fiction and his last book completed in New Orleans (but published after he had left). An apocalyptic vision of loss, this novella reconstructs the life of an island that no longer exists except in memory, only to describe its devastation. *Chita* describes a storm surge on 10 August 1856, that sweeps away L'Île Dernière, "the most fashionable watering-place of the aristocratic South," twenty miles west of Grand Isle (*Writings* 4:150). The implication is that a culture's existence depends upon its ruins, and if there are no ruins, then upon its stories. In his Creole sketches, Hearn creates a record of a culture in danger of passing away due to Americanization, and in *Chita*, of a milieu that disappears due to flood. Much of *Chita*'s narrative is topographical, the landscape serving as the protagonist. The meager human plot concerns a pampered child of a society doctor and a mother who drowns in the storm. The girl is rescued from the flood and raised in the bayous by a Spanish fisherman and his wife, who call the child Conchita, a symbolic resurrection of their own dead child of the same name. Departing from his original intention to have the child return to the island after being raised by nuns in New Orleans, Hearn simply has her live out her life happily in the bayous and islands, implying that Chita is better off in her new life as a foundling among simple folk than she would have been if she had been returned to the splendor of her former privileged life in the city. Thus, Hearn's preservationist project has less to do with a nostalgia for aristocratic antebellum society than with a romantic yearning for an even more distant Arcadian time of rustic harmony.

While the story begins in the antebellum period and ends after the war, *Chita* can be read as a post-bellum allegory of the war that swept away a civilization, a sort of *Gone with the Wind* (and Wave). By setting *The Grandissimes* in 1803, Cable had drawn a parallel between the cession of Louisiana to the United States and the period of Reconstruction; similarly, Hearn draws a parallel between the storm of 1856 and the Civil War. The dominant imagery used to describe the storm and its aftermath is borrowed from the vocabulary of war: "Ocean's cavalry;" "bannerets;" "besieging tides;" "wan battlegrounds where the woods made their last brave stand against the irresistible invasion;" "Grand Terre is going: the sea mines her fort, and will before many years carry the ramparts by storm" (*Writings* 4:152–3). Natural disaster and war are elliptically equated: "Since the war the ocean reclaimed its own" (*Writings* 4:150). From the vantage of the 1880s, the narrator points out that a similar fate came to Grand Isle after the war, invaded not by the North but by Nature.

Hearn calls the postwar period "the great decadence" (*Writings* 2: 378) in "The Post Office" (*Times-Democrat*, 19 October 1884), a contributory sketch for *Chita*.

He draws upon martial imagery to describe the destruction, but whether the decadence is due to politics or nature is left ambiguous: "when the great decadence came, the rude sea gathered up its barbarian might, and beat down the strong dikes, and made waste the opulent soil, and, in Abimelech-fury, sowed the site of its conquests with salt." Hearn looks back fondly on the "quivering splendor of sugar-cane" in "the autumn of the old feudal years" (*Writings* 2: 378) when New Orleans was the center of a thriving economy, and its surrounding plantations were enriched by the overflow of economic abundance. But the history of "the old New Orleans ends with the Civil War," writes Lyle Saxon in *Fabulous New Orleans*:

The period of Reconstruction in Louisiana is the most tragic part of its story. New Orleans had been one of the richest—if not the richest—city in the country. It became one of the poorest. Not only were men stripped of all they had, but the basis of their commercial life had been destroyed. The slave system was gone, and the commercial usefulness of the river had been destroyed by the railroads. (255)

After the war, Hearn observes in *Chita*, the plantation economy is reconstructed as a site for tourism: "the plantation-residences have been converted into rustic hotels, and the Negro-quarters remodeled into villages of cozy cottages for the reception of guests" (*Writings* 4:150). Hearn's ironic tone can be heard perhaps more clearly in "The Post Office," where "the old plantation-bell, of honest and pure tone, now summons the visitor to each repast" (*Writings* 2: 378–79), the bell that once commanded slaves now calling tourists to dinner.

Indeed, tourism sets the tone. *Chita* begins as a travelogue, inviting readers to embark from the New Orleans docks as the narrator guides them slowly through the swamps to Last Island. In the bayou landscape, trees are compared to decomposing skeletons that reach out their wounded stumps from "deepening graves" (*Writings* 4:153). The grim and hallucinatory imagery prepares us for the even more horrifying reality of the storm's strewing of actual, instead of metaphorical, corpses. Hearn collected his description on his visits to Grand Isle on *The Times-Democrat*'s company boat, but according to Arlin Turner, he found many of the details of the storm and its aftermath in newspaper archives, especially those of the *Picayune* (xxiv–v). This does not quite account for his peculiar selection of detail, such as Chita's being found with her dead mother on a floating billiard table, an example of *bizarrerie* (a word that Hearn might have Anglicized) that aspires to symbolism.

While *Chita* may today seem saccharine in its resolution, unwieldy in its structure, and overwrought in its style, it proved immensely popular with Victorians. Hearn himself later renounced its style, relegating it to his Period of Gush. The style of *Chita* and "The Post Office" seems peculiarly suited to the subject matter and completely of the time. Pre-Raphaelite in their florid and detailed descriptions of beauty and horror, as well as in their odd, antiquated, and often foreign-flavored diction, these two works suit style to subject by giving the impression that just as the landscape is composed of decomposing animal and vegetable material, so Hearn's prose contains fragments from a ruined literary tradition decomposing before our eyes. The "half-drowned" landscape, like that of

William Morris's poem "The Haystack in the Flood," paints a grim setting for a portentous event, in Hearn's case for naturalistic Gothic horror. Macabre imagery is dominant: "Grotesque roots—black, geniculated, gnarly—project from the crumbling banks like bones from an ancient grave;--dead, shrunken limbs and fallen trunks lie macerating in the slime. Grim shapes of cypress stoop above us, and seem to point the way with anchylosed knobby finger" (*Writings* 2: 374–75). The reader may pause at such words as "geniculated," "frondescence," and "anchylosed" as upon phrases from unfamiliar tongues. Hearn's English is sometimes as weird as the bayous' dialects, which is the precise effect that he is after, just as he compares the island landscape to an unfamiliar script: "those desolate islands, shaped like the letters of an Oriental alphabet" (*Writings* 2: 376). Like James McNeill Whistler and Aubrey Beardsley, Hearn later moved away from the excesses of Pre–Raphaelitism under the influence of Japanese simplicity of design. Commenting on Hearn's appreciation for Flaubert's strange novel, *The Temptation of Saint Anthony,* and for Japanese aesthetics, Guy Davenport has suggested that "such splendid accuracies of aesthetic strategy and premonition can be located in all his work. The man could *see*" ("Lafcadio Hearn," n.p.) Whatever Hearn may have thought of his New Orleans style in retrospect, it is difficult to imagine a style cleaner or leaner than Hearn's capturing the messy aftermath of the hurricane, or of the Civil War, nor the odor of post-bellum political corruption "macerating in the slime." For all its flaws, *Chita* is, as Davenport writes, Hearn's "masterpiece in fiction," achieved by fusing "French narrative" and Winslow Homer (n.p.).

The subtitle of *Chita: A Memory of Last Island* announces its subject as the reconstruction of a way of life that has been lost, *except to memory*. But *whose* memory? Hearn's ideas about cultural memory, based on Herbert Spencer's race memory (Yu 68), were not too far from Jung's theory of the universal unconscious, although for Hearn cultural memory, like myth, seems to be encoded in the spirit of place rather than the psyche. While Hearn had no direct knowledge of the storm that swept away L'Ile Dernière, he had heard the stories. Similarly, the central myth in Cable's *The Grandissimes*, the story of Bras-Coupé, was the ur story around which the novel was written after the story was rejected by the magazines on its own merits. Cable's story-within-the-story is told three times in a single day by separate narrators in separate parts of the city. Each individual telling is said to be told with its own elaborations and idiosyncrasies, but Cable acts as redactor, distilling the three versions into an essential narrative, which he admits is identical to none of the actual tellings of the story, but which serves as a sort of canonical rescension that preserves the primary substance. The essence of myth, as opposed to literature or history, is that the story can be told simultaneously, reproduced and disseminated as cultural memory, added to and elaborated upon, without damage to the narrative substance. The setting for Cable's telling of the tale of Bras-Coupé itself suggests an epic bard imparting cultural memory: "the youth and beauty of the Grandissimes were gathered in an expansive semicircle around a languishing fire, waiting to hear a story, or a song, or both, or half a dozen of each, from that master of narrative and melody, Raoul Innerarity" (Cable 216). To understand Hearn's idea of cultural memory in relation to Cable's sense of cultural myth, it is useful to know what he had on his mind when he read *The Grandissimes*.

Before writing his review of the novel, which appeared 27 September 1880, Hearn was preoccupied by the persistence of cultural memory, as seen in several essays that he wrote for *The Item*, including a pair of companion essays, Platonic dialogues called "Hereditary Memories" (22 July 1880) and "Metempsychosis" (7 September 1880). Hearn's indebtedness to Plato's idea of recognition, or "memory-echo," is clear, but while he uses a Platonic dialogue to get the idea across, he also suggests parallels in Buddhist thought about the transmigration of souls:

A Buddhist would tell you that the soul, through all its wanderings of a million years, retains faint memories of all it has seen or heard in each transmigration and that each of us now living in the flesh possesses dim and ghostly recollections of things heard and seen aeons before our birth. I am not a believer in Buddhism nor in the soul; but I attribute the existence of these vague memories to hereditary brain impressions. (*Writings* 2: 244)

The word "hereditary" implies that the phenomenon has to do less with cultural memory than with racial memory, "inherited just like a mole, a birthmark, a physical or a moral characteristic." Our brains, Hearn explains, are palimpsests, "all covered over with inscriptions written there by the long caravans of Thought" (*Writings* 2: 245). These "hieroglyphic inscriptions" are invisible but "material and real" manifestations of "hereditary impressions."

This fanciful theory wrapped in scientific terminology has several implications for Hearn's reading of Cable in post-Reconstruction New Orleans. For men like Agricola Fusilier, custom has power to perpetuate institutions; tradition is stronger than history, culture stronger than civilization, and memory stronger than objective fact. For Hearn, not all such memory is one's own. In "Metempsychosis" Hearn again takes care to put all this in scientific rather than theological terms. The transmigration of souls, he contends, is simply physics, the conservation of energy, and the recirculation of atomic particles, just Nature "refashioning the paste in her awful laboratory into new forms of being" (*Writings* 2: 260). Such refashioning, it appears, breaks down all essential identity, including personal, gender, familial, social and racial identities: "We have lived innumerable lives . . . we have been women as well as men;—we have changed our sex a thousand times like the angels of the Talmud." The result is a vision of history as layered, cyclical and ultimately illusory: "It is not the first time we have sat together on the night of September 6;—we have done so in other Septembers, yet the same; and in other New Orleanses, the same yet not the same" (*Writings* 2: 260–61).

Hearn's strongest statement about Reconstruction policies, especially as they affect relations between the races, occurs not in his writings about New Orleans but in his novella *Youma: The Story of a West-Indian Slave* (1890). As an outsider, Hearn was fairly reticent about racial matters while in New Orleans, but he must have felt freer to express his views after he left the city, especially when he was reminded in Martinique of Louisiana's post-bellum social dynamics. Speaking of the *da*, the slave nurse of white children, Hearn praises a type that he says was created by a Spencerian process of racial "selection" even more than by political action, and that likewise has become a vestige of the past through the same process: "The *da* is already of the past. Her special type was a product of slavery, largely created by selection: the one creation of slavery perhaps not unworthy of regret— one strange flowering amid all the rank growths of that bitter soil" (*Writings* 4:263– 64). Already, the *da* is taken out of the specificity of Martinique so that Hearn can generalize not only about slavery but also about the results of emancipation and universal suffrage, effects to be seen not only in the West Indies but in Louisiana:

> The atmosphere of freedom was not essentially fatal to the permanence of the type; but with freedom came many unlooked-for changes: a great industrial depression due to foreign rivalry and new discoveries—a commercial crisis, in brief—accompanied the establishment of universal suffrage, the subordination of the white element to the black by a political upheaval, and the total disintegration of the old social structure. The transformation was too violent for good results; the abuse of political powers too speedily and indiscriminately conferred, intensified the old hates and evolved new ones: the races drew forever apart when they needed each other the most. Then the increasing difficulty of existence quickly developed egotism: generosity and prosperity departed together; Creole life shrank into narrower channels; and the characters of all classes visibly hardened under the pressure of necessities previously unknown. (*Writings* 4:263–64)

Having delivered this interpolated essay on race politics in general, Hearn returns to his story of post-emancipation Martinique. I have quoted this passage at length because, although ostensibly about the effects of emancipation in the West Indies, it is an astute analysis of the social, economic, and moral effects of Reconstruction in the American South. As a preface to the narrative of *Youma*, this social analysis serves the same purpose as the topographical and climatological analysis of the Louisiana wetlands that prefaces *Chita*. Each provides an introduction to a setting and a story in terms of inexorable forces that determine the destinies of his characters' lives.

After a decade of work in New Orleans, Hearn left for New York with a sense of himself as a man of letters specializing in "weird beauty," a polished literary style that was capable of combining fact and interpretation, and a growing knowledge of ethnography that would come in handy in his travels to the West Indies and Japan. What he gave back to the intellectual life of New Orleans, a provincial city with cosmopolitan pretensions, was a breath of continental and even world culture. Tired and beaten after the war, overrun with carpetbaggers and scallywags during Reconstruction, New Orleans needed to see itself in an improved light. Hearn gave New Orleans a tarnished mirror in which to see itself as it once was, and was still, in certain enchanted pockets of the city. Such belated cultural romanticism as Hearn's might be seen as conservative or even reactionary; it is certainly preservationist. Just as Hearn meticulously cataloged and indexed his notebooks, his lifelong concern in his writing was less to create works of art than to capture and preserve what was in danger of passing away, whether in Japanese folktales and the ancestor worship of the traditional Shinto religion, or in Creole folkways and the ghosts of old New Orleans.

Paul Murray writes: "Hearn was relentlessly autobiographical in every medium in which he wrote" (22). In his later years he began increasingly to incorporate personal memories into his cultural divagations on Japan, suggesting that there was always an autobiographical impulse behind Hearn's lifelong reconstructive impulse. Like Walter Pater, Hearn was a brilliant stylist who felt the fragility of what the author of the "Conclusion" to *The Renaissance* saw as a "tragic dividing of forces on their ways." Hearn's impressionistic prose, like Pater's, was an attempt at preserving one's experience of places, objects, and people to appreciate "the passage and dissolution of impressions, images, sensations" and so combat the "continual vanishing away, that strange, perpetual, weaving and unweaving of ourselves" (Pater 59, 60). As a child who was abandoned first by his Greek mother and then by his Irish father, Hearn seems to have put all his trust into a blending of cultural with personal memory, a form of narrative self-therapy that began during his "reconstructive" years in New Orleans and ended in his championing of Japanese traditions. His funeral in Japan made him "the first foreigner ever buried in Japan with a Buddhist rite" (Murray 301), a fitting, if ironic, end for one who, in an effort to dissolve his ego, spent much of his life communing with ghosts.

REFERENCES

Cable, George Washington. *The Grandissimes*. New York: Scribner's, 1928.

Davenport, Guy. "Lafcadio Hearn." *The Art of Lafcadio Hearn*. Charlottesville: U of Virginia Library, 1983.

Hearn, Lafcadio. *Occidental Gleanings*. Ed. Albert Mordell. 2 vols. Freeport, NY: Books for Libraries P, 1967.

—. *Chita: A Memory of Last Island. Writings*. Vol. 4. 143-257.

—. *Creole Sketches. Writings*. Vol. 1. 101-208.

—. *Fantastics and Other Fancies. Writings*. Vol. 2. 195-386.

—. *Martinique Sketches. Writings*. Vol. 3. 115-390; Vol. 4. 3-141.

—. *Some Chinese Ghosts. Writings*. Vol. 1. 209-399.

—. *Stray Leaves from Strange Literature. Writings*. Vol. 2. 1-194.

—. *Two Years in the French West Indies: A Midsummer Trip to the Tropics. Writings*. Vol. 3. 1-111.

—. *Writings of Lafcadio Hearn, The*. 16 vols. Boston and New York: Houghton Mifflin, 1922.

—. *Youma: The Story of a West-Indian Slave. Writings*. Vol. 4. 259-371.

Hutson, Charles Woodward. "Introduction." *Fantastics and Other Fancies. The Writings of Lafcadio Hearn*. Vol 2. Boston and New York: Houghton Mifflin, 1922.

Kreyling, Michael. "After the War: Romance and the Reconstruction of Southern Literature." *Southern Literature in Transition: Heritage and Promise*. Ed. Philip Castille and William Osborne. Memphis: Memphis State UP, 1983. 111–16.

Murray, Paul. *A Fantastic Journey: The Life and Literature of Lafcadio Hearn*. Folkestone: Japan Library, 1993.

Pater, Walter. *Selected Writings of Walter Pater*. Ed. Harold Bloom. New York: Columbia UP, 1974.

Roskelly, Hephzibah. "Cultural Translator: Lafcadio Hearn." *Literary New Orleans: Essays and Meditations*. Ed. Richard S. Kennedy. Baton Rouge: Louisiana State UP, 1992.

Rowe, Anne. *The Enchanted Country: Northern Writers in the South 1865–1910*. Baton Rouge: Louisiana State UP, 1973.

Saxon, Lyle. *Fabulous New Orleans*. Gretna, LA: Pelican, 1995.
Skaggs, Merrill Maguire. "After the War: Northern Writers in the South." *Southern Literary Journal* 12:1 (Fall 1979): 106.
Turner, Arlin. Introduction. *Chita: A Memory of Last Island*. By Lafcadio Hearn. Chapel Hill: U of North Carolina P, 1969. xxiv–v.
Yu, Beongcheon. *An Ape of the Gods: The Art and Thought of Lafcadio Hearn*. Detroit: Wayne State UP, 1964.

"Do You Not Know That Women Can Make Money?": Women and Labor in Louisiana Literature

Tiffany Duet

Critics have classified Southern literature of the post-bellum period in numerous ways, including local color fiction,[1] the literature of plantation life,[2] and Reconstruction literature.[3] Critics attempting to define this period offer such definitions based on formulaic constructions that set Southern literature apart from other American works written during the same century. Despite the relative predictability of post-bellum literature, scholars value the synchronic depiction of works so entrenched in a time and place. Generalizing the South has proven troublesome to many of the same scholars, for even within this section of the United States, differences abound. Indeed, scholars of Southern literature often credit Louisiana authors for distinctive contributions to post-bellum literature: the abundant examples include George Washington Cable's Creoles,[4] Grace King's resistance to plantation fiction,[5] and Kate Chopin's early feminism.[6] Louisiana literature, as Barbara Ewell points out, "defines a space that is both psychic and geographic, a site where the Other—of gender, race, religion, sexuality, ethnicity—is often more clearly demarcated than in the rest of America" (9). Not only can we identify in the works of these writers a society clearly stratified on the basis of race, class, and gender, but we can also see how those socially encoded roles affect women's choices. Cable, King, and Chopin devote literary space to characters facing economic annihilation, a worry that beset most Southerners of the time. Through their texts, we glimpse a phenomenon rarely portrayed in other texts—that of women engaging in financially productive work outside the home. These authors often demonstrate the ways in which marriage stymies the power of women, reinforcing the paternalistic ideals well entrenched in late nineteenth-century Southern culture.

Much of nineteenth-century Southern literature focuses on the ornamental role of white women, who were expected to be hospitable, cheerful, beautiful, and graceful (Scott 4–5). Their passivity, Anne Goodwyn Jones notes, built up the egos and images of virile Southern men (19). Ideal Southern women, in many cases, outwardly fit these characterizations, but in addition, they were economical, practical, and hard-working. Despite these attributes, white Creole women, particularly those from the upper social classes, understood that working outside the home was out of the question. The woman's sphere of influence was limited to the domestic, and woman's employment outside the home was thought to be indicative of difficulties within the family unit. When faced with the burden of inadequate finances, women could not take on working roles and maintain their social standing. Accordingly, fictional portraits of white Creole[7] working women illustrated some kind of defect in the family. Working women resided outside of society, either living with husbands who were incapable of supporting the family financially, or worse yet, living alone as spinsters. Cajun women also fell victim to the image of the ideal woman, despite the fact that Cajuns[8] were considered social inferiors to Creoles since Cajuns descended from French peasant exiles, rather than the more socially desirable descendants of aristocracy. Even farther down on the social and economic tiers were African-American women, who were expected to labor and did so into the post-bellum era, regardless of their marital status.

Though he sets *The Grandissimes* in antebellum New Orleans, George Washington Cable's fiction contributes to the study of post-bellum literature, for as Philip Butcher explains, "only superficially is he writing about olden times. . . . He chose to depict Creoles like those he might have seen . . . in his own time" (33). Anna Shannon Elfenbein notes that Cable did substantial research on the racial injustices in New Orleans during the post-bellum era, and he tried to highlight those wrongs through his writing (27). She argues that Cable investigates problems affecting women, pointing out that because *The Grandissimes* reveals "the crushing impact of sexism and racism on women, it is tempting to assume that Cable was making a conscious attack on sexism as well as racism. . . . But whether Cable was consciously approving of the strong current of feminist protest of the period or not, his early characterizations of women reveal that he was buffeted by that current" (33). Whether or not he was an early sympathizer with women's issues, Cable does not allow his free female characters to successfully live independently from men. Some of his female characters may bemoan their situations in life, and Cable seems to imply that they can neither be happy nor remain in proper social standing without the support of male characters.

Cable also seems to follow tradition by neglecting to present the labor of African-American women. Though set in antebellum Louisiana, the novel excludes depictions of hard-working slaves. According to Susan Tracy, this omission is not surprising, for much antebellum literature slights actual working conditions of slaves (143–44). Cable only sketches for us a minor character, Palmyre Philosophe, who had once been a lady's maid before being given her freedom. In New Orleans, she is reputed for her "skill as a hair-dresser" though we never see her at work (Cable, *Grandissimes* 60). The narrator spends more time describing her voodoo skills, yet Palmyre seems to employ these skills as more of an avocation than a vocation. Cable also draws for us a picture of a bonded black woman, Clemence, who obviously must work to survive. The *marchande* peddles her cakes every morning and evening throughout the French Quarter. Cable, however, spends little time in developing Clemence's character, beyond the description of her death. Perhaps, her death indicates her insignificance in this highly structured society even though her work contributes to its survival.

Louis Rubin, Jr. notes that *The Grandissimes* should be remembered for its attempt to portray "society in transition" (79). The novel pointedly depicts women's concerns for survival, concerns which are articulated in much of post-bellum Louisiana fiction. Two of the main female Creole characters are a widowed mother and an unmarried daughter, Aurora and Clotilde Nancanou, who reside together. Though established in society's upper echelon, they spend much of their time worrying about earning a living. Always behind on their rent, only a few "picayunes," Aurora sometimes relies on voodoo for financial assistance. Clotilde attempts to raise money by teaching music; the narrator explains, "With the two music scholars whom she then had and three more whom she had some hope to get, she made bold to say they could pay the rent" (Cable, *Grandissimes* 66). She also teaches "embroidery scholars" to earn money, yet despite the pair's efforts, the women cannot make ends meet (Cable, *Grandissimes* 67). Peggy Whitman Prenshaw characterizes the Nancanou women as stereotypical Southern ladies, "shy, delicate, patient" (74), yet this reading overlooks Aurora's inclination to change the lot assigned to them by society. The most telling passage about their restricted place appears when Clotilde states that the hardest thing about being a lady is "not how to make a living, but how to get a living without making it" (Cable, *Grandissimes* 255). She further explains:

we are compelled not to make a living. Look at me: I can cook, but I must not cook; I am skillful with the needle, but I must not take in sewing; I could keep accounts; I could nurse the sick; but I must not. I could be a confectioner, a milliner, a dressmaker, a vest-maker, a cleaner of gloves and laces, a dyer, a bird-seller, a mattress-maker, an upholsterer, a dancing teacher, a florist. (Cable, *Grandissimes* 255)

However, she cannot. As Creole ladies and members of society, these women must uphold the image of the idly rich Southern lady expected of Creoles living in New Orleans, which, according to Merrill Maguire Skaggs is a patriarchal ideal (160). Although these ladies try to maintain appearances, they are realistically concerned for how they can afford to do so (Cleman 56).

Aurora and Clotilde live, perhaps, on the fringe of liberation through necessity because they choose to remain single. Their flirtation with independence may be in their blood, for Aurora's mother—also called Clotilde—became an outcast by refusing to find a husband. She numbered among the sixty women who were the "last royal allotment to Louisiana, of imported wives" (Cable, *Grandissimes* 25). When she refuses to marry anyone or to dedicate her life to the Ursuline nuns, the Grand Marquis tries to convince her that life would be much easier if she would only "submit" to the influence of the church or a husband (Cable, *Grandissimes* 26). After she still refuses, the Grand Marquis says to her, "[Y]ou are going to live on the sea-coast. I am sending an aged lady there to gather the wax of the wild myrtle. This good soldier of mine buys it for our king at twelve livres the pound. Do you not know that women can make money?" (Cable, *Grandissimes* 27). Thus, Clotilde leaves New Orleans society to earn a living in Biloxi. This banishment comments on the strict social codes of the era. Because she exerts some independence, she becomes an outcast from the community. Conveniently enough, once in Biloxi, Grandmother Clotilde immediately meets a man and is married, thus ending her struggle for survival.

Following this same Southern tradition in the early nineteenth century, Aurora and Clotilde still fear isolation from the community should they try to become financially independent. Aurora concludes:

If society has decreed that ladies must be ladies, then that is our first duty; our second is to live. Do you not see why it is that this practical world does not permit ladies to make a living? Because if they could, none of them would ever consent to be married. Ha! women talk about marrying for love; but society is too sharp to trust them, yet! It makes it necessary to marry. I will tell you the honest truth; some days when I get very, very hungry, and we have nothing but rice—I think society could drive even me to marriage! (Cable, *Grandissimes* 255)

Despite her protestations, Aurora succumbs to the influence of a man, for financial reasons, if nothing else. Cable eventually solves the ladies' problems by causing Honoré Grandissime, a Creole, to return Aurora's husband's estate to her and marry her, but not without first allowing her to balk at society's restrictions.

Aurora's and Clotilde's conversation sounds very similar to one between Madame John and her daughter in Cable's short story, "Tite Poulette," originally published in 1879. Madame John is a quadroon, and her daughter, 'Tite Poulette, also believes that she is a quadroon. Even though Madame John is an excellent yellow-fever nurse, her community, rather than calling upon her in times of need, ostracizes her because of her race. Elfenbein points out the clear comparison between these female characters and white female characters in *The Grandissimes* (41):

Living was hard work; and, as Madame John had been brought up tenderly, and had done what she could to rear her daughter in the same mistaken way, with, of course, no more education than the ladies in society got, they knew nothing beyond a little music and embroidery. They struggled as they could, faintly; now giving a few private dancing lessons, now dressing hair, but ever beat back by the steady detestation of their imperious patronesses. (Cable, "Tite Poulette" 218)

After losing the money that Monsieur John had provided her at his death, Madame John becomes a paid dancer at the ballroom on Conde Street. Every day, she discreetly slips to work at the *Salle de Condé* because "it had to be done. It brought some pay, and pay was bread" (Cable, "Tite Poulette" 220). Skaggs blames the poverty of Madame John and her daughter on their lack of skill, their lack of education, and their lack of "money sense" (Cable, "Tite Poulette" 181), but it seems that their poverty stems mostly from being quadroon women limited by a provincial society.

As non-whites, these women could not count on marriage to rescue them from penury. Madame John worries over the future of her daughter because she has "no fortune, no pleasure, no friend." She fears that she "will be lonely, lonely, all [her] poor life long. There is no place in this world for us poor women. I wish that we were either white or black" (Cable, "Tite Poulette" 220). Although 'Tite Poulette's skin is white, she does not have the opportunity to marry into white Creole society and thus acquire wealth. Though a German immigrant notices and truly does care for her, he has no intention of marrying her because it is illegal. Only after he finally discovers Madame John's secret—that 'Tite Poulette is the white daughter of a Spanish couple who died of yellow fever—are the two free to marry.

When we consider the full spectrum of castes offered by these Louisiana writers, we can see how differing values affect characters and their choices. Cajuns fare better than African Americans and fall somewhere between poor whites and Creoles. Though poor, Cajuns garner more respect than poor whites because of their industriousness. Skaggs classifies Cajuns among the "plain folk" of the South (39), sensible and hardworking. At the same time, Cajuns fall prey to the idea of Southern womanhood, especially concerning the nature of work. Still, in literature, Cajuns are more practical than Creoles. Cajun women must work, and their communities allow them to do so without humiliation, most likely because they live outside of New Orleans society.

In *Bonaventure: A Prose Pastoral of Acadian Louisiana*, published in 1887, Cable turns his attention to these rural women. After Zoséphine's husband dies, her old friend Bonaventure helps her and her children for a year until he takes mission work in another part of the state. When she returns to her parents' home for consolation, her mother says to her father, "You can go ahead and repair the schoolhouse now. Our daughter will want to begin, even tomorrow, to teach the children of the village." In the same breath, her mother says, "[I]t is certain now that Zoséphine will always remain the Widow 'Thanase'" (Cable, *Bonaventure* 72). This close pairing clearly underscores the relationship between marriage and work. Much later in the novel, Zoséphine, still single, owns a tavern and a hotel, and her daughter, Marguerite, is a tavern maid.

Marguerite, however, does not continue in this lifestyle; she moves to surrounding parishes to take music lessons and becomes a member of society in New Orleans. Soon Zoséphine sells her hotel and moves to New Orleans with her daughter. Since much of the remaining plot revolves around romantic relationships, the narrator makes no mention of what mother and daughter do to earn a living. It should be noted, however, that by the novel's end, Marguerite and Zoséphine both marry their pursuers. Cable neatly provides for their financial futures much as he does for Aurora and Clotilde Nancanou. Although beset by previous troubles, those troubles vanish because Marguerite and Zoséphine can now rely on their husbands to provide for them.

Skaggs argues that in *Bonaventure*, Cable presents a true picture of Acadian life, pointing out that "The Acadian is the only type developed entirely within the local color period . . . to fulfill the national demand for local color, for information about quaint or exotically different types. . . . as stereotypes go, the Acadian stereotype seems more reasonable and realistic than others" (Skaggs 146–47). Skaggs feels that because Cable took so much time in studying rural Cajuns before writing *Bonaventure*, his portrayals are accurate ones. However, Skaggs pays more attention to Cajun men; her only comment about Cajun women is that they marry young and are always hospitable (150). She seems to overlook the fact that Cable does not present a complete sketch of Cajun women, especially concerning the necessity of work, even within the marriage relationship, in post-bellum America.

Cable's gender, however, does not account for his inadequate portraits. White women writers Grace King and Kate Chopin also seem to support, at times, the pervasive male view of women's roles. King, a late nineteenth-century Louisiana writer, tried to realistically portray black, white, and poor women who she felt had either been misrepresented or ignored in fiction (Elfenbein 78). Struggling against editors' wishes, King wanted to offer a realistic portrait of South Louisiana instead of a romantic Reconstruction novel (Kreyling 117-19). Instead, King reinforces the conception that nineteenth-century women relied on their husbands to provide for them. For example, in King's 1916 novel, *The Pleasant Ways of St. Médard*, Mariana Talbot returns to New Orleans with her husband after living on a plantation in a swamp during the war. The Talbot family is impoverished, but Mariana relies on her husband to take care of the family, adopting the passive role of Southern lady. In fact, Mariana and her family suffer the cost of bringing with them a family of five servants in order to keep up the appearance of being financially stable. King's depiction clarifies Jones's notion that post-bellum women abandoned the industry which they had previously shown: "the southern woman after the war had to shift roles entirely in the face of man's desire to re-create a stable society" (25). That stability relied, in part, on the division of labor.

To follow social mores, Mrs. Talbot denies the power that she shows while contributing to the household finances only a short time earlier. Marie Fletcher notes that during the war, Mrs. Talbot had obviously endured "hardships on the plantation" where she "had to depend so much upon her own intelligence" (96). In fact, she had performed domestic duties such as helping the tanner make shoes for her family, spinning cotton, and knitting clothes while her servants worked in the field. However, once Mariana returns to the city with her husband in control as provider, she embraces the urban attitude that, as Fletcher describes, "being a lady is to be easy, careless, extravagant, and utterly indifferent to her money" (96-97). Her return to society impels her to abandon even domestic industry. During most of the novel, the family tries to keep up appearances, but toward the end, Mariana laments their fate. Because her husband cannot "make money during the year to pay our house rent, let alone provide food and clothing for us" (King, *Pleasant Ways* 253), she appeals to prior acquaintances for money but to no avail. She does not, however, consider taking a job for herself, and the eventual changes the family makes include everyone but Mariana.

The Talbot family is not the only impoverished Creole family in the area. In fact, when they approach the outskirts of the city, they are greeted by the sight of laboring families, "from the grandmother in her headkerchief, to little children, raking, hoeing, gathering vegetables and working the great long swinging poles over the wells" (King, *Pleasant Ways* 25). Robert Bush notes that these "Gascons" were French-speaking Creoles who inhabited a working-class district of New

Orleans, the same kind of area that King's family moved into after the war. Even though King admitted that the novel was taken from her own family's experiences (Bush 18–19), this passage contains the only references to the real economic situation of countless Creole families. Certainly, the Talbot family never works in their garden or anywhere else *en masse*. Perhaps King's privileged lifestyle contributed to her developing the same for the Talbot family.

King's depiction of African Americans, however, more truly reflects women's efforts for economic survival. The Talbots' servants work outside of the home to earn a living. When Mr. Talbot finally admits that he can no longer pay them, he advises Jerry to put his daughters to work. Even though they are not familiar with employment available in the city, they have been laboring most of their lives. The foreman of their plantation, Denis, "had them hoeing regularly with the field gang. . . . And as soon as they were large enough to balance a bucket of water on their heads they carried water to the field hands" (King, *Pleasant Ways* 135). Jerry finds work for his daughters in the barracks, and though they soon quit work to join a community of indolent blacks, it is a choice they can make now in post-war New Orleans. The choices they make do not change the fact that the option to work without shame is available to them.

Changes must also be made concerning the Talbot daughters, although Mr. Talbot says nothing about their entering the same trades as Jerry's daughters. Mr. Talbot has perhaps the most progressive attitude among the male characters under consideration, for he acknowledges that he must sacrifice some luxuries concerning his children. Still, his daughters suffer the most. Because "[h]e had seen some unfortunate young girls marry for money, some literally for the means of a living," he had planned on providing each daughter with a dower "so that she could marry or not just as she chose" (King, *Pleasant Ways* 113). He acknowledges, however, that he can no longer provide for them. Mr. Talbot's observations, like Aurore's and Clotilde's, comment on the fate of the Creole woman in New Orleans in the nineteenth century. Without dower and employment possibilities, the Talbot girls might have to marry for money, yet this idea bothers Mr. Talbot less than their earning a living through their own means.

Marrying for money, in fact, seems less gauche than earning a living as a single woman. King provides sketches of such Creole women who break social customs through undertaking labor. Like Grandmother Clotilde in *The Grandissimes*, this kind of woman often isolates herself from society or satisfies special circumstances that allow her to work. One family in King's novel meets both stipulations. When a nephew visits the Talbots, he explains how his sister and his widowed mother survived the war while living in Texas. Mrs. Talbot is shocked to find out that his mother and sister had saved fifty dollars in gold, and Harry, the nephew, quickly explains that they earned it. The conversation that follows reveals both Mariana's and Harry's attitude about women making money: "'Made it!' ejaculated the aunt in still greater amazement. 'How could they make money?' . . .'They knit, they spun, they cooked,' lowering his voice and speaking slower, 'they took in washing and ironing and they planted a little cotton, only a few rows, for the knitting, you know'" (King, *Pleasant Ways* 122). Not only were Harry's mother and sister,

Elizabeth, able to take care of themselves during the war, but upon returning to Louisiana afterward, they plan to continue providing their own livelihood. Harry explains:

They said they could put up a very comfortable cabin for fifty dollars and began at once to talk about a garden, chickens and ten acres of cotton. I suppose Heatherstone, the boy, will do the plowing when they get a plow, and I have not the slightest doubt but that Mother and Elizabeth will help in the hoeing and of course all, down to the youngest, will take a hand in the picking. (King, *Pleasant Ways* 123)

As admirable as we might find these plucky women, post-bellum society would not have agreed. King, by emphasizing that Harry lowers his voice while talking about their plight, shows that there is something embarrassing or tainted about these women and their desire to provide for themselves.

Women who embrace the challenge of menial labor seem unfeminine and perhaps threatening to the Southern way of life because they defy both gender roles and caste systems. Thus, when Elizabeth works, King dresses her to play other parts. Because Elizabeth's husband, Heatherstone, has been injured in the war, she has begun to share labor responsibilities with her mother and acts as a replacement for her husband. Harry describes her unflatteringly: "She goes stalking about in a pair of her husband's old cavalry boots and an old hat of his, and she ties her skirts up to her knees like the negro women used to do in the fields; and she wears a pistol stuck in her belt. In fact she does everything she can to make a man out of herself, except curse and smoke" (King, *Pleasant Ways* 121). In this atypical situation, the Creole family has left the state and society that deem it indecent for women to work. The new order in the family appropriately exists in Texas, a land of disorder. When they return to Louisiana to reclaim their burned plantation, they can continue the new order only because one of the men of the family cannot. By taking on physical characteristics of her husband, Elizabeth serves as a surrogate for him; she crosses both caste and gender lines. That she can work dressed like a black woman or like a man speaks to the unfair limitations placed on white women. In Fletcher's eyes, this successful change would illustrate the movement from "romantic sentimentality to . . . realistic and naturalistic fiction," which involved women doing manual labor (61).

Another working female in *The Pleasant Ways of St. Médard* is Mademoiselle Mimi, who teaches the Talbot children in a small, private school. Mimi is described as poor, ugly, and dull; hence, she is unable to obtain a husband. She must earn her own living in order to survive, and she does so by teaching dancing, languages, math, and embroidery (King, *Pleasant Ways* 48–50). Teaching seems to provide the only employment option for another of King's characters in "Le Grande Demoiselle." The main character, Idalie, once a member of New Orleans Creole society, is extremely careless with her money before the war. She never marries; in fact, she considered the idea preposterous, perhaps because she could afford to live without a husband. Her decision to remain single so repudiates the patriarchal structure of her society that she is punished for her independence. After the war, an old friend sees her in a shabby dress walking fifty miles from her mansion on her way to teach school. The narrator comments: "The old gentleman had had reverses of his own, which would bear the telling, but nothing was more shocking to him than this—that Idalie Sainte Foy Mortemart des Islets should be teaching a public colored school for—it makes one blush to name it—seven dollars and a half a month" (King, *Balcony Stories* 34). The old gentleman still adheres to the same attitudes about working women that Aurore and Clotilde Nancanou illustrate. Although he has never been romantically interested in the main character, or in any woman for that matter, he decides to marry her in order to correct her financial situation and, more importantly, to protect her honor.

Kate Chopin draws this same circle around her Creole and Cajun female protagonists. Chopin, who published her work between 1889 and 1902, is widely known for stories that illustrate the struggle of women coming to terms with their own sexuality. Additionally, many of her stories set outside of New Orleans emphasize the relationship between women and labor. For example, in "Aunt Lympy's Interference," written in 1896, the main character feels the effect of crossing social lines with her industry. Melitte, an eighteen–year–old, "had been conducting a small school which stood down the road at the far end of the Annibelle place" (Chopin, *Complete Works* 2: 511). One day, Melitte receives a visit from Aunt Lympy, an "old family servant" (2: 513), who has heard a rumor about Melitte's vocation. The following exchange reveals the popular attitudes about working women, even those who teach:

> "I yeard you was turn school-titcher! Dat ant true?"
> "Oh!" exclaimed Melitte; an utterance that expressed relief, surprise, amusement, commiseration, affirmation.
> "Den it's true,' Aunt Lympy almost whispered; 'a De Broussard turn school-titcher!" The shame of it crushed her into silence. (2: 513)

Melitte, while expressing "relief" and "amusement" at old Aunt Lympy's worries, reveals that times are changing. Melitte can be comfortable with the idea of earning an income; in fact, she feels "complete self-satisfaction in this new undertaking" (2: 513). At the same time, however, she commiserates and affirms the notion that having to work is a regrettable option.

Still, Aunt Lympy operates according to old codes and tries to remedy the situation by writing a letter to Melitte's rich uncle in New Orleans, condemning him for allowing his niece to live in poverty. Uncle Gervais Leplain offers Melitte a place in his family and sends her money. Melitte reluctantly decides to accept his offer until a young man asks her to stay because he loves her. Although many of the old and young people of the community cannot understand her decision, she decides to stay in the country and to marry the young man. The narrator ends the story by remarking, "Aunt Lympy was not altogether dissatisfied; she felt that her interference had not been wholly in vain" (Chopin, *Complete Works* 517). The old woman succeeds in remedying Melitte's financial woes by sending her straight into encircling, masculine arms.

Though Aunt Lympy shows concern for Melitte's precarious position as a single working woman, she makes no mention of the same goals for African-

American women in the community, most likely because such goals were impractical. Chopin, in fact, depicts few African-American women at work in her stories. Narrators do make reference to old servants who had worked, but few passages detail that work. Chopin's writing, like King's and Cable's, suggests that post-bellum America had no expectation for African-American women other than to work. "Beyond the Bayou" includes a short description of a black woman in her thirties who "had more physical strength than most men, and made her patch of cotton and corn and tobacco like the best of them" (Chopin, *Bayou Folk* 100). This woman, like others previously discussed, lacks a mate, but in this story, Chopin never suggests that there is something amiss with a female laborer, nor does she end the story with a wedding or an apology for La Folle. Her salvation comes in her bravery in crossing "the beautiful world beyond the bayou" (Chopin, *Bayou Folk* 110), not in finding a husband or escaping work. Perhaps, African-American characters escaped the same pressure as white characters as a result of slavery, which deemed labor their inheritance, and marriage merely a privilege often longed for and less frequently realized.

Less physically independent than African-American women, white women who attempt to use their capabilities are sometimes chastised, as in Chopin's "The Woodchoppers." After returning home one rainy day from teaching school, Léontine finds her mother shivering without a fire because Uncle Peter, who usually cuts their wood, has not yet arrived to do so. Léontine "had sometimes chopped kindling and bits of light wood" (Chopin, *Complete Works* 2: 675), so she proceeds to chop wood for a fire. A stranger approaches, appalled that this girl should be working so out in the rain. He commands her to stop, adding, "You ought to be ashamed of yourself!... What are you doing this for? Isn't there a black fellow around these diggings to chop your wood?" (Chopin, *Complete Works* 2: 678). Upon leaving, he cautions her mother against allowing her to chop wood again because "she doesn't know how" (Chopin, *Complete Works* 2: 678). Not only does the stranger think a woman incapable of work, but he also believes it is not her place. Predictably, the stranger marries Léontine, and in fact, takes the ax with them to the plantation "in a sort of triumph" (Chopin, *Complete Works* 2: 679). Surely, this symbol suggests that he has conquered her need, and perhaps desire, to work, and indirectly, her power as well. More socially powerful than African-American women, white women who showed survival skills might, in fact, usurp the white men's role in society.

In Chopin's work, as in Cable's, women are allowed to work temporarily only if the prevailing power struggle is weakened. In Chopin's "Madame Célestin's Divorce," which appeared in 1894 in *Bayou Folk*, the title character has been separated from her husband for six months without any income. Each morning, Lawyer Paxton walks by her house as she sweeps her gallery. One day he comments about her work: "It's more than human nature —woman's nature should be called upon to endure. Here you are, working your fingers off... taking in sewing; giving music lessons; doing God knows what in the way of manual labor to support yourself and those two little ones" (Chopin, *Bayou Folk* 164). The judge tries to convince her to get a divorce in order to marry Paxton, but before she can, her husband returns, promising to "turn ova a new leaf" (Chopin, *Bayou Folk* 169). Madame Célestin returns to her husband, now that he has acknowledged his error and returned to his rightful place in their marriage.

As in King's *The Pleasant Ways of St. Médard*, the female figures who work in Chopin's fiction do so in special circumstances in which a male figure has been injured or has abdicated his responsibilities or in which the family abandons its place in society. In Chopin's short story, "In Sabine," Grégoire Santien visits with an old friend, 'Tite Reine, a Cajun from Bayou Pierre in Natchitoches Parish. While her husband sleeps, 'Tite Reine tells Santien how her husband beats her and asks him to take her away with him. Her dissatisfaction with her husband no doubt concerns the beatings, but another significant factor in her situation is that 'Tite Reine also does an unusual amount of work. After she prepares breakfast the next day for her lazy husband, "Bud sent her into the field to pick cotton with old Uncle Mortimer [who] worked the crop on shares" with her husband (Chopin, *Bayou Folk* 91). She then cooks lunch for her husband, and "in the afternoon she picked cotton again; and the men played cards, smoked, and Bud drank" (Chopin, *Bayou Folk* 92). Bud's lack of motivation is attributed to the fact that he is a Texan, not a Cajun. Bud belongs to the class of poor whites, which Susan Tracy illustrates as lazy and "undisciplined" (188). Though 'Tite Rein provides an example of a working woman, she works not by choice but through coercion. By asking to be taken away, 'Tite Reine suggests that her married life is intolerable. Chopin never suggests that 'Tite Reine either enjoys doing the man's job or is resigned to it for the rest of her life; she, in fact, resists labor and seeks to escape from it.

We meet a woman who enjoys labor in Chopin's 1900 story, "Charlie." The main character, seventeen–year–old Charlie, lives with five other sisters and her widowed father on a plantation. While the girls study with a governess, Charlie wants no part of sitting inside learning "womanly" subjects. The tomboy of the family, "Charlie could ride and shoot and fish; she was untiring and fearless. In many ways she filled the place of that ideal son [her father] had always hoped for and that had never come" (Chopin, *Complete Works* 2: 644). Charlie is atypical when compared with other Creole characters. She rebels against Southern womanhood to such an extent that her father sends her away to a boarding school at a seminary in New Orleans. There, Charlie struggles to become more "ladylike." The narrator explains that "Hoeing, or chopping cane seemed child's play compared with the excruciating intricacies which the piano offered her" (Chopin, *Complete Works* 2: 658). This portrait of a woman who enjoys and even prefers manual labor to customary schooling becomes distorted as Charlie is forced to fit the image of a Southern lady.

Charlie learns to appreciate the fineries of New Orleans life and even indulges in her femininity at the possibility of love until she must return home to care for her father, after he has mangled his hand while repairing machinery at the sugar mill. There, after hearing that her romantic interest has proposed to her sister, she abandons the guise of a lady and redresses herself like the tomboy she once was. Charlie helps her father as much as she can, but his assistant, Gus, keeps her from doing more. Finally Charlie approaches her father with this complaint and suggestion: "I'm jealous of Mr. Gus. . . . I know as much as he, more perhaps when it comes to writing letters. I know as much about the plantation as you do Dad; you know I do. And from now on I'm going to be—to be your right hand—your poor right hand" (Chopin, *Complete Works* 2: 667–68). Only then can Charlie, as her nickname implies, take over the masculine role as the chief financial supporter for her family. She feels it is her duty to care for the family and even refuses a marriage proposal from Gus. This portrait of a woman as provider appears only in a broken family with a mutilated father figure.

Another such figure appears in "A Rude Awakening," also published in *Bayou Folk*. Here, Lolotte lives with her sharecropper father, Sylveste Bordon, whom she calls "the laziest' man in Natchitoches pa'ish'" (Chopin, *Bayou Folk* 126). To make matters worse, the youngest boy, Nononne is sick. Lolotte wonders aloud about the last time Sylveste brought home a pound of sugar, some meat, or even coffee. Their meals consist mostly of corn bread and pork, considered unhealthy for the ailing child. One day, instead of fulfilling his promise to take three bales of hay to the landing, Sylveste decides to go fishing. Lolotte, exasperated by her father's behavior, decides to do the work herself despite "the children's astonishment [or] Aunt Minty's scathing disapproval" (Chopin, *Bayou Folk* 130). Aunt Minty conveys society's prevailing attitude when she says, "Dat ain't no work fur a gal w'at ain't bar' seventen year ole; drivin' Marse Duplan's mules! W'at I gwine tell yo' pa?" (Chopin, *Bayou Folk* 130). Nevertheless, Lolotte attempts the chore, and when her family finds her wagon "smoshed to kindlin" near the river (Chopin, *Bayou Folk* 135), they assume that she has drowned while trying to do her father's work.

This turn of events takes on great significance in identifying post-bellum social mores. Distraught, Sylveste becomes even more aimless. One day he approaches the planter and acknowledges his uneasiness in idle activities. Finally, he begs, "By gracious! M'sieur Duplan, gi' me some work!" (Chopin, *Bayou Folk* 137). Sylveste begins to work ferociously from morning until dawn until he hears word that Duplan has found his daughter. Upon leading him to Lolotte, Duplan reminds Sylveste that never again must he neglect his children: "I want you never to forget again that you are their father—that you are a man!" (Chopin, *Bayou Folk* 142). Clearly, the line between expectations of men and women solidifies. If a man should try to shirk his responsibilities, he suffers. Only when Sylveste begins to work does he find absolution through the reclamation of his family.

While some modern critics consider Chopin's first novel unsuccessful, it includes her strongest portrait of a working woman. In *At Fault*, published in 1890, Thérèse Lafirme runs a plantation along Cane River, which she has inherited from her husband. The locals consider her management of the place somewhat of an oddity; in fact, "it was a matter of unusual interest to [her neighbors] that a plantation of four thousand acres had been left unincumbered to the disposal of a handsome, inconsolable, childless Creole widow of thirty" (Chopin, *Complete Works* 2: 741). However, unlike Charlie, Thérèse is feminine. Admittedly, Thérèse has many household and field laborers working for her. The narrator never describes her doing manual labor because she has "scores of negroes, men, women, and children [who] were dexterously picking cotton" in her fields (Chopin, *Complete Works* 2: 771). Soon, David Hosmer, who establishes a lumber mill on Thérèse's property, falls in love with her. However, David is divorced, and Thérèse, a Catholic, cannot tolerate divorce. Despite her love for David, she convinces him to reunite with his alcoholic wife. Neatly enough, Fanny drowns, thereby granting Thérèse and David freedom to marry. In her descriptions of marriage, Thérèse shows that she holds a husband more accountable for emotional support than financial support, perhaps because she is financially independent, but she does assume that her new husband, David, will "help with the plantation." When he shies away from "robbing her of her occupation," she calls him "absurd" (Chopin, *Complete Works* 2: 874). Mary Papke argues that while Chopin may have addressed controversial issues in *At Fault*, her ending is a typical one. She explains, "Perhaps because [Chopin] chose to focus on such a controversial issue as divorce ... she felt compelled to end her various plots with convenient and seemingly conventional conclusions, in other words, to make a last curtsy to propriety and popular taste" (Papke 43). Still, though Thérèse does marry, she does not relinquish all control to her husband.

Finally, Chopin shows us the stereotype on its way out. In *At Fault*, Chopin includes idly wealthy ladies, such as Lou Dawson, who passes her empty hours with illicit lovers; Belle Worthington, who "spends her time adorning herself, playing cards, attending matinees, and gossiping" (Skaggs 82); and Madame Santien, who flees Louisiana to live a "lazy life in Paris, with eyes closed to the duties that lay before her" (Chopin, *Complete Works* 2: 853). When Thérèse must write a letter to Madame Santien in Paris, she finds it " very difficult to withhold the reproach which she felt inclined to deal her; hard to refrain from upbraiding a selfishness which for a life-time had appeared to Thérèse as criminal" (Chopin, *Complete Works* 2: 853). Perhaps to underscore this moral breach, Chopin has Lou caught by her husband. According to Skaggs, Chopin places these "ladies of leisure" in contrast to Thérèse, who realizes that changing times demand that women do productive work. The critic states, "This condition of 'elegant leisure' that turns women into 'professional time-killers' Chopin regards as a potential tragedy;" women must maintain some control over their lives in order to achieve a "sense of autonomy" (Chopin, *Complete Works* 2: 853). Thomas Bonner agrees, positing that Thérèse "proves able to enter the man's world of running the plantation and to accept the changes to her land and culture that come with 'industrial progress'" (142). Through Thérèse, Chopin disproves the myth of Southern womanhood and shows us the modern woman emerging strong and diligent.

The country's movement to a market culture provides, perhaps, the greatest impetus for such change, especially for these women authors who worked for a living. Like their characters, they showed men that they could follow the popular form of the day; at the same time, they made the form change through their activity. All three of these Louisiana writers, in fact, depart from others writing post-bellum literature in their empowerment of women through work. While these authors seem to draw the Southern lady according to form, they allow for redefinition. Characters recognize their capacity for work, and some female characters even protest when they are forbidden to work. They implicitly recognize that society forbids their accomplishments through labor and hence their power in the tradition of Southern womanhood.

NOTES

1. For further discussion of local color fiction, see Thomas Richardson's article entitled "Local Color in Louisiana."

2. For further discussion of plantation fiction, see Lucinda H. MacKethan's article entitled "Plantation Fiction, 1865-1900."

3. For further discussion of Reconstruction literature, see Michael Kreyling or Jane Turner Censer.

4. For further discussion of George Washington Cable's depiction of Creoles see Elmo Howell's article entitled "George Washington Cable's Creoles: Art and Reform in *The Grandissimes*."

5. For further discussion of Grace King's resistance to plantation fiction, see Karen A. Keely's article entitled "Marriage Plots and National Reunion: The Trope of Romantic Reconciliation in Postbellum Literature."

6. For further discussion of Kate Chopin's feminist impulses, see Emily Toth's biography, *Kate Chopin*.

7. Although there is little agreement about what the term "Creole" meant in its original Spanish, *criollo*, it was first used in the United States to refer to native-born residents of foreign parentage. Today, many use the term to refer to those of mixed-racial background who are born in Louisiana. In this study, I use the term, as did those in post-bellum New Orleans, to refer to nineteenth-century whites born in New Orleans of aristocratic French and/or Spanish backgrounds. For an extended definition, see Virginia R. Domínguez, *White by Definition: Social Classification in Creole Louisiana* (New Brunswick, NJ: Rutgers UP, 1986).

8. The term "Acadian" was first used to refer to French exiles from Acadie in the Bay of Fundy in Canada who settled in Louisiana, mostly outside New Orleans in southwest Louisiana. Eventually, the term was shortened to "Cadien" and finally became "Cajun." Today, the term applies to French descendants who intermarried German and Spanish immigrants. In this study, "Acadian" and "Cajun" are used interchangeably to refer to poor, French peasant exiles.

REFERENCES

Bonner, Thomas, Jr. "Kate Chopin: Tradition and the Moment." *Southern Literature in Transition: Heritage and Promise*. Ed. Philip Castille and William Osborne. Memphis: Memphis State UP, 1983. 141–49.

Bush, Robert. *Grace King: A Southern Destiny*. Baton Rouge: Louisiana State UP, 1983.

Butcher, Philip. *George W. Cable*. New York: Twayne, 1962.

Cable, George Washington. *Bonaventure: A Prose Pastoral of Acadian Louisiana*. New York: Charles Scribner's Sons, 1887.

—. *The Grandissimes: A Story of Creole Life*. New York: Hill and Wang, 1957.

—. "'Tite Poulette." *Old Creole Days*. New York: Charles Scribner's Sons, 1888. 214–36.

Censer, Jane Turner. "Reimagining the North-South Reunion." *Southern Cultures* 5.2:

(1999): 64-91.

Chopin, Kate. "At Fault." *The Complete Works of Kate Chopin.* Ed. Per Seyersted. Vol. 2. Baton Rouge: Louisiana State UP, 1969. 741–877.

—. "Aunt Lympy's Interference." *The Complete Works of Kate Chopin.* Ed. Per Seyersted. Vol. 2. Baton Rouge: Louisiana State UP, 1969. 511–17.

—. "Beyond the Bayou." *Bayou Folk.* Ridgewood, NJ: Gregg P, 1967. 99–110.

—. "Charlie." *The Complete Works of Kate Chopin.* Ed. Per Seyersted. Vol. 2. Baton Rouge: Louisiana State UP, 1969. 638–70.

—. "In Sabine." *Bayou Folk.* Ridgewood, NJ: Gregg P, 1967. 78–95.

—. "Madame Celestin's Divorce." *Bayou Folk.* Ridgewood, NJ: Gregg P, 1967. 163–69.

—. "A Rude Awakening." *Bayou Folk.* Ridgewood, NJ: Gregg P, 1967. 126–42.

—. "The Wood-Choppers." *The Complete Works of Kate Chopin.* Ed. Per Seyersted. Vol. 2. Baton Rouge: Louisiana State UP, 1969. 674–79.

Cleman, John. *George Washington Cable Revisited.* New York: Twayne, 1996.

Elfenbein, Anna Shannon. *Women on the Color Line: Evolving Stereotypes and the Writings of George Washington Cable, Grace King, Kate Chopin.* Charlottesville: UP of Virginia, 1989.

Ewell, Barbara C. "Re-Viewing the Tradition of Louisiana Women Writers." *Louisiana Women Writers: New Essays and a Comprehensive Bibliography.* Ed. Dorothy H. Brown and Barbara C. Ewell. Baton Rouge: Louisiana State UP, 1992. 3–15.

Fletcher, Marie. *The Southern Heroine in the Fiction of Representative Southern Women Writers.* Diss. Louisiana State University, 1963. Baton Rouge: Louisiana State UP, 1963.

Howell, Elmo. "George Washington Cable's Creoles: Art and Reform in *The Grandissimes.*" *Mississippi Quarterly* 26 (1973): 43–53.

Jones, Anne Goodwyn. *Tomorrow is Another Day: The Woman Writer in the South, 1859–1936.* Baton Rouge: Louisiana State UP, 1981.

Keely, Karen A. "Marriage Plots and National Reunion: The Trope of Romantic Reconciliation in Postbellum Literature." *Mississippi Quarterly* 51 (1998): 621–48.

King, Grace. "Grande Demoiselle." *Balcony Stories.* Ridgewood, NJ: Gregg P, 1968. 23–35.

—. *The Pleasant Ways of St. Médard.* New York: Henry Holt, 1916.

Kreyling, Michael. "After the War: Romance and the Reconstruction of Southern Literature." *Southern Literature in Transition: Heritage and Promise.* Ed. Philip Castille and William Osborne. Memphis: Memphis State UP, 1983. 111–25.

MacKethan, Lucinda H. "Plantation Fiction, 1865-1900." *The History of Southern Literature.* Ed. Louis D. Rubin, Jr. Baton Rouge: Louisiana State UP, 1985. 209–218.

Papke, Mary. E. *Verging on the Abyss: The Social Fiction of Kate Chopin and Edith Wharton.* New York: Greenwood P, 1990.

Prenshaw, Peggy Whitman. "Southern Ladies and the Southern Renaissance." *The Female Tradition in Southern Literature.* Ed. Carol S. Manning. Urbana: U of Illinois P, 1993. 73–88.

Richardson, Thomas. "Local Color in Louisiana." *The History of Southern Literature.* Ed. Louis D. Rubin, Jr. Baton Rouge: Louisiana State UP, 1985. 199–208.

Rubin, Louis D., Jr. *George Washington Cable: The Life and Times of a Southern Heretic.* New York: Pegasus, 1969.

Scott, Anne Firor. *The Southern Lady: From Pedestal to Politics, 1830–1875*. Baton Rouge: Louisiana State UP, 1970.

Skaggs, Merrill Maguire. *The Folk of Southern Fiction*. Athens: U of Georgia P, 1972.

Toth, Emily. *Kate Chopin*. New York: Morrow, 1990.

Tracy, Susan J. *In the Master's Eye: Representations of Women, Blacks, and Poor Whites in Antebellum Southern Literature*. Amherst: U of Massachusetts P, 1995.

Living "Amid Romance": Ethnic Cultures in Ruth McEnery Stuart's New Orleans Stories

Joan Wylie Hall

One of the nation's most popular regionalist writers at the end of the nineteenth century, Ruth McEnery Stuart (1849–1917) was memorialized in a New York obituary entitled "Ruth M'E. Stuart, Author, Dies Here" as "interpreter of the South." Like her contemporaries George Washington Cable, Grace Elizabeth King, Alice Dunbar-Nelson, Mollie Moore Davis, and Kate Chopin, she was intrigued by New Orleans's distinctive Creole culture, a fascination that is evident in several of her short stories and particularly in *The Story of Babette: A Little Creole Girl* (1894), a book that opens on Mardi Gras and is "affectionately" dedicated "to the little girls of New Orleans" (iii).[1] Exploring this milieu in her *Ladies' Home Journal* essay "A People Who Live Amid Romance," Stuart contrasted the French-American community with "the American" in great detail, examining elements such as the Creole's "picturesque homes" and "picturesque hospitality," the French males' social conservatism, and the piety of Creole women in religious ceremonies who were simultaneously noted for their "beauty and picturesqueness" (7–8).

Despite the pronounced allure of the picturesque, Creole culture is not nearly as prominent in Stuart's fiction as it is in the works of many other Louisiana authors. For Stuart, New Orleans was a cultural patchwork whose various ethnic neighborhoods were equally colorful material for fiction, and she might have deliberately yielded the Creole terrain to Grace King, who built her literary reputation on that ground.[2] Although some recent discussions of Stuart's work have criticized her depictions as stereotypical and even racist, her stories about New Orleanians of African, Italian, German, and Irish descent were considered extremely sympathetic by the Northern press—and also by Kate Chopin, who admiringly called Stuart a "celebrity" whose "lovable" fiction was remarkable for its "sympathy and insight" (2:712) After meeting Stuart in 1897, Chopin rhapsodized on the "melting quality" of a voice that reminded her of "some soothing ointment" (2: 712). Charmed by the author's personality, Chopin concluded: "I fancy there are no sharp edges to this woman's soul, no unsheathed prejudices dwelling therein wherewith to inflict wound, or prick, or stab upon her fellow-man or woman" (2: 712). For Chopin, Stuart was a congenial reporter of quaint Southern scenes.

Besides satisfying a late nineteenth-century taste for the exotic, Stuart's portrayals of African Americans, Creole Catholics, and recent immigrants helped to offset the contemporary prejudices hinted at in Chopin's newspaper column. During a period of hostility toward assimilating such cultural others into the national economy and social structure, Stuart defused tensions with humor and sentimentality. She earned a reputation as "laureate of the lowly" (Rutherford 541) by portraying minority communities from within, a technique that Zora Neale Hurston later developed with great skill in her tales of the African-American town of Eatonville, Florida. Stuart's fictionalized New Orleans provided a multicultural model, enhanced by the artwork of E. W. Kemble, A. B. Frost, and other top illustrators. These images added a literal picturesque to King's highly visual stories, making them as quaintly appealing to the 1890s middle class as sepia-toned stereoviews of the French Market and Jackson Square.

Edwin Lewis Stephens, in his introduction to a selection of Stuart's works in the *Library of Southern Literature* (1909), especially praised her portraits of African-American life: "Although not the first to treat the negro in fiction, Mrs. Stuart has perhaps been the first to show him in his home life independent of the white man," and "never for a moment has she held him up to ridicule" (5146). The insider perspective also made it possible for Stuart's "American" readers to enter immigrant neighborhoods where they might never venture on foot. Stuart herself had traveled throughout New Orleans as a girl on daily "health walks," and her sister Sarah McEnery emphasized that Ruth saw the widely differing urban areas as communities of "friends," not as objects of a tourist's curiosity (Fletcher 15). This personal experience lent such authority to Stuart's fiction that reviewers and interviewers often treated her as a faithful recorder of Southern life. Complimenting *The River's Children* (1904), a novel set outside New Orleans along the Mississippi River, the *Reader Magazine* announced: "No one knows better than Mrs. Stuart the folk of all degrees that pay tribute to the stream" (377). In an issue of *Harper's Bazar*, which sported Stuart's full-length photograph on the cover, Candace Wheeler praised the author's "ability to feel and to present every-day phases of life in a manner inimitable for truth, kindness, humor and pathos" (1083). These last two qualities were especially attractive to popular audiences of the era, and the national media typically cited the pairing of humor and pathos in Stuart's books.

The Northern readers' perception of Stuart as a specialist on the South is reflected in the publication of essays like "A People Who Live Amid Romance" in the *Ladies' Home Journal*. The *New York Times* printed her "Value of Folklore in Literature," and—for a younger audience—the *Youth's Companion* ran the two-part autobiographical "I Remember," with its anecdotes of her childhood, first on a Louisiana plantation and then in bustling New Orleans. The most lengthy of

Stuart's non-fiction articles appeared in the *Bookman*'s "American Backgrounds for Fiction" series in 1914. Stuart had been writing regional fiction for over a quarter of a century when she was invited to contribute "Arkansas, Louisiana and the Gulf Country" as Part VI of the monthly feature. "Of course, New Orleans is the seething centre of Romance of the Gulf Country," Stuart observes (623). Three large illustrations graphically represent the essayist's dependability as a guide to even the most secluded areas of the "magnet-city" (624). The first scene fills two–thirds of a page with a balconied house rising behind a tall closed gate. Stuart's caption is placed below the stone–paved street that runs past the urban estate: "The French-American of old New Orleans built a wall of brick around his house, a potential fortress, thick, high and strong. His front gate, kept strictly locked and wide enough for only guarded welcome, was sometimes of wrought iron" (622). Such architecture might seem to hint that Stuart's Creoles are defensive and iron-willed.

Her essay explains, however, that as soon as a guest is drawn into "the charmed circle" (622), the joyful and voluble temperament of the Creole family is apparent, and "the bars [are] down" (623). Later in the article, a full-page vista of open archways, rippling water, and moss-laden trees places the reader inside the gate. The caption heightens the sensation of being on the estate grounds: "Here are even palpable ruins, reminiscent of the old order, ruins stately, gaunt and important, or dilapidated, moss-grown and picturesque in the low-browed architecture which crouches in the weed-grown rose-gardens of yesterday" (625). The final illustration once again positions the reader on the street, but this time the gaze is directed not toward a forbidding gate but toward a whole row of buildings whose front doors, carriage entrances, and windows are within touching distance of passersby on the sidewalk. "New Orleans' kaleidoscopic past is written in picturesque decay, which one, knowing her story, if he be not colour-blind and a dullard, may read as he runs," says Stuart's accompanying text (626).

With Stuart as guide, the reader is induced to pause and enter, rather than to race past, scenes that she repeatedly describes as full of "colour." The *Bookman* essay emphasizes the variety of Louisiana's people, from the Native Tchetamachis, famed for their basketry, to the "Acadian contingent," whose women are "pure and simple," but whose men have occasionally produced "such half-breeds as are found entangled in the fringes of life, so to speak" (623). Stuart also finds a rich variety in Louisiana's literature, including the histories of Charles Gayarré, folklore collections of Alcée Fortier, the fiction of George Washington Cable and Grace King, and the poetry of several women: Mary Ashley Townsend, Martha Austin, Julie K. Wetherill, Josephine Nichols, and Mollie Moore Davis. But Stuart describes her own subjects as the matter of personal discovery rather than a literary inheritance:

Realising the heterogeneous population of the Gulf region and especially of New Orleans at the time when I first took up my pen, when the city, long the Mecca of the newly freed, and still in a state of palpable transition, was a great caravansary, pictorial to a degree and pathetic in human appeal, perhaps it was but natural, in casting about for material, that my reach should first have seized upon such as, in the perspective which differences of race and class afford, made vivid appeal. (642)

Thus, her earliest fiction was not about Creole New Orleans but about the more dramatically different African-American race and European immigrant class.

The title stories of Stuart's first two collections, *A Golden Wedding and Other Tales* (1893) and *Carlotta's Intended and Other Stories* (1894), are among the best examples of her ability to immerse her audience in ethnic households alien to their own. "A Golden Wedding" opens with the sweetly "mingled perfume" of New Orleans, but the whole story is set in an African-American neighborhood, with no mingling of white characters. The rustic dialect of an elderly couple, "Sis' Garrett" and "Br'er Thormson," comprise a basic element of the tale's charm during the 1890s. With its emotional plot of love lost and recovered, "A Golden Wedding" was often a featured piece in Stuart's public readings. In a letter to Drs. Emily and Augusta Pope, Stuart accepted an invitation to direct African-American students in a dramatized version at the Hampton Institute, a very successful production that the young cast subsequently performed in Northern theatres. The popularity of "A Golden Wedding" helped to establish Stuart's lifelong reputation as an author of black dialect fiction.

"Carlotta's Intended" is another New Orleans romance, but its neighborhood is Italian instead of African American. Counterpointing the Italian voices are the speeches of a kindly, middle-aged Irishman whose love for the beautiful Carlotta drives him to defy a somewhat ineffectual branch of the Mafia. At sixteen, Lottie considers herself Pat Rooney's "intend" (30) and pledges to marry him when she is eighteen. Pat's accidental death on her eighteenth birthday frees Carlotta to marry a worthy Italian youth, incidentally strengthening her own ethnic identity. With "Carlotta's Intended," says Stuart, "I found myself in a turbulent sea of dialects in which I should have been swamped but for the fact that every one was as familiar to me as my own tongue, so that I had no more trouble in shifting from one to another than in writing such limited English as I dared essay" (Stuart "American Backgrounds" 627). She adds that, in New Orleans, "a bizarre old town of mixed traditions, . . . one may hardly escape a half dozen patois in the length of a single street" (627). Stuart's linguistic expertise in the *Golden Wedding* and *Carlotta's Intended* volumes proved her to be a keen observer of the region and practically assured the publisher of good sales.

Harper & Brothers targeted both works at the holiday gift market, including Christmas stories in each book, but the contrasting covers of the *Golden Wedding* and *Carlotta's Intended* collections suggest that Stuart did not want to typecast herself at the start of her career. Announcing a Southern motif, the brown binding *of A Golden Wedding* is decorated with darker brown and white cotton plants in four stages of development, grouped around the gold printed title. Stuart's name appears on the spine but not as part of the stylized Art Nouveau front cover. The bright red cover of *Carlotta's Intended* looks more old-fashioned. The title at the top and the author's name at the bottom (now more recognizable to book buyers than it was the previous year) imitate a neat, handwritten script in black ink. Centered on the front is a large gold cameo of a young woman in profile—Carlotta, complete with hoop earring—and a surrounding pattern of shamrocks evoking the ill-fated Irishman Pat Rooney.

Golden Wedding's embossed cover design of cotton plants anticipates the saga of Cicely Garrett and Aleck Thompson, who separately move to New Orleans several years after Emancipation with the lasting imprint of rural slavery on their memory. The Boston *Beacon* cited Stuart for effectively combining humor and pathos in portraying African-American characters in this long title story and several other pieces in the volume. Although the New England reviewer praises the tales' "verisimilitude," many scenes resemble sentimental fiction by Stuart's contemporaries by straining the reader's credulity ("Stories of Negro Life" 3). "A Golden Wedding" describes the teary Christmas reunion of the old pair who rent adjoining rooms in a New Orleans "hovel" long after they have been sold away from the adjoining plantations where they lived as newlyweds. Each finally recognizes the other as they reminisce about their youthful passions and their Christmas weddings—actually the very same wedding—while sharing a holiday dinner. Coincidentally, their son, who grew up to join the Yankees during the Civil War, is part of the congregation that gathers to celebrate his parents' renewal of vows at a golden wedding. Because "little Joe," now the tallest man in sight, has a wife and six children of his own, the ancient couple's unexpected gains offset their great losses, and, as Gena McKinley remarks, the story expresses "renewed hope for the future rather than bitterness for the past" (105).

Dedicated to "My Friend Mr. Henry Mills Alden," editor of *Harper's*, a leading New York magazine, *A Golden Wedding and Other Tales* underscores the national conciliatory aspect of much late nineteenth-century Southern regionalist writing.[3] Joe Smith has changed his surname (the name of his father's early white master) to Lincoln, after a hero of the Union. It is "a name what stood fur freedom" (38), Joe says at the New Orleans reunion, and his long-lost parents accept the alteration. As Joe reminds his father, "You 'ain't had no name what yer mought say was borned ter yer nohow" (38). While "ole marster," like many slaveowners with a sense of irony, named the father after Alexander the Great, Joe favored Yankee military leaders in naming two of his sons "Phil Sheridam an' Gineral Grant" (40). Stuart's tone is humorous, but the history of slavery is implicit in such details as the son's self-naming and the father's lack of any true name of his own. Joseph Boskin says, "More blacks were whimsically dubbed Caesar than perhaps any other classical name. Also popular were Cato, Pompey, Jupiter, and Nero" (31). Stuart's stories followed the fashion, but in the case of Joe Lincoln she also acknowledges those emancipated slaves whose choice of a new name is a bold assertion of a new identity.

Nowhere does Stuart approach the subversiveness of her African-American contemporary Charles Chesnutt in relating slaves' memories, but she is more honest about antebellum cruelties than recent critics indicate. Contrasting Stuart's tale of family separation in "A Golden Wedding" with "abolitionist" treatments of this motif in Stowe's *Uncle Tom's Cabin* and Harriet Jacobs's *Incidents in the Life of a Slave Girl*, Gena McKinley finds "no evil slavetrader here who buys husband away from wife" (104). Yet the couple's status as property is precisely the reason for their early separation and thus as much the source of sorrow for the newlywed Smiths as it is for Stowe's Eliza and Jacobs's Linda Brent. Aleck Smith does not leave his bride to fight for the Confederacy, as McKinley claims. Instead, the couple is tragically divided because they belong to different masters. Aleck's owner—who had cruelly advised him against marrying—moves from the Louisiana coast to distant Georgia not long after the wedding "and carried all his goods with him, and that had been the end" (Stuart, "Wedding," 11). These goods, of course, include the powerless Aleck.

When the Smiths later sell Aleck to the Thompsons in Georgia, and Cicely is sold by her owners, the Morgans, to the Garretts of Bayou Grôs Tete, the forced relocations and the resulting changes to the slaves' last names virtually guarantee the failure of the black family's agonizing attempts to find each other after the war. Like Rip Van Winkle returning home after his long sleep, Aleck, on his return to Louisiana, finds the old Gulf world changed: his wife gone, "an' nobody seem like dee 'membered me" (Stuart, "Wedding," 17). He finally "done give up de hunt" for Cicely, realizing that he "mought be trablin' eas' while she gwine wes'" (Stuart, "Wedding," 17). Aleck accepts the loss as God's will, and he starts a new life in an African-American section of New Orleans.

McKinley argues that, "with an all-black cast of characters, Stuart avoids the issue of interracial interaction altogether" (105). But Stuart's contemporaries believed that her depiction of black communities in "A Golden Wedding" and many other tales contributed greatly to the emotional impact of her dialect fiction. Thus, Edwin Lewis Stephens, in his early biographical portrait of Stuart, approvingly quotes Joel Chandler Harris's observation that she has "got nearer the heart of the negro than any of us" (5146).[4] Harris's authority, firmly established in the Uncle Remus stories, was taken for granted by his peers, and his assessment was often repeated by Stuart's reviewers.

Stuart compared the old couple in "A Golden Wedding" to the legendary Pyramus and Thisbe, who "conducted romance through a hole in the wall—in this instance a broken partition" on the porch of their New Orleans tenement ("American Backgrounds 624). A full-page illustration pictures the old folks companionably smoking on stools drawn up to the dividing wall.[5] Stuart, however, achieves a comic resolution for the separated lovers, not a tragic one. The joyous nuptials and restored identities at the end of "A Golden Wedding" echo the last scenes of Shakespeare's *A Midsummer Night's Dream* rather than the deadly finale of the Pyramus and Thisbe drama staged within that play by Bottom's rustic crew. Stuart's Christmas setting underscores the miracle of Cicely and Aleck's finding each other, and the sacredness of the season is emphasized when they recite their golden vows in a church where many area preachers, including their own "little Joe," have gathered for a ministerial conference. However, Cicely Garrett's passing reference to the lottery early in the story hints at the great role of chance in effecting the happy outcome. Louisiana's legalized gambling had been in the national news for a long time before the 1893 publication of the *Golden Wedding* volume. Chartered in 1868 by the state legislature for a twenty-five-year period, the Louisiana Lottery Company supported the conservative faction of Governor Samuel D. McEnery—Stuart's cousin—in 1888 against the reform candidate (and election winner) Francis Tillon Nicholls. After years of angry debate in the statehouse, the lottery became a focus of the 1892 campaign, and a proposal to extend the charter for another quarter century failed the Senate by one vote.[6]

Although the action of "A Golden Wedding" is contemporaneous with the mounting tension in the legislature, Stuart touches lightly upon the lottery, as if it were just another part of the local color, as harmless as the mockingbirds or the fresh orange blossoms that remind old Cicely and Aleck of their bridal night. Similarly, in "Carlotta's Intended," one of Carlotta's would-be suitors is described as "young Alessandro Soconneti, who won a prize in the lottery," in contrast to another of her admirers, "Joe Zucca, the peanut-vender" (57). In this second story, however, Stuart makes more serious use of another controversial element of 1890s New Orleans politics, the Mafia. The secret organization was accused of murdering the city's police superintendent in October 1890 because of his recent crackdown on urban crime. Eleven Italians jailed in the Mafia Affair were killed by a mob in the spring of 1891, and the federal government paid $25,000 in response to Italy's protests that some of the dead were not even American citizens (McGinty 235–40).

For the title story of the 1894 *Carlotta's Intended and Other Stories*, Stuart portrays the Mafia as a sinister group that bungles a murder when Pat Rooney, their assigned victim, instead drowns while rescuing a kitten on the waterfront. Two hired killers have pursued Pat to a dark wharf, stilettos "drawn and ready" to strike quickly, "for the emissaries of the Mafia are wont to use despatch" (101). Despite their ominous posturing, the narrator suggests that the Mafia frequently fails in its grim aims. The killers do not hear Pat fall soundlessly into the river on his mercy mission, and it is after midnight "when at last, despairing and mystified, they separated reluctantly, and by different routes went to report another failure to old Pietro Socola, their chief" (101). Socola's vendetta against Pat Rooney is so ridiculous that Stuart makes the Mafia look more foolish than formidable. Earlier in the story, Pat shelters Carlotta when she runs away from her mother's attempt to force her to marry the rich Mafia boss, who has been courting her with expensive gifts. To cover his humiliation at being stood up on the scheduled wedding day, Socola marries Carlotta's ugly cousin—also conveniently called Carlotta di Carlo—and spreads a rumor that the younger and more lovely Carlotta has tried to lure him to the altar. When Pat boldly defends Carlotta's honor in a crowd of Italian men, two Mafiosi in the group are bound by oath to report the insult to Socola's honor, even though they know that the middle-aged cobbler is telling the truth. The task makes one Mafia member reflect what a bad world this is: "One minute we play an organ at the corner for any beggar to dance, the next minute maybe we get orders to file our stilettos and put on a black mask" (68).[7] The organ-grinder adds that he and his now skittish monkey are both haunted by the ghost of a victim whose throat he recently slit under Mafia orders.

"Carlotta's Intended" made a lasting impression on Kate Chopin when she first read it as the featured novelette in an 1891 issue of *Lippincott's Magazine*. Instead of relating the action to the Mafia crisis that rocked the city that year, Chopin remarks appreciatively: "The character, the dialect of the dagoes with whom it deals, and of the Irish cobbler who plays so important a rôle, are singularly true to nature. Their fidelity must appear striking to anyone who has lived in New Orleans in familiar touch with the life which the author so graphically depicts in this story" (2: 711). "Fidelity" to ethnic customs and voices inclined readers to trust that Stuart's renderings of ethnic "character" were likewise faithful. In "Carlotta's Intended," the villainous and somewhat grotesque Socola stands out as an aberration in an Italian community that is more reassuringly represented by Carlotta's family. Stuart describes the children of the household as an attractive and appealing group: "A row of little black-eyed dagoes of various degrees of beauty, but all handsome, a healthy, picturesque, noisy lot, quarrelsome without pugnacity—these were the little di Carlos" (4). When the grown-up Lottie marries the handsome young Giuseppe Rubino some time after Pat Rooney's death, she, too, produces a "flock of beautiful children," who pay tribute to the Irishman every year on All-Saints' Day—a New Orleans ritual made all the quainter by the "unique inscription," of Carlotta's "own dictation," on the marble shaft in a corner of St. Patrick's Cemetery: "In Memory of Patrick Rooney, Intend of Carlotta di Carlo, Age, 42 Years" (102). The ungrammatical gravestone unites the Italian beauty and her luckless Irish suitor, evoking not ridicule but pity from Stuart's audience.

Early in the story, Stuart provides a brief history for the one-legged Pat by remarking that, before a "fearful row" at a saloon in his younger days (7), he had been "a Fenian, an American ward-politician, and a festive leader in torch-light processions, pat-riot-ism, and the like" (6). Three men almost die as a result of the shooting that destroys Pat's leg, and the violent incident ends his involvement in the secret revolutionary society of Fenians, an organization whose threat to the public order Stuart downplays by comically punning on Pat's "pat-riot-ism." His long convalescence at the home of a friendly German cobbler strengthens him on a diet of "apple-pie, cinnamon cake, *nudels*, and *smierkäse*" (8) and allows him to learn the trade that gains him a small working space in the di Carlos' fruit shop. Stuart emphasizes the city's cultural variety in Pat's bemused reflection while helping the Italians sell fruit: "Faith, an' be the time I do worrk [sic] up me Dutch thrade wud a dago's business, an' throw in a Creole *lagniappe*, I do have to run me hand forninst me flabby pockut-book to know mesilf for a Paddy" (9). Adding further to the mixture of dialects and ethnic types, African-American shoppers buy oysters from the di Carlos and bring their shoes to Pat for repairs.

The only sizable New Orleans group that does not appear in "A Golden Wedding" and "Carlotta's Intended"—and the only New Orleans audience likely to purchase the volumes of stories—is the "American" contingent. It is hard for twenty-first century readers to imagine the pleasure which these highly inflected tales of beloved characters that Stuart unblushingly called "darkeys" and "dagoes" gave to a whole generation of the white middle class. Part of the pleasure came from the opportunity to transcend—if only for the length of a story—the borders separating Northerners from Southerners, blacks from whites, and the "American" from the alien. Stuart's fictional New Orleans is, at the same time, undeniably foreign and unexpectedly familiar.[8]

NOTES

1. A photographic frontispiece of an elegantly dressed teenager contributes to an effect of realism.

2. In her autobiographical *Memories of a Southern Woman of Letters*, Grace King explains that her portrayals of Creole life were a response to Richard Watson Gilder's "rankling taunt" that she should try to improve upon George Washington Cable's Louisiana fiction. King had complained to the *Century* editor that Cable "assumed the inevitable superiority—according to his theories—of the quadroons over the Creoles" (60).

3. See, for example, Paul H. Buck, especially 196–219; and, for a much more critical analysis of this genre, see Helen Taylor. Taylor views King, Stuart, Chopin, and many of their contemporary writers as "politically conservative and—to a modern sensibility—deeply racist" (xiii).

4. Joel Chandler Harris was well known not only for his humorous Uncle Remus tales but also as the author of sympathetic race tragedies like his 1884 story "Free Joe and the Rest of the World."

5. See Ruth McEnery Stuart, "Golden Wedding," opposite page 6. The next illustration in the story, opposite page 10, is captioned "The Wedding, Long Ago" and depicts Aleck and Cicely in their youth, her veil and pretty wedding dress adorned with orange blossoms. Typical of the drawings that accompanied Stuart's short stories throughout her career, these do not caricature the African Americans in her fiction.

6. A representative account of the lottery crisis by a popular Louisiana historian is Garnie William McGinty, especially pages 233–35.

7. This scene is one of several in "Carlotta's Intended" which renders the immigrants' dialogue in perfectly grammatical English. Stuart introduces the encounter between the ruffians by explaining that they are talking to each other in Italian (66). The effect is to close the gap between the very different "discourse communities" represented by Stuart's characters and her readers.

8. I am grateful to the Earhart Foundation for a research grant in support of my work on Ruth McEnery Stuart. Thanks also to Benjamin Franklin Fisher IV of the University of Mississippi for locating several early reviews of Stuart's books in the course of his own research on Stuart's contemporaries.

REFERENCES

Boskin, Joseph. *Sambo: The Rise & Demise of an American Jester*. New York and Oxford: Oxford UP, 1986.

Buck, Paul H. *The Road to Reunion 1865–1900*. Boston: Little, Brown, 1937.

Chopin, Kate. *The Complete Works of Kate Chopin*. Ed. Per Seyersted. 2 vols. Baton Rouge: Louisiana State UP, 1969.

Fletcher, Mary Frances. "Ruth McEnery Stuart: A Biographical and Critical Study." Ph.D. diss., Louisiana State University, 1955.

King, Grace. *Memories of a Southern Woman of Letters*. New York: Macmillan, 1932.

McGinty, Garnie William. *A History of Louisiana*. 3rd ed. New York: Exposition, 1951.

McKinley, Gena. "'The Delightful Accent of the South Land': Ruth McEnery Stuart's Dialect Fiction." *Studies in American Fiction* 26 (1998): 96–114.

Review of *The River's Children*, by Ruth McEnery Stuart. *Reader Magazine* 5 (February 1905): 377.

"Ruth M' E. Stuart, Author, Dies Here." Ruth McEnery Stuart Folder, Clifton Waller Barrett Collection 8790, Special Collections, Alderman Library, University of Virginia, Charlottesville.

Rutherford, Mildred Lewis. *The South in History and Literature: A Hand-Book of Southern Authors from the Settlement of Jamestown, 1607, to Living Writers*. Atlanta: Franklin–Turner, 1907.

Stephens, Edwin Lewis. "Ruth McEnery Stuart." *Library of Southern Literature*. Ed. Edwin Anderson Alderman and Joel Chandler Harris. Atlanta: Martin and Hoyt, 1909. 11:5145–61.

"Stories of Negro Life." Review of *A Golden Wedding and Other Tales*, by Ruth McEnery Stuart. *Beacon* 18 Feb. 1893: 3.

Stuart, Ruth McEnery. "American Backgrounds for Fiction VI – Arkansas, Louisiana and the Gulf Country." *Bookman* Aug. 1914: 620–30.

—. "Carlotta's Intended." *Carlotta's Intended and Other Stories*. New York: Harper, 1894.

—. "A Golden Wedding." *A Golden Wedding and Other Tales*. New York: Harper, 1893.

—. "I Remember, Part I." *Youth's Companion* 12 July 1900: 348.

—. "I Remember, Part II." *Youth's Companion* 26 July 1900: 368.

—. Letter [January 1899] to Drs. Emily and Augusta Pope. Ruth McEnery Stuart Papers, Manuscripts Department, Howard-Tilton Memorial Library, Tulane University, New Orleans.

—. "A People Who Live Amid Romance." *Ladies' Home Journal* Dec. 1896: 7–8.

—. *The Story of Babette: A Little Creole Girl*. New York: Harper, 1894.

—. "Value of Folklore in Literature." *New York Times Review of Books* 12 Oct. 1913: 544–45.

Taylor, Helen. *Gender, Race, and Region in the Writings of Grace King, Ruth McEnery Stuart, and Kate Chopin*. Baton Rouge: Louisiana State UP, 1989.

Wheeler, Candace. "American Authoresses of the Hour: Ruth McEnery Stuart." *Harper's Bazaar* 16 Dec. 1899: 1083–84.

DEPICTIONS OF RACE AND CLASS, 1865–1945

Behind the "White Veil": Alice Dunbar-Nelson, Creole Color, and *The Goodness of St. Rocque*

Pamela Glenn Menke

Alice Dunbar-Nelson's fifteen-year-old "brown" orphan with "black eyes," "silky black hair," and "tropical beauty" cries in anguish: "Who am I? What am I?" ("Josepha," 156, 157, 160, 158, 171). She has been given the name Camille, but has no birth name or birth roots. Her lack of clear racial identity and her lush womanliness render her completely vulnerable. She becomes Sister Josepha, taking the "white veil" and, after one "swift, longing" glance toward Chartres Street, vanishes "behind the heavy door" of the [white] Sacred Heart Convent (172). "Sister Josepha" joins thirteen other stories in *The Goodness of St. Rocque*. With this 1899 publication, Dunbar-Nelson subtly, but dramatically, alters the face of Southern local color, a popular and lucrative genre that filled millions of magazine pages in the closing decades of the nineteenth century (Sedgwick). She carefully lifts aside the "white" authorial "veil" from the racially and culturally complex Louisiana that she knew intimately.

Quite likely, white readers from the Eastern U.S., who eagerly devoured stories by her white predecessors (George W. Cable, Grace King, Ruth McEnery Stuart, and Kate Chopin) saw little difference among them. Elizabeth Ammons suggests that "passing" is a primary characteristic of the *St. Rocque* collection speculating that Dunbar-Nelson intended to be free from "racial prescriptions" (60). Even so, Ammons acknowledges that the stories "either focus on race or make race an element" (61). Indeed, Dunbar-Nelson's version of Creole life, with its shaded marginality and New Orleans reality, provides a perfect local color vehicle for the well-established genre. As Violet Harrington Bryan suggests, her characters, distinguished only by racial code words that most eastern readers would not understand, appear to be "Creoles of any color" (121). Unlike her contemporary readers, whose interpretive acuity was limited by the familiar fictional portraits and plots more than two decades old, we have the capacity to peek behind the "white veil" of *St. Rocque* and to learn about passing from Dunbar-Nelson. Only then can we understand Dunbar-Nelson's distinctive achievement and the degree to which she reveals her own fluid racial distinctiveness and the complexities of "dusky-eyed" Creole reality (145). To fully appreciate her accomplishments, we will consider Cable, King, Stuart, and Chopin, who initially defined the "color" of Louisiana, and her black authorial compatriots Charles Chesnutt and Paul Laurence Dunbar, to whom she was briefly married, and *The Goodness of St. Rocque*, the first and only local-color collection published by a woman of African descent.

Commencing with the publication of Cable's "'Sieur George" in 1873, lush Louisiana provided material for the great surge of local color writing which followed the Civil War[1]. With the 1879 publication of *Old Creole Days*, Cable's depiction of the charming eccentricities of Creole and French Acadian life established an enthusiastic audience for Louisiana fiction, which was satisfied by a host of writers, including Lafcadio Hearn in the 1880s and Grace King, Kate Chopin, and Ruth McEnery Stuart in the 1890s. A complex tradition, some immensely popular local color writers like Virginian Thomas Nelson Page offered a conservative, white, patriarchal vision of a hierarchical society in which inferior beings—usually blacks and white women—knew and accepted their proper place. Other local-color stories, particularly by women writers, variously and carefully challenged white male dominance and the stultifying racial and gender codes upon which it depends.

Unlike Page's celebration of hierarchical racial relationships, Cable's fiction (as in *Old Creole Days* and *The Grandissimes*) warned against the mental and social erosion of an effete Creole past and manifested a mixture of romance and social criticism that promoted a new, if romantic, enlightened South even as he unmasked the paternalism of white Creole culture and the angered anguish of free men and women of color. In *The Grandissimes* (1880), his great novel about racial and economic tensions in antebellum, Creole Louisiana, the dying words of Creole patriarch Agricola Fusilier are "Louis—Louisian—a—for—ever!" (328). On his deathbed Cable's enslaved African prince Bras Coupé whispers,"To—Africa" (193). Unlike Dunbar-Nelson, Cable focused on the social and ideological racial tensions that, in his view, destroyed Louisiana and, by extension, the South.

With such publications and his outspoken views on racial justice, Cable became the arbiter and moral judge of Creole culture. King explicitly countered what she viewed as his distorted and unfair portrait. Even though she pursued the nuances of woman's reality (particularly in *Balcony Stories*, 1893), King was sympathetic with Page's ideological reclamation of the Old South, as was Stuart, another wildly popular Louisiana (and Arkansas) writer. Stuart employed more deliberate humor than Page and based her fiction on a realism directed toward the accuracies of dialect and careful description, but she, too, recapitulated a similar and traditional plantation mythology and was one of many, gifted white writers who provided Northerners with a sense that white Southerners "knew" and indeed could interpret African-American culture. Perhaps, the closest to Dunbar-Nelson in spirit is Chopin. In "Désirée's Baby" and "La Belle Zoraïde," she explores with surprising sensitivity the plight of mixed-race women in a racist culture; she also acknowledges the economic freedom of mulatresse Catiche, in whose garden café *Awakening* (1899) heroine Edna encounters her beloved Robert. Even so, Chopin often acquiesces, albeit poignantly, to the Page version of the loyal black servant, as in "Nég Creole," where a loyal black man defines himself through the heritage of his impoverished, failing, white Creole mistress.

Although at the time his racial heritage was unstated, Charles Chesnutt was the first to break the local color "line" that restricted the genre to white authors with "The Goophered Grapevine," Chesnutt's initial Uncle Julius story, which appeared in the prestigious *Atlantic* in 1888. Even though the Uncle Julius stories are sugar-coated by seeming adherence both to the local-color genre and to the portrait of the wily black storyteller that Joel Chandler Harris had so successfully created in Uncle Remus, they reveal the demeaning and desperate situations of blacks, whose fragile identities are vulnerable to self-betrayal and white complicity. In 1899, Chesnutt collected seven such stories in *The Conjure Woman*. The fact of Chesnutt's African heritage, first withheld, was confirmed in a review of this much-acclaimed collection and propelled the publication of *The Wife of His Youth and Other Stories of the Color Line* in time for the 1899 Christmas market.

Unlike Chesnutt, who secured his reputation as a writer of fiction, Dunbar was a prolific and popular black dialect poet. As Bruce Dickson points out, Dunbar was "America's first black literary celebrity," and until his untimely death in 1906, was the "most popular poet—black or white—in the United States" (57). With his first short-story collection, *Folks from Dixie*, published a year before *St. Rocque*, Dunbar was drawn to regional writing. It promised commercial success and, more importantly, offered a mode of writing more amenable to a realistic portrayal of blacks than his dialect poetry permitted. Even though such poetry continued to be his hallmark and livelihood, he eventually published three more short fiction collections. Dunbar's best stories, like Chesnutt's, disclose the duplicity and masking in which blacks must engage to maintain their dignity and autonomy; however, as a native Ohioan, Dunbar appears uneasy with Southern material. When he uses such material, as he does periodically, particularly in *Old Plantation Days* (1903), he draws heavily on stereotypes well established by white authors. His more effective fiction focuses on the complex circumstances which freedmen encounter as they struggle to create viable and honorable lives in spite of a continuing legacy of racial injustice. Racial nuances and interconnections of people and place are dimly realized in Dunbar's stories; in fact, he identifies the setting of his final short story collection, *The Heart of Happy Hollow* (1904), as "cities or villages, north or south . . . wherever Negroes" gather or settle (2).

Bruce articulately assesses Dunbar's conundrum:

Dunbar's ambivalence was an important sign of the extent to which his ideas of black distinctiveness ran up against assimilationist ideals in his thinking. . . . He could, and did, make a career out of black distinctiveness, as a black poet who wrote about black life using a literary form that emphasized that distinctiveness. But in a sense, this meant that he let the literary form define the meaning of blackness for him; and it was a definition—with its roots in the racist plantation tradition—that made him uncomfortable. (71)

Dunbar's desire for artistic accomplishment meant that his interest in specifying "black distinctiveness" must be ignored or suppressed, as he typically separated his art from his own passionate and often outspoken convictions about the unequal treatment of blacks. Alice praised the wisdom of his demonstration of his white canonical universal, rather than racial, talent: "Did I tell you what Gilder of the *Century* said about you in a private conversation. He said, 'Mr. Dunbar is a literary man, not a colored literary man, but one about whom there is no question.' Well, I've often thought of that and I want you to live up to it" (Boyd 177). In *Paul Laurence Dunbar: Poet Laureate of the Negro Race* (1914), Alice again reflects these sentiments, insisting that his "pure English poems" are his most substantial achievements; "he may have expressed his race in the dialect poems," she continues, but "they were to him the side issues of his work" (qtd. Bruce 59).

Dunbar-Nelson struggled with a similar desire to produce literary art, but, unlike Dunbar or even Chesnutt, the substance of place—New Orleans—and race—Creoles of color—are intricately entwined in her fiction. Dunbar-Nelson paints vivid Louisiana settings and peoples them with Creoles and Cajuns, but her Louisiana is like her Bayou St. John: "In its dark bosom many secrets lie buried . . . . it thinks unceasingly, and below its brightest sparkle you feel its unknown soul . . . Looking upon it for the first time, you would shudder because you feel what lies beneath the brown water" ("On the Bayou Bridge," III: 147). Since explicit racial indicators are absent, Dunbar-Nelson's fiction depends upon insider knowledge. It often turns on the trope of masking; secret information is offered but is available only to those who share that same secret. The most nuanced term becomes "Creole."

Eastern readers drawn to Louisiana local color would be familiar with the Creoles of Cable, King, and, to some extent, Chopin. However, with the singular exception of Cable's *Grandissimes*, published almost twenty years earlier, readers would most likely read "Creole" as white, not as potentially "colored," a fact made obvious by Chopin's designation "Nég Creole." Dunbar-Nelson, on the other hand, is clear about the subversive power and historical truths of the contested term, as she demonstrates in her 1916 discussion, "People of Color in Louisiana," published in *The Journal of Negro History*. She quickly quotes King, noted white local colorist and New Orleans social leader, who, like Dunbar-Nelson, carefully distinguishes *gens de couleur libre* from enslaved, pure-blood Africans. "The *gens de couleur*, colored people, were always a class apart," explains King, "separate from and superior to the Negroes, ennobled were it only by one drop of white in their veins" (361). After a careful history of slavery and the arrival of French West Indians, Dunbar-Nelson focuses on the historical presence of free persons of color (*gen de couleur libres*) as early as 1724 and cites governmental articles that set "a free person of color . . . as far above his slave fellows as the white man sets himself above the person of color" (371). Next, Dunbar subverts the white racial privilege inherent in King's definition. According to Dunbar-Nelson, "Creole" identifies "a native of the lower parishes of Louisiana in whose veins some traces of Spanish, West Indian, or French blood runs" (367). The key phrase is "West Indian." While she acknowledges that "Caucasians" would "shudder with horror" at such a definition, she insists that "Creole" identifies the Louisiana-born individual "in whose blood runs mixed strains of everything . . . with the African strain slightly apparent" (367). In other words, it is not King's single drop of white blood that creates a distinctive Creole, but the single drop of African blood that tempers "the inartistic complexion of the white" (364). "The true Creole," says Dunbar-Nelson, "is like . . . gumbo—a little bit of everything, making a whole, delightfully flavored, quite distinctive, and wholly unique" (367). Thus, the only "true" Creole is someone like Dunbar-Nelson herself.

Her lineage does not suggest such a heritage. Her mother, Patricia Wright Moore, was born in slavery but relocated from a southwest Louisiana plantation to New Orleans as the war concluded; she supported her family through her work as a seamstress. Dunbar-Nelson's father, a merchant marine who was probably white, had a limited presence in her life, if any. Even so, the regal, light-complexioned, well-educated, culturally refined, gifted singer and musician Dunbar-Nelson proudly claimed Creole heritage and was active in New Orleanian Creole literary and social circles. She could easily pass for white and sometimes did in order to gain access to museums and artistic performances, though for the majority of her life she identified herself as Negro and was fiercely involved in rights for blacks and for women. When Alice married the very famous, but very dark–skinned, lower–class, and less well–educated Paul, her mother disapproved. The marriage itself was a tempestuous one, and, after a short time, Alice separated from Paul while retaining his name (and a modest inheritance after his death) even after marrying journalist and soul mate Robert Nelson, with whom she lived out her mature life. She maintained her elegant and refined Creole "bearing," comments Gloria Hull, in spite of "the intimate realities" of strained "finances and private fun" (*Brave* 192).

Twenty-year-old Alice Moore's first Creole local-color stories were "Titee," "Carnival Jangle," and "Little Miss Sophie." They are repeated in *St. Rocque*, but initially appeared in *Violets* (1895), her inaugural volume of poetry, essays, sketches, and stories. Drawn to Alice precisely because of these artistic accomplishments, Dunbar declared "Little Miss Sophie," as "graceful, poignant, and charming as anything Grace King ever wrote" (Whitlow 117). Later he applauded her "determination to contest Cable for his laurels" and insisted, "Why shouldn't you tell those pretty Creole stories as well as he? You have the force, the fire and the artistic touch" (Whitlow 118–19). As these comments suggest, Dunbar-Nelson was writing within and against a clearly established white literary tradition, a tradition that Dunbar himself implicitly praised. He seems unaware of the distinction which Dunbar-Nelson herself made around the particular sort of "color" with which she invested her stories.

Dunbar's assured readership (and, perhaps, Chesnutt's huge financial success with *Conjure Woman*) must have aided Dunbar when he convinced his publishers to print *The Goodness of St. Rocque* as a companion volume to his *Poems of Cabin and Field*. The unfortunate result of that linkage made Dunbar's words prophetic. If reviewed at all, Alice's stories were considered "pretty." The *Pittsburgh Christian Advocate* (21 December 1899) chortled that: these "delightful Creole stories . . . [are] full of the true Creole air of easy-going . . . with the passion and romance of the people who will ever be associated with such names as Bayou Teche and Lake Pontchartrain" (qtd. in Hull, *Works* 1: xxxii). Reviewers saw what they expected to see: another quaint, though not particularly impressive, version of Louisiana local color. The white tradition, however, and even its important black translation in Chesnutt and Dunbar stood outside the lived experience of Dunbar-Nelson. While she might disguise her Creole heritage in her fiction, that heritage shaped her imagination. In her first published stories, we enter the mixed-blood haunts of New Orleans , such as Washington Square and the Third District, and observe Creole nobility and tragic death.

"Carnival Jangle" stands alone in the Louisiana local-color pantheon; no other story chronicles the swirling revelry of Mardi Gras with its "royal purple and golden yellow and national flags . . . with the madding dream of color and melody and fantasy gone wild" (I: 76, 77). This story leads the reader away from the "deafening clamor" (I: 77) of Canal Street to the "dingiest and most ancient-looking" disguise shop near Toulouse and St. Peter Streets where an old, "yellow," flabby–jawed woman with "eyes . . . sharp as talons" produces the disguise of a troubadour for the reluctant young woman, Flo (I: 78, 79). The young woman's racial affiliation is uncertain, but the "yellow" shopkeeper is, most probably, a woman of color and may be aware of the danger that her disguise engenders. Accompanied by her devil-disguised companion, Flo leaves Royal Street with its safe, white revelry and goes to Washington Square (a mixed neighborhood) to witness "a perfect Indian dance" (I: 81). Flo is far away from the safety of Canal Street as she watches the undulating parade of "mimic Red-men," whom New Orleans natives would recognize as the Mardi Gras Indians, black men who organize themselves in tribes and mask in sequined costumes and flamboyant headresses (81). Suddenly, the tribal chief believes the disguised Flo to be a male betrayer and, snatching a glittering knife from beneath his blanket, kills her in this maddest of "the last mad moments of Rex's reign" (I: 82). This story is indeed a disturbing "dream of color and melody and fantasy gone wild," as Dunbar-Nelson proclaims on its opening page. The story challenges the implicit safety of Carnival's multi–racial revelry, in which one can "pass" for anything that one desires. Flo leaves her safe gendered "place," becoming a young male singer, and is racially displaced as she innocently wanders into the mixed-race neighborhood. "Color," gender disguise, and place converge to produce tragedy.

"Little Miss Sophie" evokes a mixed-race woman's solitary, love-forsaken existence. Seamstress Sophie is cast aside by her white beloved, an action reminiscent of Dunbar-Nelson's seamstress mother by her father. Sophie has lived for five years in the Third District, "that nature and the city fathers seemed to have forgotten" (141). After journeying uptown on the Claiborne streetcar to deliver her stitched garments, she learns that the actual identity and, thus, claim to a rich inheritance of her former white lover, Neale, may be proven only by producing a Roman ring. "It seems," says the elegantly clad stranger whom Sophie overhears, "that Neale had some little Creole love-affair some years ago and gave this ring to his dusky-eyed fiancée. But you know how Neale is with his love-affairs, went off and forgot the girl in a month. It seems, however, she took it to heart—so much so until he's ashamed to try to find her or the ring" (147). With the phrase "dusky-eyed fiancee," Dunbar-Nelson is reflecting on the New Orleans custom of an arranged, protected, and economically supported relationship between a quadroon and her white male protector. Far from a protector, Neale represents heartless, white male dishonor. Sophie, on the other hand, is invested with Creole honor and dignity: "As a present had the quaint Roman circlet been placed upon her finger,—as a present she would return it" (148). She pawns the treasured ring to assist her dying father; she reclaims it so that she can return it and gives her life in the process. Overwork and exhaustion lead to her death on Christmas Day, with the ring on her bosom and a note to return the ring to Neale. This seemingly romantic story with its sentimental conclusion is a startling and telling reversal of other Louisiana local colorists. Cable is fond of a similar plot, but he invariably and squarely, positions the honor within the sensitive, white males of "'Tite Poulette and "Madame Delphine." Chopin, in "Désirée's Baby," reveals that the racial mixture producing orphaned Désirée's dark-featured child is inherited, in part at least, from the slave-mother of the child's arrogant, wealthy father. In "Little Miss Sophie," whiteness and maleness are the culprits. Dunbar-Nelson celebrates "dusky-eyed" Sophie but acknowledges that her honor will severely affect, even destroy her. While the white male confirms his social identity and viability, hers remains private, unacknowledged, and deadly.

"Titee" joins "Little Miss Sophie" in illustrating generous Creole nobility, although Titee, "a queer child," is an unlikely hero (I: 48). His teacher considers him an "idle, lazy, dirty, troublesome boy," but we know him as an inventive, fun-loving boy who "could dissect a butterfly or a mosquito-hawk and describe their parts as accurately as a spectacled student with a scalpel and microscope" and who knew "exactly when it was time for crawfish to be plentiful down in the Claiborne and Marigny canals" (I: 45, 46). Intimately acquainted with his boyish friends— "Creole and Spanish fellows, with dark skin and lovely eyes like Spaniels"—Titee is an informed and adventurous inhabitant of his Third District neighborhood "with its swamps and canals and commons and rail-road sections, and its wondrous tortuous streets" (I: 46, 45–6). In his adventures he discovers a sick old man, whom he keeps safe in a cave near the Marigny Canal levee. He tells no one of his new friend, whom he unselfishly feeds with his lunches and pocketed "remnants of his scanty" meals (I: 50). The bitter winter wind, rain, his famished body, and a broken leg are his undoing. His family finds him crumpled and moaning beside the railroad tracks; at his urging, they also discover the hidden old man and understand Titee's selfless generosity, but young Titee dies and is buried in the St. Rocque cemetery.

St. Rocque and his cemetery open Dunbar-Nelson's distinguished local-color collection, published five years later, and Titee, in the concluding *St. Rocque* story, survives: "he went his way as before" (I: 224). The title story and the concluding "Titee" affirm the resurgence of Creole life. Titee's generosity is celebrated; the goodness of St. Rocque conjoined with the charms and advice of the story's ancient conjure woman assist dark-eyed Manuela in defeating "dat light gal" Claralie and in wedding her beloved Theophilé (8); however, the majority of the *St. Roque* stories reflect domestic violence, working-class conflict, male deceptions, woman's economic oppression, and racial strife. With only two exceptions, as Gloria Hull points out, "women are shut in" behind a slammed door and serve as "shorthand for an almost existential female dread" (*Color* 52). Although Hull views these succumbing women as evidence of Dunbar-Nelson's separation between "herself and her actual writings," it is equally likely that they indicate Dunbar-Nelson's troubled awareness of her contemporary times (*Color* 52). Highly educated, traveled, and increasingly committed to activism even in these early years, Dunbar-Nelson was well aware that the turn-of-the-century was defined by dispiriting racial and gender turmoil. Jim Crow and other conservative Southern laws countenancing racial separation and inequality for blacks were firmly ensconced. The rampant lynching and torture of black men and women were joined by the dominant presence of the Ku Klux Klan version of virulent racism. The popular War of 1898, alluded to briefly in "Sister Josepha," defined the United States as an imperial power, and well-educated, professional, and outspoken black and white women posed an increasing threat to male presence.

The turbulent historical context and the limited tolerance among readers for stark fictional treatment of the color line must have contributed to Dunbar-Nelson's careful muting of racial and gender issues to assure the success of her fiction. That she wrote at all is a testimony to her ambition, her courage combined with youth, and her concern about the degree to which women like herself were constrained in their desires to act out authentic lives. Rather than a despairing commentary on women's passivity, the collection unmasks the destructive power of isolated and unappreciated differences. Such lack of recognition is, in Dunbar-Nelson's mind, the inability not only of whites to affirm the privilege and power of blackness, but also of blacks to affirm blood relationships with their light-complexioned sisters and brothers. Dunbar-Nelson insists, "There are a thousand subtleties of refined cruelty which every fair colored person must suffer at the hands of his or her own people" (III: 320). At one and the same time, *St. Rocque* is Dunbar-Nelson's lament and reclamation for her Creole self and for others like her. Rather than, as Hull proposes, being "separated from. . . black experience," *St. Rocque* portrays an importantly different and, in Dunbar's view, equally authentic Creole experience (*Color* 52). Dunbar-Nelson poignantly recounts the difficulties of those caught between two races and cultures because they cannot fully identify with either the black of white cultures. As a result, therefore, in most stories, intimacy is absent, and any momentary affiliation is offset by the deceptions through which it is accomplished. "Sister Josepha," for example, is a story of uncertain identity and sexual dangers for a woman on the racial margins. Sheltered for many years in the Sacred Heart Convent, Camille, at fifteen, is given an opportunity to be adopted. She feels comfortable with the Creole woman whom she meets, but not with her husband. Recognizing his "pronounced leers and admiration of her female charms," Camille instinctively understands that he is "creepy." His power and her voluptuousness serve as emblems of the unprotected mixed-race woman in an increasingly polarized racial society. Dunbar-Nelson, who had helped found the Harlem White Rose Home for Girls in the year preceding the collection's publication, knew well the unmentioned dangers that alert Camille. Camille's vulnerability is explicitly connected to her uncertain identity and to the "self-torture" that its uncertainty causes (171). In the only option which she believes available, Camille takes the "white veil" and enters the convent. This veiled whiteness anticipates the double-consciousness that W.E.B. DuBois was soon to discuss in *Souls of Black Folk*; it represents the protection of a privileged order, that of white-modeled society, through the denial and absence of racial identity. A hint of the 1898 war enters briefly as Josepha glimpses a young military man who smiles at her in the Cathedral. She considers escape to a life of romance and freedom from the closeted convent walls, but recognizing "the deception of the life she would lead," she remains "Sister Josepha" enclosed in the "pale-eyed," white-bonneted female convent (170). A celibate, woman-defined space countenanced by a male religious hierarchy becomes the only viable solution for a young woman who has "no nationality" and "cannot tell from whom or whence she came," in other words, whose racial heritage is unclear (170, 171).

With its racial markings and convent solution, the Dunbar-Nelson story implies the popular trope of passing authorially practiced by Chopin in "Désirée's Baby;" by Cable in "Madame Delphine" and "'Tite Poulette;" and by King in "Little Convent Girl." Unlike the Cable stories, Josepha's dilemma is not resolved by being declared white either through deception or fact; unlike the Chopin and King accounts, she does not wander forlorn to her presumed death in the bayou or plunge herself into the river. Josepha's is motivated to suicide by having no vibrant racial or gender identity, no intimate relationships, and no independent action. Conversely, the very protected St. Rocque Creole "Odalie" is denied simple male–female encounters by her father; her repressed sexuality leads again to a convent solution.

The dangers of transgressing gender identity as implied in "Carnival Jangle," racial identity as shown in "Sister Josepha," or sensuality as in "Odalie" hinge on male economic control (the Church, the father) and on the requirement to observe proper decorum and gender obedience. These are the subjects of the ironically entitled "Tony's Wife," which presents the abusive relationship of Italian Tony with the hard-working German woman who has lived with and supported him for years. Because of his obdurate refusal to marry her, she is denied his Prytania Street shop and any economic viability and is "sent forth in the world penniless" (33). Tony, on the other hand, is "buried" with "many honours by the Society of Italia's Sons" and his brother John inherits Tony's business (33). Quiet Creole gentlemen also stand far from the fringe of economic viability. In "Mr. Baptiste," cross-racial violence erupts in bitter and violent encounter between striking Irish and African-American dock workers. The conflict results in the death of sweet, vagrant Baptiste, who desires the almost spoiled fruit that he often secures from the docked ships, identifies with and cheers on the dock workers and is killed by an Irish-thrown brick. Only the largesse of an acquisitive, but compassionate non-Creole saves the violin and the precarious, sensitive existence of M'sieu Fortier, whose music is his life. Implicitly, Creole society cannot sustain itself; it has beauty, artistry, but no protection, no economic resources, and no recognition in the larger and more privileged world.

The *St. Rocque* storyteller Dunbar-Nelson is like her character in the superb sketch "The Praline Woman." Tante Marie sells her sweet wares for strangers' consumption, pleasing them with her regard, telling them her tales, and even sharing key events in her life just as she implicitly reveals suppressed anger and despair. Marie's abiding fear is a break in the levee that holds back a fluidity that would sweep away her reconstructed life (with her adopted daughter) and her safe place. The fluidity nibbling at the *St. Rocque* edges represents the mixed dangers of Dunbar-Nelson's racial identity and her foray into the local-color genre. In order to publish her collection, she must satisfy her readers' expectations for non-threatening, enjoyable images of Louisiana. Such containment, however, denies the authenticity of the Creole life as she understands it. In order for her to fashion a viable artistic life, she must shape her fiction into white forms, yet she knows well that her own identity is both fixed and unfixed, as are the identities of the characters that she portrays. "When the Bayou Overflows" is an explicit story about the dangers inherent in breaking with established place. A young man who goes to Chicago to seek a new life and fortune, fails. As he promised, he does return in flood season when the bayou overflows, but he returns in his coffin. The story implicitly reminds Creole and black migrants that the jubilation trains heading North become the trains of box cars, carrying dead home to be buried in Louisiana. The "native black waters" that flow through *The Goodness of St. Rocque* must be held at bay to preserve one's "place" even as they embody the authentic racial mixtures and multiplicities denied by white prescriptions and privilege. At its narrative edges flows an unfettered, free darkness represented in Dunbar-Nelson's description of the Bayou St. John as "dark and passionate like the women of Egypt . . . deep silent like their souls" (85).

Sometime during the next decade, Dunbar-Nelson wrote "Stones of the Village" in which she creates a highly educated and respected, Louisiana-born Black man who passes for white. Becoming a distinguished lawyer and judge, his reputation and agency are secured by his successful pretense of being "white" and his rejection of his rural Louisiana, quasi-Creole heritage. In this anguished and bitter story, the distinguished judge dies during a banquet honoring him. In his delirium, he believes that his childhood torture lives again when white boys, "black and yellow boys" all stoned him, shouting again and again, "White nigger! White nigger" (III: 5). Dunbar-Nelson herself had a "miserable" childhood, she later recounts in an unpublished piece, "Brass Ankles Speaks," defined by her being ridiculed as a "light nigger with straight hair" (II: 311, 312). "Stones of the Village" was rejected by *Atlantic Monthly* editor Bliss Perry because of the public's "dislike" for material on the "color-line" (Hull, *Color* 57). Both this and a third short-fiction collection, tentatively entitled "Stories of Women and Men," remained unpublished.

Although Dunbar-Nelson continued writing a few stories and more poetry and published two plays, she increasingly turned her creative energy to editorials, essays, and social commentary for periodicals specializing in black materials, such as *Crisis, Opportunity*, and the *Journal of Negro Folklore*. Insistent on bringing black voices and issues to national attention, she edited a collection of oratory, *Masterpieces of Negro Eloquence* in 1914 as well as a Paul Laurence Dunbar Nelson anthology in 1920. Beginning in the 1920s with her work on *The Wilmington Advocate*, the progressive black newspaper which she and her husband Robert Nelson edited, journalism became the primary venue for her writing talent. She also continued to be an ardent activist: an anti-lynching crusader, an organizer of the Black Women's club movement, and a champion for black people and for women's rights.

   The Goodness of St. Rocque is Dunbar-Nelson's local-color literary legacy. In it, recently married, gifted, twenty-four-year-old Alice Moore Dunbar passed on her cultural heritage. Beyond any intricate interpretation of her writing, there remain her word portraits of distinctive Louisiana Creole culture. Unlike any other local colorist, Dunbar-Nelson immerses us in a riot of colors and customs and ethnic multiplicity: Creole, Spanish, French, Irish, Black, White. As an African-descent, Creole woman, Dunbar-Nelson stands alone in her contributions to Southern local color.

NOTE

   1. I acknowledge Barbara C. Ewell's influence on portions of this essay. We have recently completed an almost seamless collaborative discussion of Southern local color, and our words and thoughts often flow together.

REFERENCES

Ammons, Elizabeth. "The Limits of Freedom: The Fiction of Alice Dunbar-Nelson, Kate Chopin, and Pauline Hopkins." *Conflicting Stories: American Women Writers at the Turn of the Century*. New York: Oxford UP, 1991. 59–85.

Boyd, Herb. *Autobiography of a People*. New York: Doubleday, 2000.

Bruce, Dickson D., Jr. *Black American Writing from the Nadir: The Evolution of a Literary Tradition, 1877–1915*. Baton Rouge: Louisiana State UP, 1989.

Bryan, Violet Harrington. "Race and Gender in the Early Works of Alice Dunbar-Nelson." *Louisiana Women Writers: New Essays and a Comprehensive Bibliography*. Ed. Dorothy H. Brown and Barbara Ewell. Baton Rouge: Louisiana State UP, 1992. 120–28.

Cable, George W. *The Grandissimes*. Ed. Newton Arvin. New York: Sagamore P, 1957.

—. *Old Creole Days*. New York: Charles Scribner's Sons, 1879.

Chesnutt, Charles. *The Conjure Woman and Other Conjure Tales*. Boston: Houghton Mifflin, 1899.

Chopin, Kate. "La Belle Zoraïde." *The Complete Works of Kate Chopin*. Ed. Per Seyersted. Baton Rouge: Louisiana State UP, 1969. 303-8.

—. "Désirée's Baby." *The Complete Works of Kate Chopin*. Ed. Per Seyersted. Baton Rouge: Louisiana State UP, 1969. 240-45.

Dunbar, Alice. *The Goodness of St. Rocque and Other Stories*. New York: Dodd, Mead, 1899.

Dunbar, Paul Laurence. *The Collected Poetry of Paul Laurence Dunbar*. Ed. Joanne M. Braxton. Charlottesville: UP of Virginia, 1993.

—. *Folks from Dixie*. New York: Dodd, Mead, 1898.

—. *The Heart of Happy Hollow*. New York: Dodd, Mead, 1904.

—. *In Old Plantation Days*. New York: Dodd, Mead, 1903.

—. *Poems of Cabin and Field*. New York: Dodd, Mead, 1899.

Dunbar-Nelson, Alice. "People of Color in Louisiana." *Journal of Negro History* 1 (1916): 361–76.

—. "Titee." *The Works of Alice Dunbar-Nelson*. Ed. Gloria T. Hull. 3 Vols. New York: Oxford UP, 1988.

—. *Violets and Other Tales*. Boston: Monthly Review P, 1895.

Elder, Arlene. *The "Hindered Hand": Cultural Implications of Early African-American Fiction*. Westport, CT: Greenwood P, 1978.

Hull, Gloria T. *Color, Sex, and Poetry*. Bloomington: Indiana UP, 1987.

—. "Researching Alice Dunbar-Nelson: A Personal and Literary Perspective." *All the Women Are White, All the Blacks Are Men, But Some of Us Are Brave: Black Women's Studies*. Ed. Gloria T. Hull, Patricia Bell Scott, and Barbara Smith. New York: Feminist P, 1982. 189–95.

King, Grace. *Balcony Stories*. New Orleans: L. Graham, 1893.

Sedgwick, Ellery. "Magazines and the Profession of Authorship in the United States: 1800–1900." Unpublished paper. American Literature Association Conference: Baltimore, MD, 30 May 1999.

Whitlow, Roger. "Alice Dunbar-Nelson: New Orleans Writer." *Regionalism and the Female Imagination: A Collection of Essays*. Ed. Emily Toth. University Park, PA: Human Sciences P, 1985.

Masking and Racial Passing at Mardi Gras in Lyle Saxon's "Have a Good Time While You Can"

Larry D. Griffin

Lyle Saxon (1891-1946) may be most noted as the Louisiana State Director of the Federal Writer's Project.[1] He is neither the first nor the last American writer to explore racial passing or to give a narrative a Mardi Gras setting. Like fiction itself, masquerade provides truth through deception, and English writers, like Geoffrey Chaucer (c.1342-1400) and William Shakespeare (1564-1616), and American writers, like Edgar Allan Poe ((1809-1949) and Nathaniel Hawthorne (1804-1864), have often recognized the value of using masquerade in their works. Saxon is not even the first to use the New Orleans Mardi Gras setting. George Washington Cable (1844-1925) in his *The Grandissimes* (1880) sets his novel at the 1803 New Orleans Mardi Gras, a century before Saxon's experience, and William Clark Falkner (1826-1889), great-grandfather of William Faulkner (1897-1962), opens his *The White Rose of Memphis* (1880) with a riverboat masquerade. As Terry Castle suggests, an engaging study might be made of the carnival and masquerade theme in Southern writing from Edgar Poe through James Purdy.[2] African-American and white passing have existed ever since there has been an African slave trade, and passing has long been a theme in American literature. Juda Bennett in *The Passing Figure: Racial Confusion in Modern American Literature* outlines the popularity of the theme from William Wells Brown's *Clotel* (1853) through James Weldon Johnson's *The Autobiography of an Ex-Colored Man* (1912).[3] In his only novel, *Children of Strangers* (1937), Lyle Saxon's Euphemie Vidal, a mulatto, has a child by her white lover who then passes for white.

Lyle Saxon's greatest achievement with a masquerading and passing theme in a Mardi Gras setting remains the purported memoir of his own experience at Mardi Gras. When he was a boy in 1903, Lyle Saxon went to Mardi Gras with his grandfather. Lyle Saxon published his two-part memoir of that event in *Century Magazine* in 1928. These two articles comprise Part I of Saxon's *Fabulous New*

Orleans, which was published later that same year of 1928. In his narrative, the young Saxon and his grandfather visit an unnamed Creole friend of his grandfather's. Saxon's grandfather transfers his parental role for the boy to that friend's African-American servant so that the child may join in the Mardi Gras festivities. If an African-American parent figure substitutes for a white parent in caring for a white child, the parent-child relationship usually takes precedence over racial separatism. For that reason, white children in the care of African-Americans may experience African-American culture in ways that white adults cannot. In Saxon's memoir, the African-American servant Robert also manipulates the opportunities that masking affords him and the boy at Mardi Gras.[4] By mask manipulation, Robert and the young Saxon character experience both the Mardi Gras of African-Americans and the Mardi Gras of whites that segregation normally prohibits. Once costumed and masked, Robert and the boy experience an early twentieth-century New Orleans Mardi Gras that permits both Robert and the boy to pass back and forth from the African-American experience to the white experience of the festival. When the boy and his grandfather meet an old beggar woman on the morning of his arrival, she tells the boy: "I hope you enjoy yourself. Have a good time while you can. . . . That's what *I* always say!'" (Saxon 6). The time is so good for the boy that as an adult, who cannot forget it twenty-five years later, he finally breaks his word not to tell of his great Mardi Gras adventure. Readers suspect no moral violation because the grandfather and the grandfather's Creole friend, those to whom he must not tell the story, are now probably dead. Furthermore, Robert, the one to whom the boy made his pledge, is also probably dead. If the boy is really Lyle Saxon, he would have been eleven or twelve years old in 1903.

When Saxon's grandfather suggests that he take the boy to some carnival parades and without a costume, the old Creole gentleman insists otherwise: "'No, the boy must mask, and he must see the thing in the way it should be seen'" (Saxon 11). The old Creole gentleman speaks to his servant in French: "I gathered that they were talking of me and soon my grandfather explained that Robert was to take me to the center of the city where I could see the maskers and the parades. He was to have charge of me for the entire day, unless I grew tired and wanted to come back to the house. In that case I was to say so. A costume would be provided me" (Saxon 12). The boy also learns that Robert is named for Giacomo Meyerbeer's opera *Robert le Diable* (1831). As they leave, Robert tells the boy: "'Us is goin' tuh have us a time'" (Saxon 13).

A playfully devilish theme permeates this memoir. The two will masquerade as devils, and they will devil the Mardi Gras of both the African-American carnival experience and the white carnival experience. With their mask manipulations, they easily pass back and forth from one cultural space to the other. At the costume shop, the boy seems amazed that two nuns rent a devil's costume. Robert orders the boy a red devil's costume. He then tells the white shop owner that he needs one like it for Saxon's older brother, but the costume is really for Robert himself: "The mystery of my 'brother' was explained, for it was Robert and none other who was to wear the other suit. He had resorted to this device, he told me, because the shopkeeper would not rent a costume to a negro" (Saxon 19). The boy also learns:

"Robert could show me things that no other man in New Orleans could show half so well. All that was necessary was that I forget it afterward and carry no tale back to his master" (Saxon 19-20). To complete his costume, Robert puts on a pair of white cotton gloves, "and now that none of skin was visible, no one could tell whether he were a white man or a negro—or a Chinaman or anything else, for that matter" (Saxon 20). Mardi Gras mask experts Carl Lindahl and Carolyn Ware suggest: "Mardi Gras masks thus fill sometimes contradictory functions of disguise and display" (15). While Lindahl and Ware suggest that the half-face mask is now associated with New Orleans, full masks were either more popular at the turn of the century in New Orleans or at least popular enough for Robert and the boy to wear them and thus conceal their racial identities (16). Half-masks have been popular in *Commedia Dell'arte* since the Middle Ages.[5] Of course, if the two devils wore only half-masks, their passing in the African-American and in the white cultural spaces would not be possible at all. Concealment of race and identity (as identity includes race) allows the two devils to pass, to blend in, and to feel invisible or unnoticed by the others in their presence.

Feeling "invisible" in his costume on the festive streets of New Orleans, the boy accompanies Robert to the grand arrival of the Zulu King, at that time, a typically African-American only experience of Mardi Gras. The Zulu King is the chosen by the Mardi Gras Indians.[6] Intrigued by the sexual innuendoes, the boy is too naive to understand them. For example, Saxon reports that the crowd kept asking the Zulu King about his queen, and the King answered that he would only have a male queen; he was through with women. Next, the two devils go into an African-American barroom on Rampart Street. At that venue, Robert pushes up his mask to drink his beer. The boy remains masked and drinks his red soda pop through his mask. To the African-American patrons in the barroom, the two devils appear to be an African-American father and his son.

From the barroom, the pair walk to the Parade of Rex. At the parade, the boy sits on Robert's shoulders and catches green beads; the crowd assumes the two masked devils are white because Robert is masked and the child is not. After the Rex Parade, the two walk streets that are lined with white whorehouses: "I wanted very much to stop and go in at each such cafe, but Robert said that we'd better not, as negroes were not allowed inside" (Saxon 43). They stroll by the whorehouses on Iberville Street:

Robert still wore his mask as many other men in the street did; and from time to time one of the red-lipped lassies would hail him with a cry: "Hello papa! Showing your boy around?" or they would wave me to say "Hey little boy, bring your daddy in to see me!" And I being a polite child, would wave back and say, "You must come see us sometime!" (Saxon 44)

The prostitutes assume that since the boy is white, the parental figure, whom they assume to be the father, must be white too. Typically, if men mask to conceal themselves, then Robert and the boy conceal their races by their masks when it is appropriate to be considered either African-American or white. While this masking reveals different cultural experiences to the two, neither one of them reveal themselves to one another or to anyone else. Furthermore, given all the first experiences the boy Saxon has at this Mardi Gras with women, wine, and song, the simple male bonding associated with Robert, his initiator, underscores the boy's ritual movement from innocence to experience. Because of Robert, the young Saxon encounters his first prostitutes, goes to barrooms for the first time, and drinks absinthe for the first time. At his first Mardi Gras, Saxon experiences a rough part of New Orleans with which he and most young white boys usually have no familiarity.

In this rough part of New Orleans, a police officer stops the two devils, and the officer says to the masked Robert: "'That kid is too young to be down here alone,' he said pointing at me with his club. 'Is he with you?' And Robert mustering up his best white-folks' voice, replied from under his mask, 'I'm taking him somewhere.' And the policeman shrugged his shoulders and walked on." (Saxon 44). They move down the street from young white to old white to mulatto prostitutes, and finally they arrive at an African-American saloon, "The High Brown Social and Athletic Club." There Robert takes the boy—both are unmasked—through the bar and back outside to a courtyard. They meet with some resistance from two African-American men: "They seemed to object to me—for some reason that I could not understand—but Robert explained that he could not let me out of his sight and that I would behave myself and say nothing" (Saxon 46). Perhaps the two African-American men do not think a white boy should be among them, but whatever the reason the boy does not understand. The reader suspects that the mature narrator, however, understands fully.

After Robert and Saxon leave the courtyard, they next enter an African-American dance hall where they again meet the Zulu King: "Then, after telling me to sit there quietly—and cautioning me not take off my mask—he was gone, promising to return in a few minutes" (Saxon 47). Robert then dances with the courtesans of the Zulu King. Again, because the boy is masked, the African-American dancehall patrons, unlike the African-Americans in the barroom courtyard previously, assume that the two devils are both African-Americans. Because the boy remains masked, the African-Americans believe he is an African-American boy with an African-American adult.

Back outside in the courtyard the two eat lunch:

Robert stood watching me until I had finished, then while I waited he ate his lunch. For Robert was a stickler for convention. Never let it be said that he let a white child eat with him. No Sir! The little gentleman could not be debased by eating with a negro—but he could be dragged into any sort of den that Robert pleased to enter himself . . . . It was a strange convention, but no stranger than many others that exist. (Saxon 49)

Only in eating lunch does Robert observe the segregation of the day, and he does so only in the presence of the white boy alone. No other persons, African-American or white, are present. In the basic human needs of sleeping, eating, elimination, and procreating, segregation takes its strongest forms. Of these, only eating remains a public activity. Because segregation manifests itself most visibly to public practice, it remains one of the strongest manifestations of segregation to both Robert and the boy in New Orleans in 1903. Food and the eating of it remain strong manifestations in any culture, African-American or white, and the sharing of food with its inevitable connections to hospitality in western culture generally remains prohibitive in racial segregation. Separatism undermines the very hospitality upon which the sharing of food depends. At restaurants and other eating venues throughout the first half of the twentieth century in the United States, segregated eating prevails. Because of its high visibility, segregated public eating becomes the focus of the forced integration protests and sit-ins of the 1960s that occurred in restaurants and at lunch counters.

Back in the dancehall after lunch, the young Saxon falls asleep only to be awakened by a fight that breaks out between the Zulu King and several other African-American men. The Zulu King cuts a man's throat, the room empties, and the police arrive. Robert spirits the boy from the room, and back on the street: "Robert had snatched off my mask and was carrying it in my hand. His own mask was in place. He did not say a word until we had gone for several squares and turned four corners. Then he sat down in a doorway and fanned himself with my mask: 'Jeese! Dat wuz a close call!' he said" (Saxon 50-51). Robert, of course, takes off the boy's mask and retains his own mask so the two will appear as a white pair of devils on the streets. Robert knows that they will be detained if the police believe he is an African-American, and he also knows that the likelihood of their being stopped at all is greatly diminished if they appear to be white. Clearly, racial profiling by police in the United States of America is not a post civil rights phenomenon.

While there very well may not be any actual record of such a violent act as the Zulu King's cutting a man's throat murder during Mardi Gras of 1903, violence most often does accompany the celebrations of carnival. Abner Cohen in his *Masquerade Politics: Explorations in the Structure of Urban Cultural Movements,* though exploring violence at London's Notting Hill Carnival of the present, reminds his readers that people "often conduct their economic struggle through the form of a cultural movement" (3). Cohen insists that "every major carnival is precariously poised between the affirmation of the established order and its rejection"(3). Saxon himself perhaps realizes the precarious balance of peace and violence in a segregated society; indeed, the last major race riot in New Orleans occurred only three years before his own childhood experience at Mardi Gras.[7] For Cohen, the attraction of Mardi Gras creates community where it would otherwise not exist: "Through interaction in primary relationships and change of role in masquerading, individuals recreate their self-identity and so are enabled to resume their demanding social roles in ordinary daily life" (3). To risk the possibility of violence demonstrates the importance of participating in a masquerade for the individual behind the mask. To the big hotels and saloons on Frenchmen Street, white establishments, Robert directs their access: "At these times he would whisper that I raise my mask, and that if any-one asked questions, I must reply that we were looking for someone" (Saxon 51). Saxon reminds readers of why and how Robert uses the mask: "Masked, he could not be distinguished from a white man—if he did not speak—and holding a small white boy by the hand, he could gain access anywhere. It is highly probable that Robert saw places that day that he had never seen in his life before and never saw again" (Saxon 52). Of course, the young Saxon too sees things himself he had never seen before or since. By manipulating the masks to pass as white, the two visit the St. Charles Hotel, and in the Ramos Bar, the boy tastes absinthe for the first time.

When the two maskers ride the streetcar to the Irish neighborhood [8] and where drunks either lie about or fight with one another, Robert explains: "'The Irish Channel'—a bad neighborhood, and that 'White mens up thisaway would jes' as soon kill a nigger eat dinner!'" (Saxon 53).[9] When the boy asks why Robert took him to such a dangerous neighborhood, "he said that he wanted me to see everything" (Saxon 53). The reader realizes that Robert himself wants to experience everything too. The paradox recapitulates itself in the act of masking, which provides focal and diversionary drama.[10] By manipulating the masks, Robert provides opportunities for the boy to pass as African-American and for himself to pass as white, whatever best suits the particular occasion of the Mardi Gras they experience. In doing so, both the white boy and the African-American servant see everything.

In the late afternoon, the two devils return to Robert's room where Robert reminds the boy "that he had promised my grandfather to show me everything" (Saxon 54) and "that he had shown me something that most white men never had seen and never *would* see. But I must promise not to tell a soul" (Saxon 54). This telling/not telling tension exists for twenty-five years before the grown man narrates his experiences of passing at Mardi Gras when he was a boy. Saxon uses the point of view of the mature narrator who recaptures his own youthful naïveté to underscore the importance of lessons he learned as a child when by passing and witnessing Robert's passing he learned some very important lessons about racism and specifically how the community required by Mardi Gras undermines separatism that segregation demands. Samuel Kinser in his *Carnival American* Style suggests that Saxon is using two eyewitnesses here, one white and one African American: "But more importantly the double eyewitness allows Saxon to carry his readers back and forth over the line between what I have called the first—elite and white— and the second—popular, both white and black—Carnival in New Orleans in ways forbidden to any single person at that time, let alone to a pair of comrades of the same age and same hue." (141). Kinser may be somewhat confused here. I read the point-of-view as the mature Saxon recalling the youthful Saxon, and not as a double narrator, white and African American. Similarly, it is the masking of the two devils and not the "double eyewitness" that allows them to pass back and forth between and sharing the elite white carnivals the popular white, the popular African-American, and the African-American elite carnival experiences of New Orleans Mardi Gras.[11]

In Robert's room, man and boy take off their masks and costumes because twilight approaches. From Robert, the boy learns about the prohibition of masks after twilight: "I gathered that the masks had been used to shield criminals in the old days, and that the rule for unmasking with the first twilight was strictly necessary"(Saxon 55). Such rules also work to prohibit African-American from passing as whites after dark. Such practice was not unique to the early twentieth century alone, for as early as 1781, Spanish authorities in New Orleans forbade free blacks and slaves from masking as whites during Mardi Gras.[12]

Unmasked and without costume, Robert and Saxon go to the Comus Parade, which they watch from the base of the statue at Lee Circle. After the Comus Parade, the boy's grandfather finds him in the crowd. Here the boy leaves Robert behind, and he joins the Creole gentleman and his grandfather as they go into the Opera House, where the boy experiences the white ball. The young white Saxon visits the strictly African-American festivities of the Mardi Gras Indians; however, Robert does not get to visit the exclusively white ball at the Opera House.

When the boy grows sleepy, the group returns to the Creole's house, and there the boy Saxon awakes in the bedroom he shares with his grandfather on Ash Wednesday. Robert soon appears with their morning coffee. Drinking his coffee, the boy asks Robert, "'Oh, wasn't Mardi Gras grand? Robert, *do* you remember'" (Saxon 69). However, Robert interrupts with "'Ah don't 'member a thing about it'" (Saxon 69). The memoir ends with the writer of 1928 recalling what concluded his great adventure in 1903: "'Oh!' I said, and was silent again'"(Saxon 69). The boy remains silent about the whole affair for twenty-five years until he writes this memoir, a story of the lessons learned from racial passing at a segregated Mardi Gras. If, as Juda Bennett suggests, the effect of the passing narrative of the Harlem Renaissance is that it "unsteadies our ontological sense of race" (112) what segregation in early twentieth-century New Orleans prohibits is exposure to and therefore understanding of diversity. The inclusive community that Mardi Gras occasions thus provides opportunities for overcoming the exclusive limitations imposed on individuals by segregation, both white and African-American. Bennett also reminds readers: "Passing is possible because definitions of race and sex rely on faulty binarisms" (113) that she characterizes as "the external and the internal, the physical and the spiritual, visual markings and inner workings"(113). While "faulty binarisms" keep the constructs of racism well within the illogical world in which they must exist, through his experiences of masking and passing, the young Lyle Saxon comes very early in his life to realize the value of others and their cultural activities regardless of the color of their skin.

NOTES

1. Saxon also served as the regional field supervisor for the project. He edited *The New Orleans City Guide* (Boston: Houghton-Mifflin [Riverside], 1938, and *Louisiana: A Guide to the State* (New York: Hastings, 1941) for the Federal Writers' Project of the Works Progress Administration. With Edward Dreyer and Robert Tallant, Saxon edited and compiled *Gumbo Ya-ya: A Collection of Louisiana Folk Tales* (Boston: Houghton-Mifflin, 1945). See Jerre Mangione, *The Dream and the Deal: The Federal Writers' Project, 1935-1943* (Boston: Little, Brown, 1972).

2. For a summary discussion of masquerade in nineteenth and twentieth century American literature, see Terry Castle's last chapter "Epilogue: The Masquerade Topos after the Eighteenth Century" in his *Masquerade and Civilization: The Carnivalesque in Eighteenth English Culture and Fiction* (Stanford: Stanford UP, 1986) 331-348.

3. Juda Bennett, *The Passing Figure: Racial Confusion in Modern American Literature* (New York: Peter Lang, 1996) 35-37. For other good discussions of passing, see Werner Sollors' *Neither Black Nor White Yet Both: Thematic Explorations of Interracial Literature* (Oxford: Oxford UP, 1997), and Gayle Wald's *Crossing the Line: Racial Passing in Twentieth-Century U.S. Literature and Culture* (Durham: Duke UP, 2000).

4. Maida Owens, the author of "The Power of the Mask," writes: "To 'mask' connotes transformation—a new face and attire allows an individual to transcend everyday life, to escape the prosaic and immerse him—or herself in the magic and power of Mardi Gras" (<http:lsm.crt.state.la.us/mgras/masking.htm>).

5. Carlo Mazzone-Clementi in his "Commedia and the Actor" (*The Drama Review* 18.1 [March 1974]) indicates the importance of the half-mask to the commedia performer: "Use of the half-mask allows greater physical freedom than a full mask. Made of leather, the commedia masks are light and flexible, permitting, rolls, tumbles and displays of skill limited only by the capabilities of the actor wearing it" (60).

6. Reid Mitchell's "Mardi Gras Indians" in his *All on a Mardi Gras Day: Episodes in the History of New Orleans Carnival* (Cambridge: Harvard UP, 1995), 113-130, provides a good history of the Mardi Gras Indians.

7. This riot is not specifically associated with Mardi Gras by William Ivy Hair in his *Carnival of Fury : Robert Charles and the New Orleans Race Riot of 1900* (Baton Rouge: Louisiana State UP, 1976). James Gill in his *Lords of Misrule: Mardi Gras and the Politics of Race in New Orleans* (Jackson: Univ of Mississippi P, 1997) reports that at the end of the riot the African-American Robert Charles, who was shot to death himself and whose body was mutilated, had killed seven policeman in a stand-off that ended with three dead, six wounded, and fifty needing medical treatment (162-163). Reid Mitchell specifically notes a violent episode at Mardi Gras the very year before Saxon's experience: "In 1902, George Purcell and Thomas Mahan, two white masqueraders, came into Allen's Barroom at Poydras and Rampart. Black maskers also patronized the bar. Purcell ... drew a revolver ... and ... killed Joe McClair" (127). Purcell announced he was there merely to kill an African-American, and that is exactly what he did—Joe McClair was an African-American.

8. According to Maida Owens in her "Louisiana's Traditional Cultures: New Orleans," Irish fleeing the potato famine in the 1840s settled in this area between the Mississippi River and the Uptown Garden District, and it became known as the Irish Channel (<http://www.crt.state.la.us/artsfolklife/main_introduction_maida.html>). Reid Mitchell characterizes the Irish Channel as "the best known white working-class neighborhood" in New Orleans (39).

9. Because Saxon reports that Robert uses the word "nigger," I have chosen to cite it here rather than deny the use of the word in its historical and textual contexts. Only through the confrontation of the unacceptable use of such words in the past can we fully enter discussion of why the term is unacceptable in today's usage. I have also not capitalized "Negro," where Saxon did not capitalize it.

10. Lindahl and Ware write: "In terms of drama, the mask is both focal and diversionary—sometimes the wearer plays a role specifically geared to fit the mask he or she is wearing, but just as often the mask is simply an opportunity, providing the freedom and anonymity that allows the wearer to adopt the role that he or she would be playing under any mask on Mardi Gras day" (56).

11. Thomas di Palma in his *New Orleans Carnival* (New Orleans: Homes Printing, 1953) relates his 1920 experience with an African-American woman who masks as a "black mammy" but with a blonde curl to suggest that she is really white. Such deception allows her to accompany her masked white mistress to white Mardi Gras festivities and yet she still can be welcome at the strictly African-American festivities, such as the court of the Zulu Queen at the Geddes Funeral Home (24-26).

12. Maida Owens in her "Mystery and History" at <http://lsm.crt.state.la.us/mgras/history.htm>. According to Lindahl and Ware in their *Cajun Mardi Gras Masks*, laws in Cajun communities of Louisiana also prohibited masking (14).

REFERENCES

Bennett, Juda. *The Passing Figure: Racial Confusion in Modern American Literature*. New York: Peter Lang, 1996.

Castle, Terry. *Masquerade and Civilization: The Carnivalesque in Eighteenth English Culture and Fiction*. Stanford: Stanford UP, 1986.

Cohen, Abner. *Masquerade Politics: Explorations in the Structure of Urban Cultural Movements*. Berkeley: U of California P, 1993.

di Palma, Thomas. *New Orleans Carnival*. New Orleans: Homes Printing, 1953.

Gill, James. *Lords of Misrule: Mardi Gras and the Politics of Race in New Orleans*. Jackson: U of Mississippi P, 1997.

Hair, William Ivy. *Carnival of Fury: Robert Charles and the New Orleans Race Riot of 1900*. Baton Rouge: Louisiana State UP, 1976.

Kinser, Samuel. *Carnival, American Style: Mardi Gras at New Orleans and Mobile*. Chicago: U of Chicago P, 1990.

Lindahl, Carl, and Carolyn Ware. *Cajun Mardi Gras Masks*. Jackson: U of Mississippi P, 1997.

Mangione, Jerre. *The Dream and the Deal: The Federal Writers' Project, 1935–1943*. Boston: Little, Brown, 1972.

Mazzone-Clementi, Carlo. "Commedia and the Actor." *The Drama Review* 18.1 (1974): 59-64.

Mitchell, Reid. *All on a Mardi Gras Day: Episodes in the History of New Orleans Carnival*. Cambridge: Harvard UP, 1995.

Saxon, Lyle. *Children of Strangers*. New York: Houghton-Mifflin, 1937.

—, ed. *Louisiana: A Guide to the State*. New York: Hastings, 1941.

—. "Mardi Gras" in *Fabulous New Orleans*. New York: Appleton–Century, 1928. 1–69.

—, ed. *New Orleans City Guide, The*. Boston: Houghton-Mifflin, 1938.

—, Edward Dreyer, and Robert Tallant, eds. *Gumbo Ya-Ya: A Collection of Louisiana Folk Tales*. Boston: Houghton-Mifflin, 1945.

Owens, Maida. "Louisiana's Traditional Cultures: New Orleans." 25 November 2000. <http://www.crt.state.la. us/ artsfolklife/main_introduction_maida.html>.

—. "Mystery and History." 25 November 2000. <http://lsm.crt.state.la.us/mgras/history.htm>.

—."The Power of the Mask." 25 November 2000. <http:lsm.crt.state.la.us/mgras/ masking.htm>.

Sollors, Werner. *Neither Black Nor White Yet Both: Thematic Explorations of Interracial Literature*. Oxford: Oxford UP, 1997.

Wald, Gayle. *Crossing the Line: Racial Passing in Twentieth-Century U.S. Literature and Culture*. Durham: Duke UP, 2000.

The "All-Seeing Eye" in Grace King's *Balcony Stories*

Susie Scifres Kuilan

One of Grace Elizabeth King's most popular works among both her contemporaries and ours is the collection of short fiction entitled *Balcony Stories.*[1] When studied as a group, the stories reveal aspects of blindness or sight in the language of the texts as well as in its themes. Many times only the character is blind to the realities of a situation, but in some instances, the reader shares this blindness with the characters until the very end of the story. These stories offer insights into social issues such as race, class, and gender that were addressed by other Southern women writers of the era. Southern women of this time are described by Anne Jones as

> physically pure, fragile, and beautiful, socially dignified, cultured, and gracious, within the family sacrificial and submissive, yet, if the occasion required, intelligent and brave. The tension between the demands of this cultural image and their own human needs lay close to the source of their creativity; that tension is expressed thematically in their fiction, often as the conflict between a public self and a private one or in the imagery of veils and masks. (xi)

In *Balcony Stories*, this conflict between King's public beliefs and the actual revelations of her stories is expressed thematically through images of blindness. Given her Southern background, King may have objected to any reading that contradicted her beliefs of racial and class superiority, yet focusing on the blindness and sight themes within *Balcony Stories* rather than focusing solely on plot and structure not only reveals her conflicting beliefs about class, race, and gender but also illustrates King's understanding that times were changing, requiring people to accept new truths about these roles. In other words, she may publicly claim to believe one way about race, gender, and class, but her stories reveal that her beliefs are actually conflicted. King's use of language and themes related to blindness and sight depicts struggles that are contrary to her own beliefs and through this depiction provide commentary on the society of King's era. Critics compare King to Kate Chopin and George Washington Cable, but the comparison to Cable is particularly ironic given that she began writing at age thirty-three as a response to what she perceived as Cable's derogatory depiction of New Orleans society in general and the Creole aristocracy in particular.[2] Many critics of King's works have focused on the "local color" aspects of her fiction, while others have discussed issues of race, gender, and class. No one has systematically studied the entire collection of *Balcony Stories* or discussed the ways in which these stories contradict her publicly–held beliefs about race and class.

Like Chopin, who lived and wrote during the same period, King also fell from favor until the late 1960s when the feminist movement helped bring increased attention to her work.[3] Grace King was born during a time when the racial crisis surrounding the designation of "Creole" and its implications were reaching a peak. Her family had to flee New Orleans during the Civil War, returning during Reconstruction to a way of life that was radically different from the one that they had left. Joan Dejean notes that King

in effect suggests that, in order for the Creoles to survive in the newly Americanized world then being created in Reconstruction New Orleans, they should admit a crucial new definition of "Creole," one rarely avowed, even by current lexicography: "creole" (with a lowercase *c*) used to refer to an individual of mixed Creole and Negro ancestry who speaks Creole French or Spanish. (119)

While most critics suggest that King felt that her fiction should portray the white creole aristocracy as superior to the African Americans and mixed-blood Creoles, DeJean suggests that King depicts this superiority as being contaminated (120), and it appears that King may have been oblivious to her own depictions since her stated purpose was to defend the Creole society (*Memories* 60–61). King may have begun writing to counter George Washington Cable's negative depictions by showing the Creoles as a superior society, but an analysis of *Balcony Stories* actually reveals a society that needs to come to terms with the changing times. As Helen Taylor points out:

While [King's] work, unlike that of her early rival Cable, remains unashamedly apologist for the "Lost Cause" South, it deserves closer examination for the insights it gives into the complexities postbellum Southerners faced *in terms of the radical redefinition of race, class, and gender to which they were forced to accommodate* [emphasis added]. ("Case" 701).

According to Jones, "Grace King wore the mask of a righteous defender of southern traditions, including the tradition that white and black cultures do not meet on the street, dancing" (120), implying that she would not accept an interpretation of her work that would encourage this type of multi–racial togetherness.

Critics support the idea that in her fiction King may have subconsciously stepped away from her beliefs about race, gender, and class roles. For example, Anna Shannon Elfenbein points out that "King created women characters whose complexity transcends sexual and racial stereotypes" (74). When an author tries to depict one class, race, or gender as being superior, he or she generally relies on negative stereotypes to portray the inferiority, so for King to transcend these stereotypes goes against her own objective of depicting the Creoles as superior.

Rather than countering Cable's depiction, Elfenbein continues that King "add[s] greater depth to the picture [Cable] had drawn" (74–75). Jones further argues: "Although King consciously and, if put to the test, politically held to this racist southern heritage, its rebellious opposite was apparent especially in her fiction" (128-129). Violet Harrington Bryan also suggests that King was not aware of the real image portrayed in her fiction, arguing that "King's ideologies of allegiance to the Old South—black loyalty and white superiority—often ran counter to what her images signified" (53). Helen Taylor implies that King was not aware of writing against her own beliefs: "although [King] never *consciously* takes anything other than a standard southern white supremacist line on questions of race, much of her work probes that line through its very choice of subject matter, narrative tone, and unsatisfactory closures" (*Gender* 28). Edward J. Piacentino calls her "an avowed southern apologist" (59) but then argues, similarly to Elfenbein, Jones, Bryan, and Taylor, that King actually had "divided loyalties." Her divided loyalties become apparent in the story "Joe," which was added to *Balcony Stories* when it was re-released in 1925 (61). Piacentino argues:

while on the one hand Grace King seems to subscribe to the views associated with the popular racial stereotype—the notions of black inferiority and the subordinate status concomitant with it as well as the slave's loyalty to and dependence upon the white man for his needs—as the most pragmatic and workable means for assuring social harmony in the South, on the other she does not fail to criticize some of the inadequacies of the slave system. (62)

This critical attitude toward slavery becomes evident throughout the *Balcony Stories* collection.

Balcony Stories begins with an introductory sketch, which explains that the balconies of New Orleans serve as the point of origin of the stories which follow. King's use of sight images begins in this introductory sketch when she describes women sitting on the balconies at night with the only light provided by the stars as "such a discreet show of light!" (1). King even makes a comment about the stories using the language of sight rather than that of hearing, which is noteworthy given that she is positing her stories as being told orally. King's narrator remarks, "Each story *is* different, or appears so to her," and the storyteller tries "to make the point visible to her apparent also to her hearers" (3). These comments are ironic since these stories are told and heard rather than seen and observed.

The first selections in *Balcony Stories* is "Drama of Three," which portrays an old Creole called the General, his wife, Honorine, and their unknown benefactor, Journel. Both the General and his wife are blind to the identity of the benefactor who is their landlord and provides them with a monthly stipend, which allows them to make ends meet. The General, in true Creole aristocratic form, would be appalled to discover that their old overseer's grandson was providing for them because having someone from a lower class, who, worse yet, is probably not even white, does not fit in with the General's view of the proper roles for one of his race and perceived class. The term overseer is also significant because of its relationship to sight. The General is blind to the ways in which class and racial structures have changed, as demonstrated by Honorine's reminders to the General that Pompey, another young man who is African American and performs favors for them, no longer works for them and is not required to do the General's bidding. King depicts this aging aristocrat as being blind to his fellow human beings, which is evident when he tries to figure out who is sending him the money every month: "Indeed, it would have been hard for the General to look anywhere and not see some one whose obligations to him far exceeded this thirty dollars a month. Could he avoid being happy with such eyes?" (18). As the story reveals, however, this obligation that others supposedly have to the General is something that only he sees. King depicts the General negatively, clearly not intending him to be a sympathetic character. He may be pitied for his lack of insight, but he is undeserving of the type of sympathy reserved for characters who have had real loss. This story reveals changing class structures, showing that only the blind, such as the General, misunderstand the implications of these changes.

"La Grande Demoiselle" also comments on these changing social structures. King demonstrates that some blindness is willful, as revealed through the character of Idalie Sainte Foy Mortemart des Islets. Idalie, a spoiled Creole aristocrat, has grown up ignoring anything that does not interest her. Things she no longer cares to own, she gives or throws away: "anything to get them out of sight" (27). Presumably during the war, her family lost everything, including their home to fire. The results of what happened to Idalie and her family are negative, but the narrator explains that "history does not relate" (30) what happened after the house burned, which indicates a blindness on the part of all characters and readers. Following her family's downfall, we meet Idalie when she is walking in a "blinding rain" (33) and wearing a veil, which simultaneously hides Idalie from herself, from the clear view of the reader, and from the sight of other characters. Idalie is the same character who in the past treated people so shabbily that when she fell from the top of her aristocratic peak, she had no one willing to help her. She resorts to teaching at the "colored public school" (33) and marries a man described as belonging to the "*nouveaux pauvres*" (32) and having an "uncomplimentary attitude toward women" (34), but the marriage provides a measure of security for her even if she now hides behind a veil. At the end of the story, even the African Americans comment about how awful she looks and how they are better dressed than she, which shows how far down the social ladder she has descended. This story, like "Drama of Three," depicts a Creole in negative terms and demonstrates the sad reality that befalls a Creole who does not accept a changing society.

Just as "La Grande Demoiselle" depicts intentional blindness, so does "Mimi's Marriage," but this story shows the ways in which people attempt to alter reality through false appearances and the insight that is gained when these false appearances are destroyed. For example, not only is the world blind to the reality that Mimi's family is now poor, but Clementine, Mimi's step-mother, even allows her husband to believe erroneously that they lost their fortune through her negligence rather than his. Mimi knows what she desires in a husband, but her papa is blind to her desires. He only values those within his class, as revealed by Mimi when she says that he never would have allowed her to marry the man she chose, and says "it was well [Papa] was dead" (40). Following her father's death, Mimi mentions that she and Clementine "could not have concealed" (46) the fact of their poverty much longer, so when a proposal of marriage comes along from someone of a lower class, she accepts. Mimi is also blind to what is good for her because she cries and cries that he is not the man of her dreams. By the end of the story, however, she tells the reader that God woke her up so that "now, you see, I prefer my husband" (53) to the man who was originally in her dreams. At the end, Mimi opens her eyes not only to what is in her best interests but also to her true desire. This desire does not fit in with the old social structure that would have viewed an inter-class marriage with grave suspicion. This story demonstrates that destroying false outward appearance and accepting the reality of changing roles can lead to insight and, ultimately, happiness.

"The Old Lady's Restoration" demonstrates the positive outcomes of accepting a changing society that includes new roles along class and racial lines. In this story, both the image and theme of blindness are initially revealed through the title because restoration is a word normally associated with sight, as in sight being restored. At one point in life, the old lady was wealthy and part of the elite class. She slowly loses her money, her status, and eventually the acquaintances within her class. The way in which she loses her money is "hidden under the many versions that had been invented" (177). Through some mistaken story in the paper, her old friends read that her fortune is being restored. After these old friends hear the story, they wait for her reappearance, but there is "no sight or sound of her" (183). Everyone—those who knew her and those who wish to know her based on her restored fortune—"began making their resolutions to capture her as soon as she came in sight of society" (183). Two women finally decide that she must be staying away so long because she is bashful after her long absence, so they go in search of her. When these old friends finally find her, they discover that her fortune has not been restored, but that she has discovered what is important. The important luxuries that she now possesses include "[a] good five-cent bouillon," "new cotton sheets," and real "friends for fifteen years" (189–190). These new friends are working men and women and their numerous children, all of whom are not considered acceptable by her old friends. Her old friends are still blind, dismissing her few luxuries as undesirable. They call her crazy because, despite the fact that her fortune has not been restored, she is happy with her life. This story also indicts the priorities that the elite class places on wealth and the ways in which this class defines acceptable acquaintances.

"Miracle Chapel" further reveals the ways in which each class is blind to the needs and desires of any class outside of its own. The poor believe the rich "do not need miracles" (57), and the rich believe the poor are closer to God (58). This story is the only one about a visually impaired character, an innocent child. The story depicts not only the child's blind hope of seeing once again but also the blind hope of those who come to this chapel seeking their own miracle. The story of the chapel has numerous references to eyes and seeing. As the story begins, a visitor asks the blind child about the chapel, and he tells the visitor the story of a miracle that occurred. In the story he mentions the miracle of the flowers and the birds seeing the Virgin Mary, even though "they ain't got no eyes,"and his story ends with the hopeful thought that maybe one day he can see the Virgin Mary, too (62–63). This visitor listens to the child's story and his desires and makes it possible for him to see again by taking him to a hospital, so a doctor can restore his eyesight. The ability to make this surgery happen suggests that the benefactor possesses wealth and, presumably, status. Through the poor, blind child, the wealthy benefactor is made to see the stereotypes that the rich have of the poor are not valid, and the wealthy benefactor as a result enables the blind child to see. Both classes now symbolically see each other with a clearer understanding.

Not having a clear understanding of human nature is also depicted in "Anne Marie and Jeanne Marie," which begins with Jeanne Marie crying and saying that "she could understand death, but she could not understand this" (91). Jeanne Marie then relates the story of the "this" that she cannot understand, which is her sister, Anne Marie. This story ends with the line, "she had never known her twin sister at all" (101), summarizing the ways in which Jeanne Marie was blind to the true nature of her sister. From the beginning of life, "Jeanne Marie was the lucky one" (93). Since her luck is not created by her efforts, we could label this success as "blind luck." Every week, when Jeanne Marie goes into town, she plays the lottery for Anne Marie and herself. One week Jeanne Marie wins forty dollars and begins dreaming of ways to use that money, such as buying new dresses for her and her sister, getting the house "red-washed," and purchasing extra food and medicine for Anne Marie (95). Later, when she takes the winnings home, Jeanne Marie tells her sister that Anne Marie was the winner instead. When Jeanne Marie goes outside to do some chores, she is very happy and feels that Anne Marie's luck has turned: "[Jeanne Marie] did not think any more of the spending of the money, only of the pleasure Anne Marie would take in spending it" (99). She looks through a knot-hole in the house in order to see Anne Marie's smile again, and instead, discovers Anne Marie hiding the money, which leads to that last key line of Jeanne Marie being blind to the true nature of her sister. Rather than sharing the money with her sister and deriving some happiness from the largesse, Anne Marie chooses to hide the money and return to her misery.

The story titled "Crippled Hope" reveals an instance in which King uses language to extend her imagery and theme of blindness because in this instance crippled is synonymous with blind. Mammy is a cripple who is never purchased because of her disability and is relegated to living in a slave trader's place of business. The surface story depicts Mammy hoping that she will be sold, so that she will finally belong to someone. While she is waiting and hoping, she begins ministering to the sick children waiting to be sold. Her skills become so valuable that the slave trader refuses to sell her to anyone. She then tries to close her eyes to the babies and their needs so that she would not be so useful, but she found herself incapable of doing this for very long. She is described as having "all-seeing eyes" (105), "eyes, attention, solely for other babies" (110) and a "quick eye . . . for symptoms" (113). When the alarm bells rang, and the slave trader "vanished" (121), she is left all alone which makes her "fear-blind" (120) since she has to venture out into freedom by herself. Her "all-seeing eyes" provide her with the ability to make a life for herself in freedom. She eventually succeeds in building a life for herself by nursing others of all races and classes, which shows her individual strength, which is not linked to race or gender. Some critics, including Linda Coleman, base their argument that King's stories depict her racist beliefs on the fact that Mammy is relegated to a life of waiting on others. Mammy has made her choice, and she made it with her "all-seeing eyes," not because that was the only thing available to her, as suggested by Coleman. Coleman says that the message in this story is one of Little Mammy's loyalty and desire for a white family. This message may be the surface story—and Mammy's early desire—but when one examines the title with its synonymous substitution "blind hope," one can begin to see King's critique of Mammy's hope—that Mammy's dearest hope is crippled. In other words, wanting to be owned or wanting to be a caretaker is not something that should be desired.

Feminist criticism may rail against women such as Mammy who seek the role of nurse, teacher, or mother, but these caretakers are to be admired when they perform these roles by choice. This desire to be a caretaker is also the crux of another story in *Balcony Stories*. "One of Us" describes a not-very-famous opera singer going to an asylum for orphaned children to request a position as a caretaker for the children. The attendant is not really listening to the singer but rather is thinking of the luxurious life that this singer must have led. As the opera singer tells of her longing to work with the children, the attendant finally begins to listen and to think of the singer as a friend: "it was the woman's eyes that drew me back to her face and her story" (134). The singer requests only food and clothing in exchange for the chance to work with the children. She says, "I could be their nurse and their servant. I would bathe and dress them, play with them, teach them their prayers," but she would only sing them only children's songs (136). The attendant awakens to her friend's need to work at the asylum and the ways in which the children and the asylum would suffer if the singer did not find a role there. This story, then, is about the initial blindness on the part of both characters: the opera singer for not realizing her true calling and the attendant for not recognizing the potential help that the singer could offer to the orphaned children.

Probably King's most anthologized story from *Balcony Stories* is "Little Convent Girl." The theme of this story revolves around the blindness of the characters and the reader, but blindness is also evident within the language of the work. In two places, King uses the word eye when she is actually referring to other senses. As the convent girl is listening to stories told by the pilot, the narrator discusses her eyes opening (155), which is an unusual expression when discussing a person listening to a story. When the narrator discusses whether anyone should have realized the girl's suicidal intentions, King suggests that the pilot may have noticed her intentions "had his eye been more sensitive" (160). In the story, the girl is blind to what real life is like and to her own heritage because she has been raised in a convent, and in much the same way as blind people have been described by society in the past, she is described as being unable to "do anything of herself" (143). She is on her way to meet her mother—a woman whom she has not seen in years and does not remember. She wears a veil, but as she becomes more animated and involved with the other travelers during the trip, she puts "up her veil, actually, to see better" (151); however, she does not truly see better, and neither does the reader because only when her mother finally arrives to pick her up from the boat do we discover that the girl's mother is black. The girl does not even know she is multi-racial. When the mother brings the girl back to the boat, the convent girl throws herself into the water: "No one was looking, no one saw more than a flutter of white petticoats, a show of white stockings, as the little convent girl went under the water" (161). This sighting of white is significant since prior to her discovery, the little convent girl took great pains to ensure that no one ever saw any white, even when she was climbing stairs. Most critics interpret this story as King's disapproval of interracial relationship and her depiction of what happens to the children of interracial relationships. I argue that the girl's discovery of her mother's race is not what drives her to suicide but rather her fears concerning society's reaction to this discovery. The crowd vocalizes their disapproval at upon discovering that the convent girl's mother is black, implying that resisting changes in racial roles creates more harm than the changes themselves.

Society's reactions and the role that readers play in ensuring publication provide another reason for King to obscure her treatment of tough issues. King may have realized that she would offend some of her readers and that she at times "ventured too far," so at the end of "Joe," she depicts the title character "yearning to be reunited with the family of his former master," which contradicts the character that she had created (Piacentino 64–65). Piacentino and Jones argue that the resolutions of King's works may have been contrived somewhat from the direction of the original narrative to ensure publication and acceptance (Piacentine 64–66, Jones 108). Jones mentions that King cannot write her stories about women "without qualification or confusion, and . . . seem[s] largely unaware of the submerged implications" (108). In a discussion of *Monsieur Motte*, a short story which King later expanded into a novel, Jones also mentions that King may have realized that she had almost ventured too far into "the imaginative exploration of black-white relations" and that she came too close to depicting these relationships as being almost equal (101). Although acknowledging that in King's writing "[c]ertain elements seem predictably, sentimentally southern," other parts "defy these conventional southern morals" (120). These commentaries could also explain why she couched the issues of the earlier *Balcony Stories* in terms of blindness because then she would have deniability when confronted with unpopular interpretations.

Katharine Capshaw Smith's article argues that King relies on the same blindness images in her autobiographical work, *Memories of a Southern Woman of Letters*.[4] Smith argues that while King may have been a Southern woman and may have intended to emphasize this in her title, most of these memoirs discuss King's travels away from this region. Smith argues that King "appears deliberately to avoid the region, using travel to escape the emotional distress, economic deprivation, racial tension, and literary and historical ignorance that characterize her home" (133). She supposedly intended her trips to educate Europeans about the South, but in *Memories*, she never discusses race or any issue with the vehemence that she was known for in her letters. For example, Smith maintains that King "largely avoids honest description of the South before the Nook Farm men, and in doing so perpetuates her ladylike mask and advances her literary aspirations" (138). Masks earlier create the illusion of blindness or inhibit the ability to fully see; therefore, King creates an illusion about her own feelings on those issues that had fully engulfed the South. Smith argues that "the overwhelming emphasis on King's gracious and polite persona in and of itself suggests a need to conceal details of her experience, for one does not need a mask unless there is something to hide" (138). Clara Juncker also uses the imagery of hiding behind a veil, thus enhancing blindness, when she points out that King "hid her 'improper' anger and militancy behind a becoming imaginative veil ("Feminist" 20). These critics agree that King uses masks and veils in connection with blindness images to address the tough issues of race and class in *Balcony Stories*. King uses blindness as a way of discussing wrongs perpetuated against people on the basis of race, gender and class. As Juncker points out, "King's fiction speaks as eloquently, if more discreetly, of sexual and social discriminations against (southern) women and subtly posits alternatives to existing gender arrangements. As a result of a unresolved conflict between a conservative and militant self, Grace King preferred her pen to the picket line and advocated change in a way befitting a southern lady" (16). Juncker and other critics do not point to specifics in the text that lead them to suggest that King was experiencing these conflicts. King experiences these conflicts not just in "gender arrangements" but also in class and race arrangements, and these conflicts are revealed by the theme and language of blindness and sight and are seen by a close reading of *Balcony Stories*.

While King may not have set out to comment upon her beliefs about race, gender, and class roles, Elfenbein posits that, "the achievement of King's fiction exceeded her conscious grasp of social issues, confirming the transgressive and transformative power of literary art" (75). Falvey says, "On the 'interlocking' issues of race and gender, she does not crack the old codes, but enough seismic rumblings can be felt in her work to convince a 'listener' of King's troubled confidence in the system she supported" (xxii). King may have intended to perpetuate her racist attitudes, womanly Southern values, and aristocratic Creole elitism through her fiction, but through the use of language associated with blindness and sight, she achieves the opposite effect. Just as Little Mammy is "all-seeing," these stories are "all-seeing," and they tell the true tale—the tale that is revealed when the surface veils and masks are pushed aside.

NOTES

1. The selections in *Balcony Stories* were originally published individually and then collected into a volume in 1893. I am using a reprint of the 1914 edition, which included fourteen stories. Subsequent editions included two additional stories.

2. Although not a Creole by birth, King was raised and educated with Creoles.

3. Although the interest in Grace King has increased, it has not reached the proportions of Kate Chopin scholarship. Only two scholars have written full-length works on her: Robert Bush, her biographer, and David Kirby, who wrote a psychological study entitled *Grace*

King, which compared her to Henry James. She has been the subject of numerous recent articles, and Anne Goodwyn Jones, Helen Taylor, and Shannon Elfenbein include her along with other writers in their books.

4. Bush is a King apologist—if I may borrow the term from Piacentino—and his view of her tends to be a romantic or idealized depiction. His primary negative comment about King's *Memories* is that she held back much of her true self.

REFERENCES

Bryan, Violet Harrington. *The Myth of New Orleans in Literature: Dialogues of Race and Gender.* Knoxville: U of Tennessee P, 1993.

Bush, Robert. *Grace King: A Southern Destiny.* Baton Rouge and London: Louisiana State UP, 1983.

—. *Grace King of New Orleans: A Selection of Her Writings.* Baton Rouge: Louisiana State UP, 1973.

—. "Grace King: The Emergence of a Southern Intellectual Woman." *Southern Review* 13 (1977): 272–88.

Coleman, Linda. "At Odds: Race and Gender in Grace King's Short Fiction." *Louisiana Women Writers: New Essays and a Comprehensive Bibliography.* Ed. Dorothy H. Brown and Barbara C. Ewell. Baton Rouge: Louisiana State UP, 1992. 33-55.

DeJean, Joan. "Critical Creolization: Grace King and Writing on French in the American South." *Southern Literature and Literary Theory.* Ed. Jefferson Humphries. Athens and London: U of Georgia P, 1990. 109-126.

Elfenbein, Anna Shannon. *Women on the Color Line: Evolving Stereotypes and the Writings of George Washington Cable, Grace King, Kate Chopin.* Charlottesville: UP of Virginia, 1989.

Falvey, E. Catherine. "'Furnished Real and Gratis': Grace King and the Romance of Story." *Balcony Stories.* By Grace King. Albany, NY: NCUP, 1994. vii–xlvii.

Jones, Anne Goodwyn. *Tomorrow is Another Day: The Woman Writer in the South, 1859–1936.* Baton Rouge: Louisiana State UP, 1981.

Juncker, Clara. "Grace King: Woman As Artist." *Southern Literary Journal* 20 (1987): 37–44.

—. "Grace King: Feminist, Southern Style." *Southern Quarterly* 26.3 (1988): 15–30.

King, Grace. *Balcony Stories.* New Orleans: L. Graham, 1914.

—. *Memories of a Southern Woman of Letters.* New York: Macmillan, 1932.

Kirby, David. *Grace King.* Boston: Twayne, 1980.

Piacentino, Edward J. "The Enigma of Black Identity in Grace King's 'Joe.'" *Southern Literary Journal* 19 (1986): 56–67.

Smith, Katharine Capshaw. "Conflicting Visions of the South in Grace King's *Memories of a Southern Woman of Letters.*" *Southern Quarterly* 36.3 (1998): 133–45.

Taylor, Helen. "The Case of Grace King." *Southern Review* 18 (1982): 685–702.

—. *Gender, Race, and Region in the Writings of Grace King, Ruth McEnery Stuart, and Kate Chopin.* Baton Rouge and London: Louisiana State UP, 1989.

Bleaching the Color Line: Caste Structures in Lyle Saxon's *Children of Strangers* and Zora Neale Hurston's *Their Eyes Were Watching God*

Suzanne Disheroon-Green

The era between the end of Reconstruction and the beginning of the modern period in Southern history was one of extensive turmoil throughout the region, especially with regard to race relations. This era, stretching from roughly 1878 to 1965, is marked by events such as the *Brown v. Board of Education* decision by the United States Supreme Court, the integration of the U. S. Armed Forces in 1948, and the passage of the Civil Rights and Voting Rights Acts. History demonstrates that prior to these landmark events, racial attitudes in the South were not just the subject of abstract debate; they led to persecution, discrimination, and violence against people of color. Individuals of mixed racial heritage found themselves caught in a no-man's land which typified this tempestuous era. Those whose heritage included European ancestry felt themselves ethnically superior to full-blooded members of the African-American community, yet these free people of color were unwelcome as equals in the white community. The net result of such social constructions of race was that people of mixed race—especially women—found themselves, in many cases, even more disenfranchised than members of the African-American community. Women of all races learned early that "social distinctions based on gradations of color *were* significant for free women of color and for women slaves" (Elfenbein 17), and that the choices open to them varied based upon the lightness of their skin.

The difficulties faced by individuals of mixed racial heritage are pointedly examined in two novels from the pre-Civil Rights era of Southern history: *Children of Strangers* by Louisiana writer Lyle Saxon and *Their Eyes Were Watching God* by Zora Neale Hurston, who was not only a novelist but also an astute folklorist and anthropologist. Saxon and Hurston share numerous commonalities in their backgrounds, which, not surprisingly, inform their attitudes toward race and toward the creation of their literary works. Both were highly educated and were active collectors of regional folklore. Both spent a portion of their adult lives in the environments about which they write. Further, each author produced a novel addressing the plight of a woman of mixed heritage during the post-Reconstruction era. *Children* and *Their Eyes* each appeared in 1937, shortly after *I'll Take My Stand*, the Agrarian intellectual treatise which argued for a return to the antebellum way of life. Inextricably bound up in this argument was the necessity of reviving the racial roles inherent in the plantation system. Given the synchronous timing of the appearance of each of these works—works that were hailed as the writers' best efforts during and after their respective lifetimes—each novel offers insight into the racial attitudes prevalent during this tempestuous era.

Perhaps more compelling than the parallels between the life stories of these authors is the fact that each novel features a female protagonist who rejects the choices available to a woman of her race. Both Famie Vidal of *Children of Strangers* and Janie of *Their Eyes Were Watching God* exist on a plane that is both separate from, and hierarchically superior to, that of other members of their respective communities. Famie's choice of a black lover at the end of the novel places her at odds with her Creole community, forcing her to choose between her lover and her family. Her community holds itself above the African-American community, refusing to have any social or fiscal interaction with those who are considered inferiors; members of the Creole community as depicted by Saxon "regarded [themselves] as apart from the black field hands" (Saxon, *Children* 76). Rather than giving in to the demands of her family that she not forfeit her position in the more privileged middle caste, Famie chooses to become absorbed into the African-American community so that she can remain with the man that she loves. Saxon seems to intend readers to perceive his final portrayal of Famie as overtly degrading, as he makes it clear that outsiders identify her as an African American. We realize that she, in fact, transcends societal impediments to her happiness rather than being degraded by her choice.

Janie, Hurston's "mulatta who refuses to accept the righteousness of the position, 'Queen of the Porch'" (Christian 73) shares with Famie an isolated status which is revealed in large part by her white features. Her appearance drives men to seek to possess her and which evoke jealousy from other women. She is placed on a pedestal by her second husband, Jody, who sees her as a well-deserved sign of his success and importance and also as a precious possession that must not be contaminated by mingling with the common folk. Janie, too, makes a choice that is met with suspicion in her community when she takes up with a man much younger and much darker–skinned than she. Rather than bowing to public opinion, Janie builds a relationship with Tea Cake which is based on love, passion, and companionship. Like Famie, she rejects the social constructions of race which dictate the age and skin color of the men with whom she can become involved. Despite societal constraints on behavior and lifestyle choices, each woman lives life on her own terms, defining morality according to her standards rather than those dictated by social convention. Only when each woman finds love with a man of substantially darker skin than she, does she find happiness, security, and a sense of wholeness. By rejecting societal definitions which assess a person's value based exclusively upon skin color, each woman comes to embrace a new moral standard that is not motivated by the racist notions so prevalent in the post-Reconstruction South.

A major element contributing to the racial unrest of the Southern region during the pre-Civil Rights era derives from the different perceptions of race within its subcultures. A common fallacy applied to Southern culture is the idea that the region is homogeneous and that it may be defined through the application of stereotypical criteria: for example, manor houses and sharecroppers' shanties, flirtatious belles, grinning slaves, and poor white trash. Despite these misperceptions, important differences exist between the racial attitudes and conventions of Louisiana, where Saxon's novel is set, and the larger Southern region, where Hurston places her narrative. Despite these differences, however, each author demonstrates the sliding scale of social standing, challenging the notion that the lighter an individual's skin is, the more desirable he or she is to society at large.

The primary differences between Louisiana's racial hierarchy and that of the Southern region as a whole derive from the French and Spanish influences upon colonial Louisiana and the growth of a large, financially independent, free, and influential Creole culture.[1] Unlike neighboring states, Louisiana did not view race as an either/or proposition until well after the colonial era, which ended in 1803 with the Louisiana Purchase. Generally, Southerners viewed individuals as white, and accordingly welcome at any level of society that their breeding and financial situation would support, or as black, and thus hopelessly and irrevocably consigned to lower levels of the social hierarchy. The legal and social realities of the deep South were such that the "one-drop rule" effectively allowed blackness to be used as a social weapon which excluded people with the slightest "taint" in their lineage. Louisiana, however, based its racial codes on a tripartite system. The basis of this system was a third racial caste, comprised of *les gens de couleur libre*, or free people of color. *Les gens de couleur libre* came from a variety of economic backgrounds and under colonial law were allowed substantially more freedom than their full-blooded African counterparts. Creoles of color could own property, enter into business arrangements with whites, marry a Creole woman of their choosing, and bear children without risk of their being sold (Mills 192). Creoles of color often owned slaves of their own, a practice which clearly placed them at odds with the African-American community, both before and after emancipation.[2] As Mills points out, "[p]reservation of this third racial class in Louisiana society was contingent upon strict adherence to the caste system by its members. Just as the whites entertained feelings of superiority to Negroes, so did Louisiana's *gens de couleur libre*" (Mills xiv). Following the Louisiana Purchase and the transition to American governance, the situation of the *gens de couleur libre* was compromised by the hardening of racial attitudes on the part of the white community following the end of the Civil War and the onset of Reconstruction. Individuals of mixed heritage who had been considered "elite," especially in Louisiana, "lost [their] status as far as whites were concerned" (Elfenbein 13). They fell victim to epithets which described them as "'neither fish nor fowl,'" and found themselves in a position in which they "had no race . . . and hence no identity. . . . By the end of

Reconstruction, white Southerners were able to condemn the whole of the Negro community as a body, out of hand and without regard to variations in color" (Williamson 92). Following this paradigmatic shift which effectively disenfranchised all people of color, a clear disparity, which had always existed, grew into a chasm which even today has not been completely bridged.

Hurston and Saxon portray women of mixed racial heritage in terms of the stereotypical trope of the tragic mulatto, a voiceless, powerless victim of her parentage, her beauty, and her naïvete. During the antebellum period, and even stretching into the Civil War years themselves, "reading or retelling the standard story of the woman of ambiguous race had been considered a betrayal of Southern loyalties" (Elfenbein 13). Writers of the post-Civil War period, however, defied this convention, seemingly adopting the "Northern view that interracial sex in the South had caused God to forsake [the South's] cause" (Elfenbein 13) and accordingly, typified the archetypal tragic mulatto not only by her amazing beauty but also by her brushes with threats to her innocence—threats which all too often came to fruition. Her beauty attracted the unwanted attentions of unscrupulous men who wanted to possess her physically, but who paid no heed to the consequences of such attentions to the woman. As Barbara Ladd has pointed out, the woman of mixed racial heritage in literature is portrayed as "a tragic kind of American geisha" (1). Further, the tragic mulatto, both in "the literature of abolition, as well as in historical novels written long after emancipation" possesses "connections to 'aristocracy' through her white father, and sometimes through her African mother as well. [She is] virtually indistinguishable from the idealized white heroines" (Ladd 2), except insofar as her "taint" of blackness excludes her from unequivocal acceptance by either the white aristocracy or the African-American culture. Despite the seeming advantages of beauty and desirability, the tragic mulatto is "wretched because of the 'single drop of midnight in her veins,'" wishing for "a white lover above all else. For this she 'must go down to a tragic end'" (Zanger 63; Brown 144). Literary examples of the trope abound, including pieces such as Kate Chopin's "Désirée's Baby" and "La Belle Zoraïde," George Washington Cable's *Madame Delphine*, and Grace King's "Little Convent Girl."[3] Each of these writers demonstrates the pathetic fate dealt to women of mixed heritage who dare to overreach that which society deigns to allow them.

These literary depictions of the tragic mulatto are, in fact, rather misleading. Whereas the *literati* tended to portray mixed-race women as victims of circumstance who had no control over their destinies, their relatives, in fact, had a significant hand in their barter. An attractive woman of mixed heritage could form a "permanent or semipermanent alliance with a wealthy white man. . . . For this reason, these women strove to please" (Elfenbein 17). Elaborate balls were hosted by shrewd mothers who, realizing that their daughters faced futures marked by financial uncertainty, would place them on display before wealthy white men. They "bargained for extramarital alliances with white men who would become their daughters' *maris*. These alliances, which were called *plaçages*, in many instances became lifetime quasi-marriages, with the white man devising a means for his children to be educated as ladies and gentlemen in Paris and for their inheritance of his wealth" (Elfenbein 17). Despite the fiscal advantages of such arrangements, however, the *plaçage* system was degrading to its core, as women of mixed heritage were "forced to barter for an advantageous arrangement" (Elfenbein 17), in which they assumed "as a merit and a distinction what is universally considered in the civilized world a shame and a disgrace" (King 348). In the final analysis, women of mixed racial heritage were "as enslaved as their slave sisters and as their truly white sisters, who were coerced to maintain their chastity both before and after marriage by a standard of conduct that applied only to them" (Elfenbein 18). The options available to women of mixed ancestry frequently left them with little choice but to submit to the type of concubinage so prevalent during this era.

The trope of the tragic mulatto depicts female characters stereotypically, as part of a marginalized group. As Violet Harrington Bryan has pointed out, "the 'tragic mulatto' theme, which became so popular in literature during the late nineteenth and early twentieth centuries did not include the free man of color. He was not a pathetic figure, but more of a threat to the white reader. . . . The Creole men of color were shadows, too ethereal and undefined to interest writers or readers of the period" (160). P. Gabrielle Foreman has argued that the "'tragic mulatta' is simply a mediating device" which allows "undifferentiated 'white readers'" to identify with the character. Saxon attempts to depict Famie as a tragic mulatto, as indicated when her family rejects her, telling her pointedly that she has chosen to lose caste through her refusal to denounce her black lover, as well as through her decision to sell her family land to the white plantation owner. Her fate, however, can be viewed as more than a simple failure to adhere to the strictures of a rigid caste system. By showing Famie in a situation in which she can make a free choice, Saxon unwittingly provides the means of her empowerment and the means by which she demonstrates her redefined racial code. Famie subverts the attempts to victimize her by constructing a life that suits her, regardless of whether society considers it suitable for a woman of her caste. Famie further rejects the pre-Civil Rights racial code when she aids her son in his attempts to pass, literally giving up everything of value to give him the chance to live his life as a white man. Famie realizes that passing will lead to the only truly acceptable life for her son, but she demonstrates that she herself will not live by this code. Saxon draws upon the trope of the tragic mulatto to tell his story, yet in allowing his sense of his own superiority to color the representation of his protagonist, he unwittingly raises her to the level of spokesperson for personal choice and racial equity.

Hurston also draws on the tragic mulatto stereotype but uses the attributes of the trope to subvert its oppressive ideology. In an effort to protect her early in her life, Janie's grandmother barters her to a man who has relative wealth. Flying in the face of the tradition which forces young girls to seek the financial and legal protection of wealthy men, such as that found in the New Orleans *plaçage* system, Hurston shows Janie escaping from her enslavement to a man whom she does not love, her first husband. Unlike her naive predecessors who suffered the ignominity of being traded as prizes in return for relatively secure futures, Janie takes her future into her own hands when she runs away with Joe Starks, who becomes her second husband.

The novels of Saxon and Hurston deal with the treatment of a mixed-race woman in the context of her specific Southern culture, and each remarks on the status of women of mixed heritage in those cultures. We might expect Saxon's point of view to be more modern, given his familiarity with Louisiana customs, but he, in fact, relies heavily on stereotypical representations of people of color which, while contributing to what is arguably an engaging story, appear designed to relegate the female protagonist to the status of a voiceless victim. Famie is depicted alternately as a victim of oppression at the hands of the white community and as a victim of her family's prejudice against the members of the black community. Hurston, on the other hand, creates a story out of these same stereotypical conventions in which her protagonist is empowered—she makes her own choices, regardless of social pressure to do otherwise, and develops her own voice. These differences in the characterization of Hurston's and Saxon's protagonists derive from their divergent perspectives on the communities about which they write. These divergences may be traced, in part, to the backgrounds of their creators. Although each author worked for a time gathering folktales, Saxon was not a part of the community that he attempted to preserve, and in many ways his narrative demonstrates his perceived superiority to a "foreign" sub-culture. On the other hand, Hurston was a member of the community whose stories she collected, despite the fact that her education at times acted as a barrier when she went into her native community to gather data. She admits in her autobiography, *Dust Tracks on a Road*, that she experienced difficulty in gathering the folk stories that she sought because "the glamor of Barnard College was still upon me. I dwelt in Marble Halls. I knew where the material was, all right. But I went about asking, in carefully accented Barnardese, 'Pardon me, but do you know any folk-tales or folk-songs?'" (127-28). Her preliminary results were "unsatisfactory and dispiriting" (Hemenway 90), but she eventually mastered data-gathering techniques which would allow her to "keep a keen eye out for the behavioral characteristics" of a performance taking place "among childhood friends" (Hemenway 92). Ultimately, both of these writers demonstrate the prevailing attitude of their own ethnic groups toward the communities whose traditions they sought to preserve—one as a means of personal sustenance during the Depression as a director of the Federal Writer's Project, and the other in a scholarly effort to document important parts of her cultural heritage.

Further, *Children of Strangers* was Saxon's only novel. He expressed the desire to write novels on more than one occasion, and considered writing his primary vocation; secondarily, he was a collector of native folk materials who then embellished and fictionalized his data. He spent some time as member of Cammie G. Henry's colony of writers and artists at Melrose Plantation, a place which he found "restful and stimulating," and where he "was able to write again . . . for the first time in several months" (Thomas 51-52). He found Melrose a "haven from the hectic social life of the Quarter . . . where he could compose the kind of stories he really wanted to write" (Thomas 52). Melrose was certainly an attractive place to attempt such a transformation, as creativity abounded and was openly appreciated. In fact, after one of his early visits to Melrose, Saxon begins an article published in the *Times-Picayune* (22 April 1923) by saying that upon his death, he will surpass heaven in favor of "spend[ing] his time instead on Melrose plantation" (1). Room and board were provided *gratis* to the members of the colony, provided that they produced some kind of work in their area of interest each day, an arrangement which allowed a great deal of creative autonomy. Writers needed only to write a few pages; artists might work on a painting or sculpture. Members of the colony would share their work with the community on a regular basis, and presumably improve as a result of the constructive feedback. Saxon wrote much of his novel in this sheltered environment, as a pampered guest on a working Southern plantation. Because of his privileged status and because of the largely elite, white audience for which he wrote, he represents the caste system so rigidly and so stereotypically.

Janie is equally unable to fit into the black community because of her mixed heritage, which lends her a beauty that makes her an attractive target for unscrupulous men. Her grandmother, fearing that her own imminent demise may leave Janie unprotected, marries the girl off to a man that she does not love. Logan Killicks is financially stable, but Janie's early marriage to a man whom she sees as one of the "folks [who] was never meant to be loved" (Hurston, *Eyes* 22) leads Janie to run away with another man. However, her hasty departure from her first husband does not bring Janie any more happiness, as her new husband places her upon a pedestal because she is desirable to other men. Hurston makes it clear that Janie's beauty is perceived as deriving from her white blood—she has long, flowing hair and delicate, white features. The members of her community are jealous of her beauty, remarking that a woman of forty should not let "her hair swing down her back lak some young gal," and hoping that "she might fall to their level some day" (Hurston, *Eyes* 2). They detect a difference in Janie that they want for themselves, and they demonstrate their own feelings of inferiority by peevishly asking "why she don't stay in her class?" (Hurston, *Eyes* 2). They are further aghast when her third—and most adored—lover is a man half her age with coal-black skin, and this choice causes her to be further marginalized by her home community because of her lack of attention to racial boundaries. Ironically, only when Janie becomes involved with Tea Cake does she have the opportunity, for the first time, to experience a sense of community. She accompanies him down to the Florida muck to pick citrus for a living. Tea Cake

repeatedly rejects the definition of male/female relationships that Joe had internalized and forced on Janie. In teaching Janie to play checkers, to shoot, to drive, and in inviting her to work alongside of him, Tea Cake breaks down the rigid gender definitions Joe sought to impose, bringing Janie into the cultural life of the black community and building a relationship with her grounded in reciprocity rather than hierarchy. (Meisenhelder 68)

When she returns to her hometown sometime after Tea Cake's death, Janie meets the same suspicion that she has experienced all of her life. As she strolls through town, the neighbors stare and speculate, but only her closest friend, Phoebe, actually comes to greet and welcome her. Janie has been an irritant to the members of the black community for several reasons: because of her association with whiteness itself, because she does not deny the part of her that *is* white, and because she does not deem it necessary to prove her whiteness through an alliance with a light-skinned man. Janie shares her experiences with Phoebe, demonstrating that she has left the community's expectations behind her, that she has formulated her own version of morality which, much like Famie's, is no longer restricted by racial boundaries.

Ultimately, because these female protagonists are not fully accepted as members of either race, they are equally unable to fulfill the role that is socially prescribed for them. Rather than allowing society to dictate her proper place, each protagonist chooses to reject the socially mandated role for women of color. One of the results of this racial stratification is the relegation of women of color to supporting roles which divest them of autonomy while burdening them with excessive responsibilities. Janie's grandmother articulates this prevailing theme in Hurston's fiction, saying that

de white man is de ruler of everything as fur as Ah been able tuh find out. Maybe it's some place way off in de ocean where de black man is in power, but we don't know nothin' but what we see. So de white man throw down de load and tell de nigger man tuh pick it up. He pick it up because he have to, but he don't tote it. He hand it to his womenfolks. De nigger woman is *de mule uh de world so fur as Ah can see*. Ah been prayin' fuh it tuh be different wid you. (Hurston, *Eyes* 14, emphasis added)

Hurston later makes bitter sport of the mule trope, telling a great yarn of a dead mule in a field upon whose corpse clothing is hung. Even in death, the mule is expected to carry its burden. However, despite the fact that Jody tries to separate Janie from these expectations, his actions do not serve to release her from the role of the mule. He expresses his intent to protect her, promising to set her up "on de front porch," to "rock and fan yo'self and eat p'taters dat other folks plant just special for you" (Hurston, *Eyes* 28), yet he precludes any possibility that she may develop relationships with the members of her community. For example, Jody does not allow Janie to go out to see the dead mule, claiming that her presence at such an event is unseemly for the mayor's wife, despite the fact that it is the biggest event to hit the town in months: "de mayor's wife is somethin' different again . . . *you* ain't goin' off in all dat mess uh commonness. Ah'm surprised at yuh fuh askin'" (Hurston, *Eyes* 56). Jody claims to be protecting Janie's public image and treating her more like a white woman than other women in her community are typically treated, yet he victimizes her by not allowing her to make her own decisions. She ultimately rebels against his restrictions, verbally emasculating him in front of the entire town. Upon his death, she takes up with exactly the type of individual with whom Jody would never allow her to associate and quickly learns that this man cares more for her needs than anyone ever has. By rejecting the code which prescribes that lightness is superior to darkness, and that a light individual should eschew a relationship with a darker one, Janie is able to find a loving relationship and her moral compass is recalibrated accordingly.

Saxon's Famie also loses caste within the middle racial category through her choice of a mate, a man of purely African-American heritage, yet we know from the beginning of the novel that this is to be Famie's fate. Because Saxon portrays Famie as a failure, an outcast from membership in her native community, her fate is pre-determined. In the paradigm of the tragic mulatto—a paradigm within which Saxon goes to great lengths to place Famie—she must be taken advantage of and experience a loss of face as a result of this experience. Accordingly, early in the novel Famie rejects the Creole man who loves her blindly in favor of a white, red-headed escaped convict named Joe who treats her as a possession whose role is to obey his every command. The convict takes her innocence, her honesty, and her virginity, then is murdered as a result of his crimes, leaving her with a bastard child who grows to feel resentful of, and humiliated by, his non-white mother. However, Famie loves the child unconditionally because he looks white and can pass, even when she knows that he is going take her life savings and leave her forever. Famie loves her son *because* he is part white, just as she is attracted to the red-haired man because of his whiteness. As she comes of age, we know that she is interested in white men, dreams of them. She is curious about the ways of more worldly girls, which leads her to dream "of a man . . .with a bare chest. . . . His skin was white" (Saxon, *Children* 51). When she initially becomes aware of Joe's presence, she is intrigued, wondering, "Was he a white man?" (Saxon, *Children* 53). After her first sexual experience with Joe, she continually reflects on his appearance, focusing upon "his whiteness" (Saxon, *Children* 67). While the other attributes that Famie recalls in her private moments are specifically tied to one of Joe's features—his "crisp red hair, his steel–blue eyes" (Saxon, *Children* 67)—her first and most compelling descriptor of the man focuses upon his color, becoming one of his two primary identifying attributes. Further evidence of Famie's attraction to whiteness is found in her reaction to his prejudices. Joe treats Famie as an object, telling her, "You belong to me, understand that. To nobody else. And you'll do as I tell you. . . . From now on, you'll do as I say" (Saxon, *Children* 63). Despite his possessiveness and brutality, Famie adores him and becomes embarrassed when she realizes that he does not know that she is a person of color. Joe makes a derogatory remark about the "Cajun" who has been assisting him in obtaining supplies, and Famie finds herself with a "burning face. She realized then that the man did not know she was a mulatto. He thought she was a white girl. She was proud and afraid" (Saxon, *Children* 69). Early in her life, then, Famie is clearly pleased by her ability to attract the attention of a white man because she feels that it raises her stature.

Famie's perception that others will not denigrate her actions is confirmed when she learns that she is pregnant with Joe's child. Her family is disappointed, but there is no talk of disowning her or rejecting the bastard child. Her fiancé, Numa, still loves her and marries her, knowing that he will have to care for another man's child. Famie exhibits a distinct lack of enthusiasm for her marriage to Numa, despite the fact that she clearly cares for him at the outset of the novel. On the night of their wedding, Famie's son is born, and the truth about his wife dawns on him: "Numa stood forgotten. His shoulders sagged and his eyes were sad as he looked at the figures beneath the tree beside the well, for at that moment he realized that, in Famie's affections, the white man's child would always come first" (Saxon, *Children* 135). Famie has her child before she and Numa consummate their marriage, and this delay is indicative of Famie's priorities.

Numa is correct; the focus of Famie's existence is the happiness of her son, Joel, and her focus is noticeable even to outsiders. The white plantation owner, for whom Famie and her grandmother work on occasion, remarks that "she was obsessed about this white child of hers. I used to see her here, watching my children. She noticed what they said, what they ate, what they wore . . . and then her child did the same thing" (Saxon, *Children* 229). Famie sacrifices everything for her son—her husband's happiness, her family heirlooms, her place in society. She places each of these sacrifices on the altar of whiteness, in the interest of allowing her son to pass in white society. Like Janie, Famie comes to reject the societal expectations placed on a woman of her caste. She places the selfish demands of her son above convention, and in so doing, sacrifices her own position in that society. After losing everything, however, she comes to the realization that value does not derive from skin color. The realization hits her following the interview with the elders of her family, during which they literally cast her out of the family:

it was all finished, done with. She was insulted, shut out, and they had not let her answer. But, after all, what could she say? . . . Suddenly she was proud. She shook the tears from her eyes. Let them look at her now.

She broke a sprig of red quince flowers from the bush beside the gate. Slowly she put it in her hair, adjusted it, squared her shoulders. With steady step, and with her head held high, she walked through the gate and down the road. (Saxon, *Children* 275)

Famie has sacrificed every possession of value so that her son may be white and has gained the serenity of one who has placed the care of a child above all else. Her focus has shifted away from her race and its implications and toward a revaluation of human qualities.

After her connection to the white community, in the form of her troubled son, is gone, Famie takes refuge, not in the Creole community of which she is a member, but in the Black community. Saxon attempts to portray her choice as a descent into darkness, a punishment for her poor choices. While Hurston's presentation culminates in Janie's triumph, Saxon's presentation attempts to show Famie as a down-trodden failure who has lost caste, and thus lost face, because of her choice of a full-blooded African-American man as her lover. In the context of the tragic mulatto paradigm, this loss of face would seemingly be the result of the woman's innate promiscuity or naïvete, which blinds her to outcomes of her actions until it is too late, and certainly it could be argued that Famie's fall is the result of both. She chooses to become part of a culture which is reviled by her own community because it is considered beneath her. However, in his overt attempt to place Famie within the tragic mulatto paradigm, Saxon unintentionally provides the means to empower her. Rather than ending up beaten down and alone, she is with a man that she has freely chosen. She does not remain alone or settle for a Creole man whom she does not love merely because it is what is socially acceptable. She makes choices which are right for her, defying Southern morality with its emphasis on stereotypical race and gender roles. Unlike the archetypal tragic mulatto, Famie chooses her destiny. That choice results in her loss of caste, but it is a choice that she freely makes. She may be a "cracked plate" (Hurston, *Their Eyes* 19), as Hurston terms the abused African-American woman, but she determines where she will be placed, cracks and all.

The final image of Saxon's novel is that of Famie riding behind her lover, Henry, on a mule. A wealthy white tourist is charmed by the rustic picture and demands that her husband allow her to take their picture. She tells Henry, "I want to take your *picture*. . . ask your wife to look at me . . . well, never mind, you'll look coy with your head down. Maybe it will be *better* that way, more natural. . . . There, I've *got* it. But I never did see the woman's face" (Saxon, *Children* 294). Famie has lost her caste and, according to her relatives, her face as well, so not surprisingly, she is faceless in the picture. She sits on the back of a mule, like the prototypical servant woman, belonging now to the caste that must carry the load for others. The tourist is thrilled with her picture nonetheless; she speculates that she has taken "the *grandest* picture. They were so *typical*" (Saxon, *Children* 294).   The irony is, however, that neither Famie, nor Janie, is typical.

In the end, both Janie and Famie defy attempts to characterize them exclusively in light of their mixed racial heritage and as a result are alienated from their native communities. Hurston's prevailing theme holds true that the African-American woman is the mule of the world, and Saxon unwittingly supports Hurston's position. Each woman is cast in the role of the tragic mulatto but overcomes its restrictions to make her own choices about her life and to accept the consequences of those choices.

NOTES

1.   The Creole colony of Isle Brevelle has its roots in the manumission and financial success of Marie Thérèze Coincoin. Of African descent, Marie Thérèze was a slave to Sieur Louis Juchereau de St. Denis and demonstrated her intelligence, loyalty, and work ethic at an early age. She quickly became indispensable to the St. Denis family and ultimately saved the life of her mistress when she appeared to be terminally ill. Marie Thérèze applied her knowledge of folk and natural remedies and helped Mme. St. Denis fully recover. In gratitude for her assistance during her mistress's health crisis, as well as for many years of faithful service, Marie Thérèze was granted her freedom and assisted in obtaining a land grant which provided the basis for the Isle Brevelle colony. She also began work on her plantation with the assistance of two slaves given to her by the St. Denis family. She became the founder and matriarch of what grew into a very sizeable community of *gens de couleur libre* in the Cane River region of northwestern Louisiana. This community continued to grow and prosper until the end of the Civil War, at which point, as Virginia Domínguez aptly points out, the abolition of slavery caused "the legal distinction that had always existed in Louisiana between the slave and the free-colored [to] disappear. Whereas three legally defined social strata had existed in antebellum society, only one was legally recognized in the immediate postwar years" (134).

2.   According to Gary Mills, it was not an uncommon practice for *gens de couleur libre* to own slaves themselves. Marie Thérèze Coincoin, the founder of the Isle Brevelle colony, set out to purchase the freedom of all of her children following her own manumission and inheritance. By 1816, she had accomplished this goal and had purchased at least twelve other slaves as well (44). Although Marie Thérèze did make use of slave labor, she "always treated her slaves with gentleness, never forgetting that she herself had been a slave" (45).

Marie Thérèze was not the only member of the Creole community to own slaves; Sybil Kein remarks that "before the Civil War, [Creoles of color] also participated in the plantation system, owning large estates and slaves" (xx).

3. Kate Chopin's "Désirée's Baby" tells the story of a woman of unknown racial heritage who attracts the fancy of a local aristocrat, Armand. The couple marries against the warnings of the girl's parents. Upon the birth of their first child, who appears to be of mixed racial heritage, Armand casts out both Désirée and their child. The story ends with Désirée walking forlornly into the bayou with her child, never to be seen again. The reader learns that Armand is of mixed heritage; Désirée's heritage is never clearly established. "La Belle Zoraïde" relates the experience of a beautiful young woman of mixed heritage who makes the grievous error, in the eyes of her mistress, of falling in love with a man who is much darker-skinned than she. Furious that Zoraïde does not want to marry the unkind, but much lighter–skinned, man that her mistress has picked out for her, the mistress forbids the two to see each other and causes Zoraïde's lover to be sold. When Zoraïde's child is born, she is told that the child has died. Grief over this dual loss drives Zoraïde insane. Grace King's protagonist fares little better in "A Little Convent Girl," a narrative in which a young girl, who has spent her life sheltered in a convent, learns that she is of mixed racial heritage. Rather than attempting to negotiate a world in which she is denigrated because of her race, she chooses to quietly commit suicide.

REFERENCES

Brown, Sterling. *The Negro in American Fiction*. Washington, D.C.: n.p., 1966.

Bryan, Violet Harrington. *The Myth of New Orleans in Literature*. Knoxville: U of Tennessee P, 1993.

Christian, Barbara. *Black Feminist Criticism: Perspectives on Black Women Writers*. Elmsford, NY: Pergamon P, 1985.

Domínguez, Virginia. *White by Definition: Social Classification in Creole Louisiana*. 1986. New Brunswick, NJ: Rutgers UP, 1997.

Elfenbein, Anna Shannon. *Women on the Color Line: Evolving Stereotypes and the Writings of George Washington Cable, Grace King, Kate Chopin*. Charlottesville: UP of Virginia, 1989.

Foreman, P. Gabrielle. "'Reading Aright': White Slavery, Black Referents, and the Strategy of Histotextuality in Iola Leroy." *Yale Journal of Criticism* 10 (1997): 327-54.

Hemenway, Robert E. *Zora Neale Hurston: A Literary Biography*. Urbana: U of Illinois P, 1980.

Hurston, Zora Neale. *Dust Tracks on a Road*. 1942. New York: HarperPerennial, 1991.

—. *Their Eyes Were Watching God*. 1937. New York: HarperPerennial, 1937.

Kein, Sybil, ed. Introduction. *Creole: The History and Legacy of Louisiana's Free People of Color*. Baton Rouge: Louisiana State UP, 2000.

King, Grace. *New Orleans: The Place and the People*. New York: Macmillan, 1904.

Ladd, Barbara. *Nationalism and the Color Line in George W. Cable, Mark Twain, and William Faulkner*. Baton Rouge: Louisiana State UP, 1996.

Meisenhelder, Susan Edwards. *Hitting a Straight Lick with a Crooked Stick: Race and Gender in the Work of Zora Neale Hurston*. Tuscaloosa: U of Alabama P, 1999.

Mills, Gary B. *The Forgotten People: Cane River's Creoles of Color*. Baton Rouge: Louisiana State UP, 1977.

Saxon, Lyle. *Children of Strangers*. 1937. Gretna, LA: Pelican, 1989.

—. "Easter at Aunt Cammie's." *Times-Picayune* 22 Apr. 1923: 1.

Thomas, James W. *Lyle Saxon: A Critical Biography*. Birmingham: Summa, 1991.

Twelve Southerners. *I'll Take My Stand.* 1930. Ed. Louis D. Rubin, Jr. Baton Rouge: Louisiana State UP, 1977.

Williamson, Joel. *New People: Miscegenation and Mulattoes in the United States.* New York: Free P, 1980.

Zanger, Jules. "The Tragic Octoroon in Pre-Civil War Fiction." *American Quarterly* 18 (1966): 63.

The Irreducible African: Challenges to Racial Stereotypes in George W. Cable's *The Grandissimes*

Robert Allen Alexander, Jr.

"We ought to be grateful that any one of us is alive": thus concludes Mary Boykin Chesnut, writing in her diary on 7 October 1861, as she contemplates the murder of her cousin Elizabeth Boykin Witherspoon at the hands of African-American slaves. At this particular time, Chesnut refuses to see African Americans as anything other than "horrid brutes—savages, monsters," yet in the very same paragraph she claims that "nobody is afraid of their own negroes" (Chesnut 211). In this brief entry, Chesnut encapsulates the paradoxical attitude toward African Americans that dominated the white Southern—and to a large degree, Northern— mind in the nineteenth century. For the vast majority of white Americans, the presence of African Americans conjured up two distinct images: that of the dark, bloodthirsty savage only slightly removed from the jungles of Africa or that of the carefree, non-threatening, pitiable "darkey." African–American writers who might have righted this wrong were effectively silenced by periodicals and publishing houses who showed little interest in their works. Thus, the fate of African-American characters was left almost entirely in the hands of white writers, who, more often than not, created fictional worlds devoid of black characters or employed only token black characters in stock roles. Even writers sympathetic to the plight of African Americans tended to depict African-American characters as helpless victims or bumbling clowns, as exemplified by Harriet Beecher Stowe's famous representation of Uncle Tom. One of the few exceptions to this tendency was George Washington Cable, a native of New Orleans and an outspoken proponent of civil rights for African Americans. Although Cable fell back on racial stereotypes in some of his fiction, in *The Grandissimes*, his best known and most highly acclaimed novel, he develops African-American characters who are fully realized human beings. With his depiction of Bras-Coupé and Palmyre Philosophe, Cable presents black characters who exhibit the full range of human emotions and motivations: intelligence, shrewdness, nobility, power, arrogance, revenge, passion, heroism, treachery. These characters are irreducible, in that they resist reduction to weak, helpless, servile, non-persons despite the overwhelming political and social powers that call for their systematic dehumanization.

Cable is a master of complexity who demonstrates to us that little about America is simple, whether it is the thoughts, motives, and actions of an oppressed people or the cultural practices of a particular region. Why is it that Cable could recognize this complexity while most of his contemporaries continued to oversimplify the African-American experience? In part, his complex vision is derived from New Orleans, the city in which he was raised and lived for the first forty-one years of his life. Cable's black characters are African American, but they are also African, and they reside in a unique cultural environment—New Orleans— a city that blends European, African, and Native American traditions to form a hybrid society distinctive from the rest of the United States. In *The Grandissimes*, set in 1803–1804, Cable explores the American frontier, with regard to both geography and the evolution of human consciousness. He may seem to be working at the edges of American society in *The Grandissimes*, but he is effectively digging to the core of America, a hot and messy mixture of experimental democracy and dehumanization, of sameness and difference, of the Age of Reason and an age marred by the irrationality of human commodification.

Cable seems like the unlikeliest of candidates to have challenged the racial status quo in the American South. As was typical of a young, white male growing up in the antebellum South, he inculcated the racist notions that dominated his culture and became an ardent defender of slavery. As a mere teenager, he rode as a Confederate cavalryman and fought valiantly for a cause upon which he staked his very life. His mother and sisters refused to swear an oath of loyalty to the Union after General Butler took control of New Orleans and were subsequently exiled into Mississippi. Cable and his family were also dedicated Presbyterians who were much more socially conservative than most of their New Orleans neighbors. In short, there is hardly anything in Cable's background that would suggest that one day he would become one of the South's most outspoken proponents of civil rights for African Americans.

So what led this son of the South, this scion of the old order and institutionalized convention, to challenge his region's most dearly held beliefs through fictional works such as *The Grandissimes* and essays such as: "The Freedman's Case in Equity" and "The Silent South"? This question cannot can be answered simply, for both Cable and the place that he called home, New Orleans, are immensely complex entities. While it is true that Cable was born and raised in New Orleans, his family, due in part to their Protestant beliefs and Anglo-American roots, remained outsiders in a city dominated by French Creole Catholics. Consequently, he had a natural tendency to view his community from the perspective of an outsider, a stance that perhaps allowed him greater freedom to question the status quo. However, due to the complex cultural history of New Orleans, the status quo that he questioned was quite dissimilar to what was standard in most other Southern communities. New Orleans was evolving into a community which had much in common with the rest of the South. Though still quite different in character from other Southern communities, New Orleans had undergone a process of Americanization, beginning with, as Cable describes in "Jean-ah Poquelin," "that first wave of the Anglo-American flood" after the Louisiana Purchase (*Old Creole Days* 88) and escalating after the Battle of New Orleans. Having been a boy in the New Orleans of the 1840s and 1850s, Cable had tasted the flavor of the city while the French Creole culture still played a dominant, but diminishing, role. By the time Cable returned to his hometown after the Civil War, he encountered a city substantially different from the one that he had known as a boy. While still retaining much of the exotic charm that Cable so effectively documented in his short stories, New Orleans had nonetheless become a thoroughly Americanized community.

As Cable began to write, one of his potential audiences was composed of his fellow New Orleanians, many of whom had witnessed and supported the Americanization of the city. While Cable certainly acknowledged some of the benefits resulting from this process—after all, he was not reluctant to criticize what he saw as the outworn and ridiculous traditions of the French Creole community— he also understood that much was being lost, including a more complex view of race that had been replaced by the Anglo-American insistence on a rigorous and irrational separation of black and white. This severe racial dichotomy differed fundamentally from what Jerah Johnson describes as the French assimilationist impulse, one that played a prominent role in the development of the racial social order in the years during which the French Creoles dominated New Orleans. This impulse "offered far greater freedom for individuals to associate not only with members of their own corporate group but, more important, with members of other groups as well" (Johnson 16). Consequently, up until the time that the Anglo-American model became the dominant paradigm, the races had not been consistently segregated in New Orleans. Cable's hometown also had the distinction of being a city that supported the institution of slavery even as it was the domicile of the largest population of free African Americans in the antebellum South. Numbering nearly 20,000 in 1840 and 11,000 as late as 1860, these free people of color "composed a fully articulated community, with a complex class structure, that occupied far more than the fringes of society" (Hirsch and Logsdon 192). But with the rising tide of Americanization in the decades following the Louisiana Purchase, that political and economic clout came to an abrupt end, especially after 1852, when the "consolidation of the three separate municipalities [of New Orleans] coincided with a new serge [sic] of racial repression," and "the state legislature began an assault on [African-Americans'] rights of manumission and began transferring enforcement of existing restrictions from local to state authorities" (Logsdon and Bell 208). Thereafter, New Orleans came to resemble other Southern communities in ways that it never had before as its civic leaders boiled down complex and sometimes unclear racial distinctions into the simplistic black-white dichotomy favored by most white Southerners. Consequently, the ruling white elite now saw the city's destiny as more closely aligned with the fate of the rest of the American South.

Even with these changes, New Orleans still retained much of its unique flavor, much of which is evident today in what may well be "the most African city in the United States" (Hall 59). Cable was amply aware of this uniqueness, with regard to both the French and Spanish Creole and the African and West Indian influences. As he began to dig into the city's archives in the late 1860s and early 1870s, partly because of his job as a journalist but also out of insatiable curiosity, Cable supplemented his firsthand observations of New Orleans life with historical documents. Already suffering from a profound sense of loss, as were many of his white Southern contemporaries in the years after the war, he may have been drawn to his study of the city's past out of a hopeless romantic belief that he could somehow help to restore that which had passed away. Of course, this emotion overpowered most white Southerners in the post–war years as the cult of the Lost Cause came to dominate the political and social landscape of the South. Even if Cable had started his investigations with the same motives of his contemporaries, he drew dramatically different conclusions, inspired largely by his readings of the *Code Noir* of Louisiana (Turner 94). Much like the white Honoré in *The Grandissimes*, who says the death of Bras-Coupé "changed the whole channel of [his] convictions (Cable 48), Cable was so profoundly appalled by the horrific penalties prescribed by the Black Codes that he was moved to question the racist assumptions upon which he had based his most deeply held beliefs. This experience compelled Cable to write, and perhaps that is why, as his critics have consistently charged, his fiction so often devolves into didacticism.

The critical consensus concerning Cable's oeuvre is that his best work is his earliest fiction, most notably *Old Creole Days* and *The Grandissimes*, and that his reform impulse overtakes his artistic sensibility thereafter, thus effectively ending his career as a serious literary artist. While there is no denying that some of Cable's fiction appears to be driven more by a social message than aesthetic concerns, it is in that very same early fiction praised by most critics that we find his reform impulse most evident. In contrast, *The Cavalier*, Cable's best-selling 1901 novel, is devoid of any social critique but is one of his worst efforts, seldom rising above the level of sentimental romance.

Is it possible that it was Cable's editors' preoccupation with quelling his social message and not his insistence on incorporating it that squeezed the life out of his fiction? Edmund Wilson draws that conclusion, arguing that "the slow strangulation of Cable as an artist and a serious writer is surely one of the most gruesome episodes in American literary history" (579). "Bibi," one of Cable's earliest stories, and the model for the Bras-Coupé episodes in *The Grandissimes*, grew directly out of Cable's desire to address the horrors that he had uncovered in the archives of New Orleans and to redress the wrongs that still persisted in his day. Prior to his encounter with the *Code Noir* in those historical records, he apparently had no serious aspirations as a creative writer. He was a young man with a limited education and a modest economic background. *Belles-lettres* and fine art were not among his passions. Now with his passions inflamed and his youthful idealism boundless, he began to look for a way to make a difference.

How could Cable, with few political and social advantages, especially as an ex-Confederate soldier in Reconstruction New Orleans, effect social change? He was already a practicing journalist, and he indeed would make use of that venue to make his views known, but he knew that his audience would necessarily be limited to the boundaries of his newspaper's circulation. Later in his career, after he had established a national reputation, he turned to the essay as a means to promote reform, with regard to both African-American civil rights and Southern penal reform. However, as an obscure journalist in the early 1870s, he lacked the name recognition to secure a platform for essay writing. Cable also knew enough about his native region and its entrenched conservatism to know that the sort of outright denouncements of the racial status quo that he could incorporate into an essay would be met with much resistance. Later, after his literary reputation had provided him with some economic and professional security, he employed the essay as a tool to promote reform and met with the sort of hostility which he had earlier feared. Undaunted by these limitations and filled with the hubris of youth, Cable began experimenting with the short story form, perhaps because he saw it as his best shot to reach a large regional, if not national, audience, but also because he, like Melville, must have sensed that he would have to present his message "covertly, and by snatches" in order to retain an audience (Melville 542).[1]

When Edward King arrived in New Orleans in 1873 to conduct research for a series of articles for *Scribner's Monthly Magazine*, he met Cable, who proved to be an invaluable resource because of his knowledge of Louisiana history culled from his archival readings. King departed with two of Cable's manuscripts, "'Sieur George," which would become Cable's first published piece of fiction, and "Bibi," a story that King claimed "'rode [him] as a nightmare" (Turner 54). King was so taken by "Bibi" that he predicted Cable's imminent literary fame (Turner 54). King was correct in predicting Cable's quick rise to fame in the next few years, but he missed the mark with regard to "Bibi." King's editor, Richard Watson Gilder, who would later publish much of Cable's fiction before Cable and he severed their working relationship in the early 1890s due to irreconcilable differences, refused to publish the story, probably because it "was too grisly to have the ironic and picturesque charm" desired by the genteel Gilder (Stephens 395). George Parson Lathrop, editor of the *Atlantic Monthly*, confirmed Gilder's assessment, claiming that the story failed "'on account of [its] unmitigatedly distressful effect'" (Turner 54). Thus began a battle that Cable would wage with his editors for the next two decades as he attempted to reconcile his reform impulses with the literary establishment's desire for aesthetically pleasing and supposedly apolitical stories.

Despite the rejection of "Bibi," Cable continued to work on socially relevant fiction, as is evident from several of the stories that he published in the 1870s. He also began work on *The Grandissimes*, a novel structured around his reworking of "Bibi." It is not surprising that Cable would be persistent in pursuing his goal of producing fiction that would promote his reform agenda. After all, as a young man he had risked his life in combat for a cause, albeit one which he no longer supported; in comparison, dealing with the fickleness of editors must have seemed like a holiday. More than courage and stubbornness compelled Cable to keep working social criticism into his fiction. Much like his future touring partner Mark Twain, Cable was aware that the Compromise of 1877 and the effective end of

Reconstruction opened the way for the re-institution of white supremacy and the rolling back of civil rights legislation. Like most Confederate veterans, embittered by defeat and Northern occupation, Cable probably initially opposed many of the laws passed during Reconstruction to guarantee the rights of African Americans, but as his views evolved, he must have begun to see the worth of the sorts of changes called for by the 1868 Louisiana Constitution, which "mandat[ed] universal desegregated education and prohibit[ed] racial discrimination in public places" (Tregle 170). Like Twain, as he observed white backlash and the implementation of legalized segregation, he began to detect disturbing similarities between the post-Reconstruction and the antebellum South. Twain would present his searing social critique of American racism in *The Adventures of Huckleberry Finn*, masterfully masking his satire by choosing an antebellum setting. Four years before Twain's great achievement, however, Cable brought forth *The Grandissimes*, an equally ingenious narrative, one that criticized the contemporary South through the setting of antebellum New Orleans.

Like Edward King, who could not get "Bibi" out of his mind, contemporary reviewers of *The Grandissimes* could not ignore the impressive power of Cable's portrait of Bras-Coupé. Those early reviewers recognized the centrality of the Bras-Coupé story to the novel, and since most of them were from the North, they were much impressed with the novel's critique of the institution of slavery. Some of them were quick to point out that such a critique, however laudable, seemed irrelevant since the issue of slavery had already been settled. The fact that these Northern critics did not see that Cable's critique also could be applied to the post-Reconstruction South reflects "a desire to put the Negro problem out of mind following the Compromise of 1877" (Stephens 396). Of course, Twain would be damned by similar faint praise when he published *The Adventures of Huckleberry Finn*, which did little to stir debate concerning racism because most readers were more preoccupied with Huck's bad grammar.

Among Cable's early fans was Twain, who undoubtedly recognized that the New Orleans native was much more than a local colorist, that in fact he was weaving texts of considerable power. Though Twain was a decade older than Cable and already established as a platform performer and comic writer before they met in the early 1880s, the elder writer learned much from his younger friend with regard to using fiction as a platform for social critique, a technique that he did not fully master until he began revising *The Adventures of Huckleberry Finn*. In Cable, Twain saw a fellow "desouthernized Southerner" (Howells 35), a Southern writer who "[did] not write in the southern style;" that is, he saw beyond the cult of the Lost Cause and its preoccupation with "the sham chivalries of a brainless and worthless long-vanished society" (Twain 327–29). As that sort of perceptive and critical observer of the South, Cable did not want to oversimplify his African-American characters and reinforce the racist stereotypes upon which much of Southern society had been based. To that end in *The Grandissimes*, he develops African-American characters of remarkable depth, most notably, Bras-Coupé and Palmyre Philosophe, neither of whom fits easily into the two categories—barbaric savage or docile servant—identified by Mary Chesnut.

Agricola Fusilier—an elderly French Creole who serves as the chief antagonist for all three of these African-American characters, and an individual whose views are somewhat representative of the South's reactionary response to social progress—cannot reconcile his feelings of racial superiority with his mixed feelings of admiration and dread concerning both Bras-Coupé and Palmyre. When he first encounters Bras-Coupé in the slave market, he is "struck with admiration for the physical beauties of the chieftain" (Cable, *Grandissimes* 220), but such a response fails to acknowledge that the African is anything other than an object, a commodity to be bought the way that one would purchase a fine horse or bull. Agricola is willing to "'kindly and generously tolerate'" the presence of blacks as long as they "'can be of any service in a strictly menial capacity'" (73–74), an attitude not that different from the ones harbored by so-called Northern progressives who, like Richard Watson Gilder, could tolerate stories about blacks as long as they were picturesque and tasteful. The old Creole remains in the dark throughout the story, refusing to acknowledge the fundamental humanity of any black character, though he continues to pride himself on his tolerance. Even when he acknowledges his fear of Palmyre, that feeling is not based on any recognition of her cunning and subversiveness, qualities that are recognizably human and political, but on his belief in her supernatural abilities and her inhuman nature.

In contrast to Agricola is Raoul Innerarity, on the surface not the brightest of the French Creoles but who nonetheless, as his last name suggests, has an inner rarity, a capacity for insight that his more sophisticated brethren lack. At one point Raoul asks Joseph Frowenfeld, a German-American immigrant whose ideals and values consistently clash with those of the French Creoles, if "'it would be hanny disgrace to paint de pigshoe of a niggah?'" (Cable, *Grandissimes* 149). After receiving Frowenfeld's approval, Raoul declares "'Ah, my soul! what a pigshoe I could paint of Bras-Coupé!'" (149). It is not a great leap here to see Cable speaking through Raoul with regard to his own frustration over the rejections of "Bibi." Frowenfeld, whose ideals are noble but not always pragmatic, is eager to support the painting of a "'niggah,'" for that appeals to his sense of fairness and his identification with the downtrodden. Likewise, Cable's editors, as well as most writers, editors, and critics of the post-Reconstruction era, were not averse to, and in fact, sought out stories that featured African-American characters, but they still expected those stories to match their preconceptions, the same ones voiced by Mary Chesnut in 1861. Cable, like Raoul, desires to paint the portrait of Bras-Coupé because that would be something new, something shocking, something subversive.

Of course, one of the chief problems for the writer who employs irony as an element of social critique is the risk of being misinterpreted, and *The Grandissimes* proved to be unexceptional in this regard. Most readers of Cable's time missed the full thrust of his satire, with the detractors declaring that the work misrepresented the culture that it supposedly portrayed, and the supporters reducing the work's complex themes to the simple dictum that "all Slavery is maiming" (Cable, *Grandissimes* 221). While Cable certainly agreed with that dictum, he did not intend for his audience to pity Bras-Coupé in the same way that so many readers had pitied Stowe's Uncle Tom. Cable systematically underscores the complexity of

Bras-Coupé, pointing out that as an African prince and warrior he had been and could be as cruel as the worst of the French Creole slave masters, that despite the injustices done to him, "not a whit broods he over man's inhumanity, but, taking the affair as a matter of course, casts about him for a future" (*Grandissimes* 237). He accepts his captivity as "the fortune of war" and acknowledges the power wielded by his master not because he will allow himself to be reduced to a commodity but because he is essentially a prisoner of war (Cable, *Grandissimes* 226). After he is punished according to the laws of the *Code Noir*, he is "mutilated but unconquered" (Cable, *Grandissimes* 249). And he is always African, for in his hold on that identity rests his hold on the essence of his humanity. His ears can be shorn from his head, his hamstrings can be cut, his muscles branded with the fleur-de-lis, his life literally torn from his body, but he refuses to be appropriated by another. "'To— Africa'" are his final words, spoken to a Catholic priest armed with European notions of heaven and hell (Cable, *Grandissimes* 252). Similar to the flying Africans of African-American folklore, Bras-Coupé circumvents American slavery by rising above it with his indomitable spirit and incomparable character.[2]

Cable's novel is not primarily about rising above the fray or escaping through open rebellion. "Our nights are the keys to our days" (*Grandissimes* 118), proclaims Cable's narrator, suggesting that darkness, mystery, silence, and subversion are the threads that hold together the narrative. Palmyre is the clearest embodiment of these qualities, for she speaks most powerfully through her eyes, through which she earns the respect of Frowenfeld, the fear of Agricola, and the political alliance of Bras-Coupé. Unlike Frowenfeld, she does not always voice her disapproval. She is most often silent; "and so, sometimes, is fire in the wall" (Cable, *Grandissimes* 227). Bras-Coupé also speaks through his gaze and his silence. "His words were all in his eyes," thus subverting the power of the master to silence (Cable, *Grandissimes* 250). Just as the eyes of the severed head of Babo gaze down relentlessly in Melville's *Benito Cereno*, the eyes of Bras-Coupé and Palmyre effectively subvert the physical and psychological boundaries imposed by their supposed masters.

While the attention of most readers is readily drawn to the larger-than-life figure of Bras-Coupé, whose persistent resistance to commodification wins our admiration, Palymre remains as a living and perhaps even more lethal threat to Agricola and the defenders of brutal racial oppression. In the end we tend to see Bras-Coupé as a martyr, shorn of his physical strength and beauty but defiantly adorned with his humanity. As is ultimately the case with martyrs, Bras-Coupé dies, and with his death comes the possibility that what he represents—defiance, independence, subversion—could be swallowed up by the oppressive forces enforcing the status quo. However, Palmyre, who had seen in Bras-Coupé "the gigantic embodiment of her own dark, fierce will" (Cable, *Grandissimes* 228), continues as a potent psychological force, haunting the nightmares of her oppressors and compelling them to lash out at those within their grasp, such as the unfortunate Clemence. Unlike Bras-Coupé, who accepts his status as a prisoner of war even as he refuses to be reduced to a commodity, Palmyre refuses to give Agricola and his fellow racists the satisfaction of her acquiescence. Aware of the slave insurrections of San Domingo, she had hoped that Bras-Coupé would lead an open rebellion in Louisiana. Of course, his mutilation and subsequent death ended such speculation, yet she remains "fifty times the mutineer she had been before— the mutineer who has nothing to lose" (Cable, *Grandissimes* 239). Even the irreducible Bras-Coupé has been corralled, his body and capacity to lead bounded by physical mortality. Only Palmyre, consistently eluding the psychological and physical enclosures established by the white authorities, is boundless.

Cable subverts other boundaries in the text, challenging conventional narrative structures to add additional layers of complexity to his social critique. At the beginning of the Bras-Coupé story, we are told that the narrative is actually a compilation of three different versions told to Frowenfeld by the white Honoré, Honoré, the f.m.c., and Raoul (Cable, *Grandissimes* 219). Why does Cable make this point concerning the story of Bras-Coupé? A meticulous craftsman not prone to throw in insignificant detail, Cable obviously deemed this detail crucial, especially since it consumes the entire opening paragraph of what is perhaps the most important chapter in the novel. Barbara Ladd concludes that this narrative that does not "exactly follow the words of any" single version suggests "that the story of Bras-Coupé, as Cable tells it, is something very different from the story of Bras-Coupé as it might be told" ("Atmosphere" 73). In other words, Cable is making the point that he cannot tell the story entirely as he would like to due to the conservative standards of his editors. Consequently, he recognizes that his version may prove ineffective, that his readers may miss the point just as "the Grandissime beauties" who hear Raoul's version of the story agree "that it was pitiful" but can "suggest no alternative," preferring instead to remain "confirmed in this sentiment" (Cable, *Grandissimes* 253).

As Barbara Ladd and Robert O. Stephens have pointed out in separate studies, Cable drew much of the inspiration for his story of Bras-Coupé from numerous antebellum sources in New Orleans, including historical, journalistic, and personal accounts of figures that closely resembled the central character of Cable's text.[3] Several of those accounts were based on subversive figures associated with the San Domingo revolution or other slave insurrections, as well as with the practice of voodoo. Even though Bras-Coupé may have struck Northern readers of *The Grandissimes* as a picturesque and somewhat pitiable figure, within New Orleans and its surrounding parishes the legend of Bras-Coupé filled the popular imagination with images of rebellion—a frightening notion to ruling whites but an empowering thought for oppressed blacks. Cable, who had acquired an in-depth knowledge of Louisiana history by the time he began his writing career, understood that the history of his native region was deeply intertwined with the West Indies. He knew that "no firm distinction between West Indian rebels and Louisiana fugitives would have been drawn" during the years that form the setting of *The Grandissimes* (Ladd, "Atmosphere" 71). Consequently, the subversive figures within his narrative transcend not only the boundaries imposed by their white protagonists but also the borders of the text. Cable's fiction spills over into history even as history informs the fiction. His editors preferred that his novel be a pristine environment which would romanticize reality and thus confirm white readers in their beliefs.

Cable subverts that preference by "construct[ing] a dialogue with his editors about the relevance of history in the United States" rather than "enact[ing] their reconciliationist agenda" (Ladd, *Nationalism* 77), thus suggesting once again that Cable at this point in his career sees his fiction as a means to accomplish social and political ends.

The easiest target for Cable to attack in *The Grandissimes* is slavery and its apologists, but to see the novel as nothing more than an irrelevant critique of an already defeated and discredited institution, at least in the eyes of Northern readers, is comparable to claiming that Twain's chief target in *The Adventures of Huckleberry Finn* is Huck's father. Anyone could make fun of Pap Finn, but the real genius of Twain's narrative is present in his satire of the hypocrisy of the educated, the sober, and the religious. Cable's target in *The Grandissimes* is much the same. He certainly had plenty of Miss Watsons and Aunt Sallies lining up to "sivilize" his writing (Twain 321). With the end of Reconstruction and the North's increasing infatuation with Southern local color, the chief arbiters of taste deem serious discussions of racial matters unseemly and unnecessary. Whether from exhaustion or a lack of nerve, Cable eventually acquiesced to their demands, producing in the 1890s and early 1900s literature almost entirely devoid of African-American characters. Like so many white Americans of his day and ours, he concluded that "ignoring race is understood to be a graceful, even generous, liberal gesture" that protects us from a painful confrontation with the past and present (Morrison 9–10).

As long as we insist on regarding *The Grandissimes* as nothing more than a finite world encased within the covers of a book, we will see it, at best, as "a minor masterpiece," as the one text in which "Cable transcended his usual limitations" (Chase 167). If we insist that it is a work of art to be judged by the standards of genteel editors residing in plush Victorian offices or the principles of New Critics entranced by delusions of the decontextualized work, then we will conclude that its author is a failure, as "if 'failure' is an intelligent term to apply to any fiction" (Morrison 18). If we recognize that Cable's novel cannot be reduced to itself, that it must be understood within the historical, social, and political milieu in which it was produced, then we can begin to understand it as a text, which, after all, is a fabric, a tapestry, woven of finer thread than we had heretofore imagined.

NOTES

1. This citation is drawn from a passage in which Melville reveals his frustration with the reading public and its reluctance to embrace literature that unabashedly probes controversial metaphysical, social, or political questions. Unlike most of his white contemporaries, Melville made a serious effort to address race and cultural differences, especially in *Moby Dick* and *Benito Cereno*.

2. The legend of the flying Africans plays a prominent role in Toni Morrison's *Song of Solomon* and has been included in numerous collections of African-American folklore. For a version of the legend, see Julius Lester's *Black Folktales*.

3. See Ladd's "'An Atmosphere of Hints and Allusions': Bras-Coupé and the Context of Black Insurrection in *The Grandissimes*" and Stephens's "Cable's Bras-Coupe and Merimee's Tamango: The Case of the Missing Arm."

REFERENCES

Cable, George Washington. *The Grandissimes*. New York: Charles Scribner's Sons, 1880.
—. *Old Creole Days*. New York: Charles Scribner's Sons, 1879.
Chase, Richard. *The American Novel and Its Tradition*. Baltimore: Johns Hopkins UP, 1957.
Chesnut, Mary Boykin. *Mary Chesnut's Civil War*. Ed. C. Vann Woodward. New Haven, CT: Yale UP, 1981.
Hall, Gwendolyn Midlo. "The Formation of Afro-Creole Culture." Hirsch and Logsdon 58–87.
Hirsch, Arnold R. and Joseph Logsdon, eds. *Creole New Orleans: Race and Americanization*. Baton Rouge: Louisiana State UP, 1992.
—. "Franco-Africans and African-Americans: Introduction." Hirsch and Logsdon 189–200.
Howells, William Dean. *My Mark Twain*. 1910. Mineola, New York: Dover, 1997.
Johnson, Jerah. "Colonial New Orleans: A Fragment of the Eighteenth-Century French Ethos." Hirsch and Logsdon 12–57.
Ladd, Barbara. "'An Atmosphere of Hints and Allusions': Bras-Coupé and the Context of Black Insurrection in *The Grandissimes*." *The Southern Quarterly* 29 (1991): 63–76.
—. *Nationalism and the Color Line in George W. Cable, Mark Twain, and William Faulkner*. Baton Rouge: Louisiana State UP, 1996.
Lester, Julius. *Black Folktales*. New York: Grove P, 1969.
Logsdon, Joseph and Caryn Cossé Bell. "The Americanization of Black New Orleans 1850-1900." Hirsch and Logsdon 201–61.
Melville, Herman. "Hawthorne and His Mosses." 1850. *Moby Dick: A Norton Critical Edition*. Ed. Harrison Hayford and Hershel Parker. New York: Norton, 1967. 535–551.
Morrison, Toni. *Playing in the Dark: Whiteness and the Literary Imagination*. New York: Vintage, 1992.
Stephens, Robert O. "Cable's Bras-Coupe and Merimee's Tamango: The Case of the Missing Arm." *Mississippi Quarterly* 35 (1982): 387–405.
Tregle, Joseph G., Jr. "Creoles and Americans." Hirsch and Logsdon 131–85.
Turner, Arlin. *George W. Cable: A Biography*. 1956. Baton Rouge: Louisiana State UP, 1966.
Twain, Mark. *The Adventures of Huckleberry Finn*. 1884. New York: Penguin, 1985.
—. *Life on the Mississippi*. 1883. New York: Penguin, 1984.
Wilson, Edmund. *Patriotic Gore: Studies in the Literature of the American Civil War*. 1962. New York: Norton, 1994.

LOUISIANA DURING THE
MODERNIST PERIOD, 1919–1945

Cakewalks, Cauls, and Conjure: Folk Practices in Arna Bontemps's *God Sends Sunday* and "A Summer Tragedy"

Lisa Abney

Arnaud (Arna) Wendell Bontemps lived his life as one of the leading figures of, and authorities, on the Harlem Renaissance. Bontemps's critical pieces focus upon urban literature and culture, and within the context of the Harlem Renaissance, few would think of categorizing him as a Southern writer, nor, even more specifically, as a Louisiana writer. The time in which he lived and his experiences with the Harlem Renaissance movement lead many to think of Bontemps as a modernist. His works, however, such as *God Sends Sunday* (1931) and "A Summer Tragedy"(1933) illustrate the kind of verisimilitude that leads readers to view Bontemps as a realist rather than a modernist. Many of Bontemps's fictional works reflect elements of his early life in Louisiana, and he set several of his fiction works in that state. *God Sends Sunday* illustrates the worlds of central Louisiana, New Orleans, St. Louis, and Los Angeles while "A Summer Tragedy" focuses upon central Louisiana and New Orleans. Bontemps not only sets his works in Louisiana, but he also imbues his characters with folk practices and traditions which provide readers with vivid depictions of Louisiana's people. Bontemps allows readers to glimpse both the traditional rural and modern urban aspects of African-American culture of the early half of the twentieth century. The traditional is exemplified by Leah of *God Sends Sunday* and Jeff and Jennie Patton of "A Summer Tragedy" in contrast to the modern African-American culture, illustrated by Augie and Terry of *God Sends Sunday*.[1] In the lives of both the traditional and modern characters, the influence and importance of folk traditions remains clear.[2] Specifically within the texts, Bontemps illustrates the importance of folk traditions relating three specific areas of African-American life—belief systems, recreation, and occupation.[3]

In order to fully understand Bontemps's depictions of Louisiana, something must be said of his life. Bontemps was born on 13 October 1902 in Alexandria, Louisiana. He lived there for only a short time before his family decided to move to California. From the early part of the twentieth century until the 1950s, several

Creoles from the Cane River Region in Natchitoches Parish, some fifty miles north of Alexandria, left seeking new opportunities in California (Ravare). Bontemps's family may have been familiar with the California journeys of many of these Cane River residents. The lure of better opportunities and Bontemps's father's brush with some racist whites on his way home from work one evening, likely spurred Paul Bontemps's decision to leave Louisiana (Canaday 163).[4] The family successfully settled in Los Angeles and lived well, as Bontemps's father was a talented brick mason. Arna's mother passed away when he was just twelve years old, but from her influence, he gained a love of reading and education (Jones 12).

After his mother's death, Bontemps spent an increasing amount of time with his grandmother and her younger brother, Buddy, who provided the model for Augie of *God Sends Sunday*. Buddy encouraged Arna's desire to write, and even though Buddy did not possess a strong formal education, he was well read for a person of limited resources. Buddy worked as a chef and lived a life of drinking and carousing, which horrified Arna's conservative father. However, because of the his father's need to work, Arna was often left in the care of Buddy and Arna's grandmother, who shared their tales of Louisiana life with Arna. Though Arna Bontemps had left his native state at a young age, he developed an extensive knowledge of the region and its culture through the tales of his family.

Paul Bontemps hoped that Arna would become the fourth generation of Bontemps's family brick masons and arranged for Arna to become an apprentice in the trade. Arna Bontemps rebelled, for he wanted to pursue his education, and he did so, with the hard-won blessing of his father. In 1917, his father agreed to send Arna to a white, private boarding school, San Fernando Academy. Bontemps then enrolled at Pacific Union College and was graduated in 1923 (Jones 14). In 1924, Bontemps moved to New York to teach at Harlem Academy. During his time in Harlem, Bontemps encountered and worked with all the major cultural and literary figures of the era—Carl Van Vechten, Langston Hughes, Jean Toomer, Claude McKay, James Weldon Johnson, Countee Cullen, and James Baldwin. In 1926, he married Alberta Johnson with whom he produced six children. During this time, Bontemps wrote many poems and published several fiction pieces. In 1931, Bontemps left the Harlem Academy and published *God Sends Sunday*. From 1931-1934, Bontemps taught at Oakwood Junior College in Huntsville, Alabama (Jones 16). Bontemps's Alabama life was characterized by a continual lack of money and insufferable climate changes from blazing heat to freezing cold. Because of the lack of space in the house, Bontemps wrote his works outside under the shade of the house's eaves. Ultimately, his persistence produced results. During this time, Bontemps turned his attention to juvenile literature, for he felt that young people's hearts had not yet been hardened by the inhumane, adult world and that they would be a better audience for his work. His efforts yielded many significant children's books. In 1943, Bontemps completed a Masters degree in Library Science from the University of Chicago; he became librarian at Fisk University in Nashville, Tennessee, until 1965, when he retired. Bontemps continued to write poetry, literary criticism, and fiction throughout his career until he died at age seventy-one in 1973. Bontemps's work as a librarian was crucial to scholars of his day and contemporary scholars as well since he accrued one of the most complete collections of Harlem Renaissance and other African-American writing in the world for Fisk University. During Bontemps's life, the author played a variety of roles—poet, prose writer, literary critic, librarian, and author of children's literature, and his writing reflects his Louisiana roots—replete with African-American cultural and folk traditions, which are vividly depicted throughout his works.

Bontemps illustrates the belief system of African Americans in Louisiana during the early twentieth century. Belief systems generally incorporate the interpretation of signs in order to ascribe meaning to, or to provide explanation for, a variety of events or occurrences. Noted folklorist, Alan Dundes, argues that folk beliefs and traditions represent "a people's image of themselves. . . . Folklore as a mirror of culture provides unique raw material for those eager to better understand themselves and others" (vii). For many cultures, births and deaths provide members of societies with the opportunity to express beliefs and to offer interpretations of these events. In the American South, in both white and African-American cultures, when a child is born with a filmy covering over its face, called a *caul* or veil, many interpret this to mean that the child will lead a charmed life or will have the powers of clairvoyance (Radford 92). Bontemps's text, *God Sends Sunday*, illustrates this widely held belief through the life of Lil Augie, whose veiled birth deeply affects his life. From the first page of the novel, the importance of the caul is shown: "He was a thin, undersized boy, smaller for his years than any other child on the place, and he had round pop-eyes. But he enjoyed a certain prestige among the black youngsters, and older folks as well, because of the legend that he was lucky, a legend that had attended him since birth, due to a mysterious veil with which he had entered the world" (Bontemps, *God* 3). This paragraph sets forth the importance of the belief in luck as an integral part of the novel. Augie's mantra throughout the novel is that he is lucky and will always have good fortune because of the circumstances of his birth. The opening paragraph of the second chapter of the work thus begins: "Little Augie believed in conjure and 'signs.' Having been born with a caul over his face, he was endowed (he believed) with clairvoyant powers. For example he was able to see spirits, he could put curses on people and he could remove them, and, above all, he was lucky—unfailingly lucky" (Bontemps, *God* 10). Augie's unfailing belief that he is infinitely lucky remains true until his final encounter with Florence, the lover, whom he has sought for several years.

After many attempts at trying to make other women refashion themselves to become the image of Florence, Augie seizes the opportunity to make Florence his paramour. He leaves his old friend Bad-foot and joins Florence. This passage marks the last time that Augie's luck is described as good. Bad-foot and Augie have the following conversation.

> "Us ain't gonna bus' up, Bad-foot. Us is always gonna be lak dis." He held up his first two fingers.
> "I gonna miss you jes' de same," Bad-foot said. "You is ma luck stone, son."
> "You is good luck yo' black self," Augie smiled. (Bontemps, *God* 102)

Life with Florence, however, is less than what Augie expects because once they become united, Augie's usual good luck ebbs. The light-skinned Florence is forced to move from her house because of her alliance with the dark-skinned Augie. Because Florence has traditionally allied herself with white men, her white neighbors refuse to tolerate the relationship with Augie.

All of a sudden bad days came upon Little Augie. An accumulation of bad luck, reserved from many, many days past, fell at once upon his head. For years a successful gambler, he was now unable to draw a single pair from a deck of cards. All the dice that had been so responsive to his cajoling now seemed loaded against him. . . . Augie began drinking more than usual. He could not bear to confront his wretched fortunes with a clear mind. . . .He was a race-horse man. A woman was like a fine suit of clothes to him, something to please his vanity, to show him off well in the eyes of his friends. "Damn 'em all, all de womens! I b'lieve Florence is bad luck to me anyhow."

But that was just mouth-talk. He had hardly spoken the words when he wondered if he were actually losing his mind about her. How otherwise could he have imagined such an outlandish lie! (Bontemps, *God* 103–104)

Florence and Augie live in squalor. Meanwhile, Augie struggles to find ways to restore his good luck. He seeks the aid of conjurers who give him charms to change his luck: "All that winter Augie fought off bad luck. He carried a good-luck 'hand' in his coat pocket and a money 'hand' in his pants—small wads of cloth containing loadstones and other magic ingredients mixed by a conjurer and sewed up tight" (Bontemps, *God* 105). These talismans, however, have little effect upon his luck, and ultimately, he endures another losing season at horse racing and gambling. Florence, who can take no more of the squalid living, leaves Augie with little except a few of his worst clothes and his accordion. In their final scene, he realizes how completely his enchanted life has changed when Florence tells him that she is leaving.

"I'm gonna quit you, Lil Augie," she said.
"How come dat, yella gal?"
"Yo' luck done change, Lil Augie. It's leavin'-time. . . ."
"I'd fight 'bout you; I'd fight ma daddy 'bout you. But ma luck is done gone down."
(Bontemps, *God* 111– 12)

Defeated, the aging and past his prime, Augie leaves to find his sister, Leah, in California. All the while, he curses his wretched luck. Once settled at Leah's, Augie begins to scheme about breeding Leah's old horse in order to produce a racing foal which can renew his luck. Unfortunately, Augie's luck has run out, and his plan goes unfulfilled, as does his hope of staying at Leah's and successfully settling down. Ultimately, he must leave Leah's because of a nasty fight in which he renders a near fatal blow with a beet knife to Lissus. Augie's final leave-taking illustrates his despondence as he embarks upon his relocation to Tia Juana, where he has heard that there is horse racing and "plenty of liquor" (Bontemps, *God* 197). Augie has undergone a dramatic change of fortune which can be expected if the Greek and Renaissance ideas of *hubris* and the wheel of fortune come to mind while reading the novel. A reader almost expects Augie to fail because of his excessive pride and arrogance. Augie's unrealistic belief in the power of the caul to provide luck stands as an illustration of the significance of this belief within his culture.

While the power of the caul illustrates an important element of Augie's belief system, the interpretation of signs also figures into this novel. After Augie moves to California to Leah's house, two specific events occur which presage death or bad luck. An owl lands on Leah's gate and hoots loudly while Terry (Augie's nephew), Beulah and Azilee (Leah's neighbors), Augie, and Leah are relaxing one evening. In response to this bad omen, Leah shows fear and repulsion:

Leah stood in the middle of the floor panic-stricken. Her eyes glowing with terror, she angled her ear to hear it again. She turned to Augie with a frightened whisper. "Looka yonder. Ain't dat ma ole shoe behind de stove?"

Augie gave the shoe a kick but didn't stop playing.

"Turn it up, Terry," the old woman said. "Quick." Then she hurried to the door and began sprinkling salt on the ground.

"How come you do that?" Beulah asked.

"Make him go way. Owl hootin' mean bad day comin'."

The owl went away, but Leah was troubled the rest of the evening. . . .

Terry had seen his grandmother fighting bad luck before, crossing sticks and burning hair, and Augie had understood and obeyed the signs all his natural life. But no harm ever threatened Leah's home; so these things had come to receive only a small attention. This time, however, Augie and Terry were both impressed. That devilish little owl sounded bad outside on the fence post, terribly bad. (Bontemps, *God* 174–75)

In many contexts, the owl can symbolize wisdom, but it can also be a harbinger of doom. While the Greeks viewed the owl with awe, the Romans felt that its appearance and hooting signaled a coming death, and even today, if an owl "hoots or hollers near your house disaster is not too far off. It may even be foretelling a death in the family. So wear your clothes backward, pull out your pockets, throw salt over your left shoulder, and put a knot in your handkerchief" (Potter 147). While the presence of owls often terrifies many people, birds, in folklore, are associated with grim events. Carole Potter describes the role of birds in death beliefs: "Birds were thought to be messengers of departed souls. When a bird tapped on a window or flew into a house, it was assumed that a spirit was in search of another to join it; in other words, it was a messenger of death" (24). In *God Sends Sunday,* after the incident with the owl, one morning when Terry, Augie, and Leah are eating breakfast, a sparrow flies into the house. Leah immediately springs into action to rid the house of the bird.

"Lawd Jesus!" Leah cried. "Come heah quick, y'all. Come heah an' help me shoo dis bad-luck bird outa ma house."

Augie dropped his fork. . .and sprang up as if the house were on fire. . . .

"He done flew in heah in de broad daylight. I sho to Gawd b'lieve it's a sign. Bad luck done come at us. Our luck done change."

"Hush dat moanin' an' shoo," Leah commanded. "Get him outa heah." (Bontemps, *God* 187).

Shortly after the bird's appearance in the house, Augie encounters the evil Lissus, whom he ultimately cuts with a beet knife. This incident leads to Augie's departure from Leah's house. Indeed, the owl and the sparrow signal more bad luck for Augie.

Bontemps once again incorporates birds into his work in "A Summer Tragedy." While birds sometimes connote evil, in other cases, they fend off evil, as illustrated in "A Summer Tragedy." In this short story, the elderly Patton couple deals with the decision to end their lives because of their rapidly advancing physical deterioration. While reviewing his life, Jeff Patton thinks about his livestock, of which only three "frizzly chickens" are left. These frizzly chickens are said to possess special powers, as Bontemps shows through Jeff's passage.

There were three frizzly chickens in the yard. All his other chickens had been killed or stolen recently. But the frizzly chickens had been saved somehow. That was fortunate indeed, for these curious creatures had a way of devouring "poison" from the yard in that way protecting against conjure and bad luck and spells. But even the frizzly chickens seemed now to be in a stupor. (Bontemps, "Summer" 2)

Throughout Bontemps's work, the incorporation of these folk elements into the belief system of these communities indicates the importance of these traditions. Bontemps's use of elements common to the culture of Southern African Americans indeed brings verisimilitude to the text and serves to strengthen the connection between reader and text by providing a vivid and accurate depiction of the lives of the Pattons.

While folk beliefs play a role in the realistic depictions of African-American culture in the text, so, too, do the recreational practices in the novel. In *God Sends Sunday*, the sporting life is vividly portrayed. Bontemps's depictions of the macks and their behavior indicate much about this segment of society during the time period of the novel.[5] Cakewalks, music, Juneteenth celebrations, and Mardi Gras festivities are specific elements of recreation, which appear in Bontemps's fiction. The cakewalk is a folk practice that occurs across the South even today, yet it rose to prominence during the 1920s and 1930s. Folklorist and fiction writer, Zora Neale Hurston, documents this important element of African-American culture in her work, *Their Eyes Were Watching God*. The cakewalk of Bontemps's era was an elaborate dance contest in which the winner literally took the cake as prize for a stellar performance. Contemporary cakewalks, though derived from these earlier dances, bear little resemblance to their predecessors. The cakewalks depicted in *God Sends Sunday* show contests which test participants' abilities to strut and dance in an elegant, yet flashy, manner. In the novel, Bontemps depicts two cakewalks and illustrates the changes in the activity through Augie's eyes.

Augie's first cakewalk with Della is shown as a sparkling event in which brightly colored dresses and suits bring attention to the stylish movements of their wearers (Bontemps, *God* 74–5). Bontemps creates an almost photographic impression of the Cotton Flower Ball, of which the cakewalk is the high point of the evening. Bontemps describes the food vendors, the music, and the colorful dress of the macks and their women. Bontemps's most descriptive passage chronicles Della and Augie's entrance into the cakewalk:

With so many impressive pairs on the floor, it became apparent that selecting a winner was to be no simple task. The room buzzed. . . .Suddenly the buzzing ceased. There was a hush, then a burst of cheers and furious applause. It was so wild and sudden that all arguments ended. Every head was turned, every neck strained. Little Augie had taken the floor with Della Green.

He wore a full dress suit made of leaf-green satin, with a cape and top hat to match. His lapels were gold, as were also his pumps and the knob of his green cane, and his hair was oiled and pressed to his head like patent leather. Della's dress was plum-colored, her petticoats gold; she too wore gold slippers. Their walk was simply an elaborate strut, but it was effective enough.

"Tha's it," the crowd shouted. "Tha's de one."

"Yes, suh, Lil Augie takes de cake."

"Lil Augie is It. There ain't no flies on him." (Bontemps, *God* 78–9)

Clearly, the elegant and colorful couple has won the event, and Bontemps's illustration of dance provides readers with a clear view of the cakewalk and all that it entails. Later in the text, when Augie goes to the California cakewalk, he sees new manners and new dances, and he feels utterly left behind. He thinks back to the Cotton Flower Ball, where he and Della had been king and queen for a night.

The denizens of Mudtown were seeing the shimmy for the first time in a public place. In those days it was regarded as a low, unseemly dance, and the young country girls felt a little outraged at seeing it done there so badly. . .But Augie watched it calmly from the sidelines. He had nothing but scorn for the modern nigger dances. He thought of the night he walked with Della Green at the Cotton Flower Ball. That had been a real come-off. That was what he called a dance. It was fancy. (Bontemps, *God* 161)

Indeed, the advent of new social mores and styles takes Augie aback and serves to remind him of how old he truly is and of the changing times in which he is living. He ponders the changes in recreation and in the manners of people of his nephew's generation in opposition to the more elegant ways of his past.

While dance styles change for Augie, music remains a stable element for him. He relies upon his accordion and its music for comfort. Blues music plays a major role in this text, which may be in large part due to the increasing popularity of blues music made more accessible by musicians such as W.C. Handy.[6] Throughout the work, Augie sings the blues, and the influence of the city of St. Louis becomes apparent when he re-creates songs that he has heard while in the area and in New Orleans. Throughout the text, Augie and Della sing various blues songs. At the end of the novel, Augie sits in the back of a truck and plays his accordion. He has no other possessions remaining, yet seemingly, he needs no others as he moves toward another difficult chapter of his life. His previous view regarding the importance of material goods has been altered by his many life experiences. The one constant element is the music which flows through his mind and springs out of his accordion.

Dance and music are two folk activities which appear in this novel and other novels by African-American writers. Few authors, however, have depicted June 19th celebrations in literature of the 1920s or 1930s.[7] The Juneteenth celebration which Bontemps portrays becomes a raucous event in which two men are killed, yet prior to the murders, he illustrates the customary manner in which the holiday was celebrated at the time with picnics in the country. Augie puzzles about why he has come to the event since "he had never been inside a church and he did not know how to behave in the presence of girls who had religion" (Bontemps, *God* 27). The picnic, sponsored by a church, draws a number of, as Augie calls them, "sinners" (Bontemps, *God* 27) who carry with them their fighting tools "knives, brass knuckles, razors, and in some cases, pistols" (Bontemps, *God* 27). Ultimately, the event concludes in tragedy, yet the mention of the event in the text marks the practice of the celebration of Juneteenth in New Orleans in the 1920s and 1930s, thus documenting an important cultural tradition and providing another element of realism within the novel.

While dancing, music, and a Juneteenth celebration appear in this novel, the folk tradition of Mardi Gras is depicted in "A Summer Tragedy" when Jeff Patton thinks back to his younger days when he and his friends attended Mardi Gras in New Orleans.

Young Jeff Patton was among them, the Jeff Patton of fifty years ago who went down to New Orleans with a crowd of country boys to the Mardi Gras doings. The gay young crowd-boys with candy-striped shirts and rouged brown girls in noisy silks was like a picture in his head. Yet it did not make him sad. On that very trip Slim Burns had killed Joe Beasely—the crowd had been broken up. (9)

The use of these folk elements provides realism in the text and helps to convey the culture and the times of these characters. Bontemps, in his fiction, re-creates the world of African Americans of the early twentieth century, offering both the violent and joyful sides of this complex culture.

While deeply seated beliefs and recreational activities include folkloric elements, so too, does occupation in Bontemps's texts. In Augie's occupation as jockey, each day is filled with the unknown. When animals and humans work together, humans rarely have complete control. Augie's life as a jockey is based upon his own lucky nature, yet within his life as a jockey, there are many folk traditions that he calls upon. The racing life calls for jockeys to live transient existences, following the racing season from city to city. Because of an early experience with what Augie calls a "jack-ma-lantern," he feels that he is doomed to be a wanderer. Bontemps's telling of the "jack–ma–lantern" story in *God Sends Sunday* echoes a popular tale which circulates in the Port Neches/ Beaumont/ Port Arthur region of Texas in which a ghost figure carries his head or a jack-o-lantern under his arm and wanders throughout the area looking for the person who has decapitated him (Abney). However, most of the Texas variants do not report luck as a consequence of seeing the headless man. This area of Texas contains a high number of residents whose families hail from western Louisiana, and many of them, as late as the 1990s, tell variants of the jack-ma-lantern/headless wanderer story. The occurrence of the story in Bontemps's fiction documents the presence of this tale in Louisiana during the early twentieth century. The wanderer is a frequent folk motif and can be found in the Aarne Thompson tale type index, as can the phenomenon of the "jack–ma–lantern." The wanderer and headless ghost figure have been cataloged as E422.1.8: Headless Revenant and E413.1 Execution Victim

Cannot Rest in Grave, and have been further documented in such works as *Swapping Stories: Folktales from Louisiana*. Indeed, Augie's feelings after his experience with the "jack–ma–lantern" lead him to become a jockey, and when his luck turns, he realizes that the prophetic stories about the "jack–ma–lantern" have come to pass in his life:

Augie believed that he was bound to wander all his natural days, that there would be no rest for him any place until he had exhausted his luck and met the final disaster that awaited him. For a jack-ma-lantern was an unreal light, a brightness that appeared in the dark thickets and swamplands, that seduced its victims by leading them on and on to destruction. The usual victims were men caught after dark in the woods, and the end was generally direct and speedy, but in Augie's case it had not been the same. The jack-ma-lantern that he saw came out of the pine woods after nightfall, hovered along the fence near the quarters and traveled off toward the swamp. (Bontemps, *God* 10–11)

Augie's life as a jockey fulfills his fate to wander, moving from one city to another over the course of the racing season: "He followed the retinue to San Antonio and to Louisville and Mobile as the racing seasons shifted, and learned to amuse himself like the other Negro hands, drinking whiskey, gambling with dice, and clog dancing. Augie could sing too, and in his spare time around the stable he learned to play an old accordion that he found there" (Bontemps, *God* 15–16). Bontemps's depictions of the racing life illustrate the folk traditions of its practitioners through the images associated with the sporting life. The life of gambling, dancing, and drinking coupled with horse racing lures many like Augie into its den. While Augie's life as a jockey appeals to his need for excitement and surprise, when he needs to regroup and to collect himself, he goes to his sister, Leah.

His final trip to Leah's house lands him in the country. This rural setting brings his life full circle—he finds an uneasy peace in rural California, yet tending the animals uplifts him and helps him to find hope in his unlucky time. This section of the novel vividly illustrates rural farming traditions and further shows agricultural practices of the time. In chapter nine, Bontemps uses the example of feeding beets to cattle as winter fodder. This example shows the ingenuity of those who make use of every available resource in order to survive—a practice integral to folk traditions. In an earlier chapter of the section, Augie leads Leah and Terry in the planting of a new garden. Within this chapter, the kinds of beans planted are addressed, as is the issue of breeding Leah's two heifers. The depictions of farm life, like those of the racing life, illustrate the importance and the place of occupation in the lives of these characters.

In the same way, Jeff Patton of Bontemps's "Summer Tragedy" thinks of his life of toil and describes the difficulty of raising a crop for Major Stevenson.

He could not help reflecting that the crops were good. He knew what that meant, too; he had made forty-five of them with his own hands. It was true that he had worn out nearly a dozen mules, but that was the fault of old man Stevenson, the owner of the land. Major Stevenson had the odd notion that one mule was all a share farmer needed to work a thirty-acre plot. It was an expensive notion, the way it killed mules from overwork, but the old man held to it. Jeff thought it killed a good many share farmers as well as mules. (4)

Bontemps depicts the world of the sharecropper in Jeff and Jenny Patton's story, and his accurate illustrations of the days before mechanized agriculture show the struggles of many farmers in this arduous occupation.

Bontemps is decidedly a writer of the Modernist age, yet he crafts his fiction in a manner, which does not rely solely upon the literary techniques of the Modernists. Bontemps's narratives are linear, and the narrative voicing that he employs in his works does not feature the kinds of stream-of-consciousness writing that so many of his colleagues adopted. While the Modernist themes of isolation, angst, universal inhumanity, hopelessness, fragmentation of community, and alienation appear in his fiction, his work transcends these themes and depicts realistic characters and situations. The literary world that Bontemps creates is enhanced by his use of folkloric elements relating to belief systems, recreation, and occupation.

NOTES

1. Modern in this essay refers to the time period from 1919–1965 which is considered to be the time period for the Modernist movement in literature.

2. Folk traditions are those elements of everyday life, which pass from one person to another, usually across generations. Folk traditions include religious or occupational practices, activities, foodways, arts, stories that are shared by members of a family or a community which are learned within a family or group. Material culture practices would include activities such as quilting, weaving, needlework, foodways, carving, and whittling. The practice of these activities in true folk tradition is learned through other people, not from a kit or an instructional video.

3. These three elements of folk practice have been selected for examination in the text since folklorists and anthropologists often select these elements along with two others to review when studying various groups: recreational activities, occupational practices, religious beliefs, ethnic identification, and gender.

4. Canaday asserts that the Bontemps's family were Creoles. This term has many definitions; in the eighteenth, nineteenth, and early twentieth centuries, the term meant born in the New World of European parentage. As time passed, and more racial miscegenation occurred during and after slavery, the term sometimes meant born of one European and one African parent. Some researchers, such as Gwendolyn Midlo Hall, use the term to mean anyone born in Louisiana regardless of parentage or heritage. Hence, Hall terms children of Africans who were born in Louisiana, Creoles. Most residents of the Cane River area in Natchitoches Parish use the term to describe a person who is either bi-racial or mono-racial of French descent. In a footnote in Canaday's article, he states that he learned much about Bontemps's life through a series of interviews and experiences with Bontemps while Canaday was studying with the author. Canaday's use of the term Creole could be any of the three earlier described definitions. However, Bontemps's family's occupation as stone masons may connect them to the Cane River Creoles, many of whom are of mixed heritage and who migrated to California later in the twentieth century. For more information on this topic, see Malinda Ravare's essay or the book-length studies by Virginia Dominguez, Gary Mills, and Sybil Kein.

5. The term mack is short for mackerel, which means one who ministers to sexual debauchery—a bawd, a pimp, or a procurer. The term has also been used to mean someone who is a person of considerable status in the street hierarchy, who by his lively and

persuasive rapping has acquired a stable of girls to hustle for him and give him money. Bontemps's usage seems to indicate a similar meaning with an element of the sporting life mingled into the definition. He depicts them as young men who dress in a flashy fashion, gamble, drink, and engage in sexual exploits. Augie, while a mack, does not prostitute his women, nor does he take money from them as the earlier definition suggests.

6. Bontemps knew Handy's work well and edited Handy's autobiography, *Father of the Blues: An Autobiography by W. C. Handy.* The influence of the blues and Bontemps's knowledge of this kind of music could hardly be separated from his writing.

7. 19 June 1865 was the date on which news of the Emancipation Proclamation arrived in Texas. The celebration of this date began in East Texas and spread to Louisiana and Arkansas. By the late 1800s, the free people of color who left Louisiana and Texas took the practice of the celebrating with them. Because of the 1979 official State of Texas recognition of the Emancipation celebration, the commemoration of this event has now spread to many other states (Wiggins 420).

REFERENCES

Aarne, Antii and Stith Thompson. *The Types of the Folktale.* Folklore Fellows Communications. Helsinki: Suomalainen Tiedeakatemia, 1961.

Abernathy, Edward Francis. *Legendary Ladies of Texas.* Dallas: E-Heart Press, 1981.

Abney, Lisa. "The Legend of Sarah Jane Lane and Other East Texas Stories." Unpublished manuscript.

Bontemps, Arna. *God Sends Sunday.* New York: Harcourt, 1931.

—. "A Summer Tragedy." *The Old South.* New York: Dodd, Mead, 1933.

Canaday, Nicholas. "Arna Bontemps: The Louisiana Heritage." *Callaloo: A Journal of African-American and African-American Arts and Letters* 4.1–2 (1981): 163–69.

Domínguez, Virginia. *White by Definition: Social Classification in Creole Louisiana.* 1986. New Brunswick, NJ: Rutgers UP, 1997.

Dundes, Alan. *Interpreting Folklore.* Bloomington: Indiana UP, 1980.

Handy, W. C. *Father of the Blues: An Autobiography of W. C. Handy.* Ed. Arna Bontemps. New York: MacMillan, 1941.

Hurston, Zora Neale. *Their Eyes Were Watching God.* 1937. New York: HarperPerennial, 1989.

Jones, Kirkland C. "Arna Bontemps." *Dictionary of Literary Biography, Volume 51: Afro-American Writers from the Harlem Renaissance to 1940.* Ed. Trudier Harris. Detroit: Gale, 1987. 10-21.

Kein, Sybil, ed. Introduction. *Creole: The History and Legacy of Louisiana's Free People of Color.* Baton Rouge: Louisiana State UP, 2000.

Lindahl, Carl, Maida Owens, and C. Renee Harvison, eds. *Swapping Stories: Folktales from Louisiana.* Jackson: U of Mississippi P, 1997.

"Mack." *Oxford English Dictionary On-line.* 1 February 2001. <http://dictionary.oed.com/>.

Mills, Gary B. *The Forgotten People: Cane River's Creoles of Color.* Baton Rouge: Louisiana State UP, 1977.

Potter, Carole. *Knock on Wood and Other Superstitions: An Encyclopedia of Talismans, Charms, Superstitions, and Symbols.* New York: Bonanza Books, 1983.

Radford, E. and M.A. Radford. *The Encyclopedia of Superstitions.* 1961. Ed. Christina Hole. New York: Barnes and Noble, 1961, 1996.

Ravare, Malinda. "Louisiana to California." Natchitoches/NSU Folk Festival Program. Natchitoches: Louisiana Folklife Center Publications, 1998.

Wiggins, William H., Jr. "Juneteenth." *American Folklore: An Encyclopedia.* Ed. Jan Harold Brunvand. New York: Garland, 1996.

Wiggins, William H., Jr. "Juneteenth." *American Folklore: An Encyclopedia.* Ed. Jan
   Harold Brunvand. New York: Garland, 1996.

William Faulkner's Two-Basket Stories

Jo LeCoeur

The content of William Faulkner's fiction has been enriched by Central Mississippi Choctaw and Northern Mississippi Chickasaw, so critics have noted,and Faulkner acknowledged.[1] Until now, however, the Choctaw hand imprinted in his style has gone undocumented. Yet the structural design of *The Sound and the Fury* (1929) and the multi-listener-tellers in *Absalom, Absalom!* (1936) were traditional storytelling concepts among the Choctaw of Southeast Louisiana at least by the early 1900s if not long before. Malcolm Cowley's complaint that "Faulkner is incapable of telling the same story twice without adding new details"(xv) misses the point of an oral history tradition that retells matters of importance, accumulating detail from stipulated perspectives designed to build intensity with each retelling.

Writers' current doctrine on narrative method owes more to critics such as Cowley and to commercially conscious publishers than it does to William Faulkner's art. Writing texts advise novices to keep the narrative moving and avoid distractions that invade the intimate space between the writer and the reader. Repetitious storytellers and talkative listeners, both standard features in an oral culture, translate well to paper, say writers on the lecture circuit. One cannot structure art for a literate audience, say the teachers, on a method that evolved in a pre-literate culture, when cultural survival depended on word of mouth, and oral language itself was only one generation away from extinction upon the death of the last speakers of a language.

Before I learned to read, I listened to Choctaw stories. I listened on into my early adolescence, unconscious of the structural guidelines, thinking then in terms of content only. As an adult I found Choctaw stories in print.[2] They read like flat synopses of the powerful, wise, and funny stories that I remembered. Seeking an explanation for this discrepancy, I encountered an essay by Grayson Noley that lumps all Choctaw tales into three categories: (1) ancient legends "popularly accepted as being historic," (2) myths "involving spiritual explanations for some alleged fact," and (3) moralistic fables "which assign human roles to animals" (Noley 83–84). Noley's descriptions overlooked the elements that gave the stories life. Where were the comedies that had made me laugh my sides sore? Where was the history not yet ancient—"The Natchez Attack," "Dancing Rabbit Creek," "The Hanging Child"? Noley concedes that the categories are "somewhat intertwined," that stories were "perhaps...recorded without the proper context," and that "possibly some stories were and are interrelated, each depending for its effectiveness on being told in conjunction with others" (84). No clue is offered as to how stories might be related. No context is suggested other than the statement that in a council meeting, old men spoke first about their nation's history. Even the scholarly *Choctaw Genesis 1500–1700* scarcely touches upon oral tradition and oral history; summaries of migration and origin legends fail to indicate that a story is more than plot outline (Galloway 24, 324–27).

Finding nothing in print on the method of storytelling, I decided to find my Choctaw storyteller Rebecca Boyd and ask her how much of what I remembered was real. The fact that the same story was never the same had many explanations, as did my recollection that the story grew better and funnier with each telling. I recalled how she always said no when I asked for an immediate retelling, but her explanation that I had to wait until "next time" because she could not "buck the one-a-day installment plan" sounded more like Sears Roebuck than Choctaw. I had not known then that she was training me, until ultimately, after several tellings, she would say that the story was not finished until I told it. Later I would learn that the story must be told a fourth time by a listener relying solely upon the memory of having listened to the first three versions, though it still amazes me how, without my conscious awareness, Rebecca Boyd guided my retelling with her promptings and her questions. I can recall equating the memorable with the valuable—if certain elements stuck in my mind from her earlier versions, they must belong in mine. I had forgotten her different voices and that where we sat or stood had mattered, as the stories were often told while we did chores.

The spot where Andrew and Rebecca Boyd's cabin had stood was now overgrown pasture, and they were not among the phone listings in the small town where I grew up just inside the 1830 Choctaw Cession Line. Most of the townspeople were born there, except those like my mother (now ninety-three) and like Rebecca Boyd. Both women had moved there when they married, Rebecca Boyd from Manchac, Louisiana, where she had learned storytelling as a child in the early 1900s. My mother asked around, then told me where Rebecca's husband lived. From him I learned of Beka's death and that I could come back tomorrow. The next day I brought him a pack of cigarettes, the *nan isht aiokpachi* (token of respect) that I should have brought the day before, and he began telling me about the four-voiced, four-part stories with at least one sleep between each telling. Sitting outside to get the breeze from the south, we talked again the next day, and again on my subsequent visits home. His rationing of information showed me the value of a time lapse of at least one day, for as I wrote and slept and thought about the *anoli talbal tuklo* (two-basket stories), more memories came back to me. A logic governing the structure emerged as I began to perceive the educational principles guiding this process designed not only to entertain while preserving history but also to pass on knowledge and to train sensory awareness, memory, observation, and judgment as well as a sense of humor and the ability to speculate upon logical consequences for the future.

The metaphor in the name became clear. The Choctaw weave a doubleweave-doublewall basket. Its interior wall and exterior wall form a seamlessly woven structure capable of the extra strength that was needed for carrying the bones of ancestors as related in the tribal migration legend. The rough undersides of cane strips face each other in the two walls so that only the shiny side of the cane shows in the finished basket. Two doublewall baskets add up to four walls, thus making an apt metaphor for the two-basket story which redoubles its weave into four walls or four versions. Each version requires a different teller who faces a different direction to reinforce the different point of view. The first teller emphasizes sensory impressions, the second historical background, and the third comic elements. The last storyteller, chosen from among those listening to the earlier versions, must not have participated in, nor witnessed, any of the story's events and is therefore unable to rely on previous knowledge or firsthand experience. The last teller must depend upon listening skills, memory, and judgment in order to recap significant points from the first three versions and must conclude with a forecast.

As testament to adaptive skills born of necessity, Rebecca Boyd would make her voice sound different as she told each of the first three versions, her way of keeping the tradition of different tellers. She assumed a youthful, sensory voice for *Anolahpi* (the first teller), an old man's historical voice for *Anolituklo* (the second teller), and her own natural comic voice for *Anolituchina* (the third teller). As the first teller, she faced east, regardless of the time of day because what matters to the rising sun is the physical world—its colors, shapes, and smells. Ancestry, precipitating events, and accuracy of recall were important to the second teller, who faced the other side of what is where the sun sleeps, dreaming of what was. The third teller, chosen by the listeners for either a sense of humor or the need to cultivate one, faced the home of the south wind whether or not it was blowing in from the Gulf. Salty air tickled the nose, Beka would say laughing, the way some words tickled the lips. *Oka-mali*, the word for south—literally water wind—was a lip-tickler. So was *oka-mali-mali*, the word for south wind, literally, water wind wind.[3]

Listener participation in the form of questions, commentary, information, and/or clarification was encouraged, though optional, in the first three tellings. Participation was built in during the last. *Anolushta*, the fourth teller, had to tell what was important in the first three stories strictly from having listened to the storytelling rather than from having seen or done. The fourth teller faced *fichik faluhmi*, the North Star, whether visible or not, for guidance to synthesize and prophesy.[4]

Mr. Boyd did not explain how the fourth perspective's "whole including what will be" is the other side of laughter. "Is the ability to see the whole picture the other side of the ability to see what is funny?" I asked. His response was laughter, not mocking but merry. Was he delighted that I was right, or was I so wrong that it was funny? Was my own sense of order presuming to create the same neat balance between perspectives three and four that I had perceived in one and two? Mr. Boyd's inability or refusal to clarify answered a question I had not thought to ask: is education the only reason for including a teller who has neither participated nor witnessed? Questioning my own biases (partial knowledge and a participant's unconscious expectations) made me see that a fresh listener without those blind spots could better serve the story. Mr. Boyd was clear, however, that the accumulation of detail was calculated to strengthen impact.

Storytelling served not only as entertainment but also as an apprenticeship in listening, remembering, questioning, judging, and responsible learning—an educational experience and simultaneous cultural preservation without camera, computer, blackboard, book, or tape. No logical mind could recreate such a multipurpose experience and make it work in writing. That would take something beyond logic, such as praying to a good south wind. Making the unworkable work in writing takes an imagination such as William Faulkner's. It takes his faith to freely salt the paper with his words. Analytical critics attempting to take the measure of Faulkner's unruliness remind me of Mark Twain's humorous critiques of the fiction of James Fenimore Cooper. Realist makes fun of Romantic's lack of Realism; the stimulus of idealization upon the psyche and the power of mystery upon the imagination are lost on Twain, at least so Twain pretends.

Faulkner's readers learn to read as if reading were a listening experience, staying alert to the moment, allowing the storyteller to control pace and detail. We learn to lean into that power of mystery, resisting the urge to turn back and reread in an effort to play it safe and keep facts straight, trusting that we will be told what we need to know when we need to know it. We will be reminded if we need reminding, freeing us simply to listen, intensity building as Faulkner weaves a sturdy, two-walled basket. Then he weaves another one, strong enough to carry the bones of our imaginations on a long, long journey home.

Aware that variation is a given in an oral culture, we hear the two-basket design in *The Sound and the Fury* with its four storytellers and four perspectives: (1) what is, (2) what was , (3) what's funny, and (4) the whole, including what will be. The story is told four times. Dates in lieu of titles on the four sections show the time lapse of at least one sleep between each telling. Questioned about the dates' significance, Faulkner denied "writing any symbolism of the Passion Week...I'm sure it was quite instinctive that I picked out Easter" (Gwynn 68). Cultural bias influences whether the dates draw our attention to the time lapse, to Christian holy days, to the chronological disorder, or to the fact that the Compsons' story is told in perfect, two-basket order beginning with Benjy's "what is."

Benjy is in the moment the day before Easter, mornings still cool in Northern Mississippi. He is a grown man hanging onto a wrought iron fence looking out through the "curling flower spaces," watching Luster "hunting in the grass by the flower tree" (Faulkner, *Sound* 3). Benjy is all sensory impression in the white glare of sunlight; the light is important because its presence is how we learn that we have moved inside the house. The light changes to firelight jumping to the diamonds on

Mother's hand. Benjy loves light, and he loves rain—on the roof, against the glass, pelting leaves. Benjy loves the smell of "bright cold," and he loves Caddy, the sister who always "smelled like leaves" (Faulkner, *Sound* 5).

Section two is dated eighteen years earlier than the other three sections. The day of Quentin's suicide is listened to from inside his consciousness, from the watch ticking in his pocket, from the remembered voices in his head. Twenty-year-old Quentin's voice sounds like an old man's as his memory takes us back even further, to the riverbank with his sister "lying in the water her head on the sand spit the water flowing about her hips" (Faulkner, *Sound* 94). It is still Quentin's voice, but the voice sounds different when it takes us back again, this time into their lives as children, to the "day damuddy died when you sat down in the water in your drawers" (96). Quentin's view of "what was" balances on the other side of Benjy's "what is."

Jason's comical comeuppance is section three. It is on Good Friday that whiney-voiced Jason tells the joke on himself, and part of what makes it funny is that Jason, desperately in need of a sense of humor, fails to see the humor. We laugh not with, but at him: Jason, humorless, taking himself so seriously, chasing around after his niece, keeping his sister from her daughter, threatening to rent Benjy to a sideshow; Jason, the grown man, teasing a child; Jason, cruel and greedy, investing in the stock market in 1928.

Faulkner, neither participant nor witness, tells section four as omniscient voice. He recaps "the whole," having learned the structure, perhaps, as well as the content, from having listened to his fictional storytellers, to his own imagination, and to non-fictional storytellers. Jason's loss is discovered, his niece has escaped, and Benjy is in church with Dilsey. Though we get no prophecy from Faulkner's lips on Easter Sunday, it is clear that in the omniscient view Dilsey is the future.

Sixteen years after the original 1929 printing of *The Sound and the Fury*, Faulkner added an appendix. His voice continues. His subject is genealogy and historical background: specifically the 1746 battle in Northern Scotland notorious for the slaughter afterward of wounded Highlanders and 1833, when the stars shook loose and flew across the sky of the Indians' world broken apart by the 1830 Treaty of Dancing Rabbit Creek. The appendix extends the whole picture, finally says the word "castration," answers the incest question, and laughs again at Jason: "robbed not only of his thievings but his savings too, and by his own victim . . . [so he] couldn't even go to the police; because he had lost four thousand dollars which did not belong to him he couldn't even recover the three thousand which did . . . [and he] didn't dare pursue the girl himself because he might catch her and she would talk" (Faulkner, *Sound* 214). Looking into the future at Jason's lack of possible redress and having seen his past cruelties add to readers' satisfaction at seeing him in the present as cheater cheated. Our laughing at the whole picture of Jason's past, present, and future illustrates how meaning builds as detail accumulates. The perspectives of present-focused Benjy, past-focused Quentin, self-focused Jason, and omniscient Faulkner make two Choctaw baskets carried one on either side, the balanced load of one basket's "what is" and "what was" offsetting the other basket's weight of laughter in light of the future implied in the omniscient's total picture. Two balanced structures balance against each other with a familiar order beneath the surface detected in, rather than imposed upon, this four-part, four-voiced book.

All four of the stipulated Choctaw perspectives that balance voices in *The Sound and the Fury* are not in *Absalom, Absalom!* In this Civil War tale, Faulkner sacrifices balance to truth in his fidelity to a culture blinded by inherited loss and guilt to the first Choctaw perspective. "What is" is buried in the South's obsession with the past. Half a century later Quentin, born thirty years after the surrender, says he knows "at last why God let us lose the War" (Faulkner, *Absalom* 6). Laughter, the third Choctaw perspective, is sadly missing: "'Well, Kernel, they mought have whupped us but they aint kilt us yit, air they?'—This was not flippancy either. It too was just that protective coloring of levity behind which the youthful shame of being moved hid itself, out of which Quentin also spoke, the reason for Quentin's sullen bemusement, the (on both their parts) flipness, the strained clowning" (225). The balance is off when the laughter is sullen, when the whole story is "what was," defeat and occupation not forgotten in the South, the past not yet passed.

What links *Absalom, Absalom!* to southeastern Louisiana Choctaw storytelling is the way that the story bends and twists like the Mississippi itself in a weave of listening and storytelling. Although the perspectives do not match up and the tellers are not sectioned off, still four voices tell this story which ends with prophecy: (1) Quentin, (2) Miss Rosa, (3) Sutpen, and (4) Shreve. Father and Grandfather are sources of information, but their storytelling voices are not heard. It is the interwoven pattern of listening and telling that matters here, not the individual strips of cane. Quentin's college roommate, Shreve, hears the story of Confederate officer Thomas Sutpen from Quentin, who had the story from Miss Rosa, the ancient spinster whom Sutpen had been engaged to marry fifty years before she begins to tell Quentin about "a man who fled here and hid, concealed himself behind respectability, behind that hundred miles of land which he took from a tribe of ignorant Indians, nobody knows how, and a house the size of a courthouse where he lived for three years without a window or door or bedstead in it and still called it Sutpen's Hundred as if it had been a King's grant" (Faulkner, *Absalom* 10). Quentin is telling Shreve, but it is Miss Rosa's voice that we hear and through her eyes that we see Sutpen arriving larger-than-life out of nowhere to carve his house literally out of the Mississippi wilderness in 1833, the year that the stars flew. Quentin hears more of Sutpen from Father, who had heard it years before from Grandfather, who had learned of Sutpen's childhood from Sutpen himself on a hunting trip. Sutpen had a

woodsman's instinct . . . acquired from the environment where he grew up or maybe had been bequeathed him by the two brothers who had vanished . . . bequeathed him along with the worn-out buckskin garments . . . left in the cabin when they departed the last time for good . . . But that was past now, the moment when he last could have said exactly where he had been born . . . he became confused about his age and was never able to straighten it out again. (Faulkner, *Absalom* 183–84)

Quentin had learned Sutpen's story from having listened to Father who had listened to Grandfather who had listened to Sutpen. Quentin tells Shreve Sutpen's history behind the history of the South's defeat from Sutpen's point of view. Then two-thirds of the way into the book, Quentin's role changes:

"Your father," Shreve said. "He seems to have got an awful lot of delayed information awful quick, after having waited forty-five years. If he knew all this, what was his reason for telling you that the trouble between Henry and Bon was the octoroon woman?"

"He didn't know it then [says Quentin]. Grandfather didn't tell him all of it either, like Sutpen never told Grandfather quite all of it."

"Then who did tell him?" [Shreve asks.]

"I did." [says Quentin]. (214)

Quentin's knowledge has exceeded that of listener-only. He and Miss Rosa had ridden out and seen fire destroy the house that Sutpen built, with Sutpen's bloodline surviving in Jim Bond, a descendant of slaves. Having seen Sutpen's Hundred destroyed, Quentin is now a witness, and a witness must not tell the end. A listener-only fourth voice must take on that final duty. In the guise of a questioning, speculative voice, Shreve the listener begins telling: "'Wait,' Shreve said, 'You mean that he got the son he wanted, after all that trouble, and then turned right around and—'. . . it was Shreve speaking . . . both thinking as one . . . the two of them creating between them, out of the rag-tag and bob-ends of old tales and talking, people who perhaps had never existed at all" (234, 243). Shreve recaps the whole story, and then prophesies "that in time the Jim Bonds are going to conquer the western hemisphere . . . and so in a few thousand years, I who regard you will also have sprung from the loins of African kings" (302). There is an intensity inherent in the objectivity of a prophecy delivered by a listener without the participant's blind spot. The inevitable contrast of perspectives works with the accumulation of detail to build power with a vengeance in *Absalom, Absalom!*

By contrast, the sensory beauty of Benjy's voice in *The Sound and the Fury* is so original and so powerful that it outweighs the accumulation of detail in subsequent voices, making the design toward intensity work in reverse. "What design?," said Faulkner in interviews, introductions, taped classes at the University of Virginia, and international lectures. In response to a question posed in his 1955 "Interviews in Japan," Faulkner said, "I wrote that same story [*The Sound and the Fury*] four times. None of them were right, but I had anguished so much that I could not throw any of it away and start over, so I printed it in the four sections. That was not a deliberate *tour de force* at all, the book just grew that way" (147). Quite a coincidence that out of failure to get it right, the book just grew into four stories told on four different days by four narrators with four stipulated perspectives. In *Absalom, Absalom!*, four voices just happen to tell the same story from four perspectives with time lapse, prophecy, and intricate listener-teller relationship intact. Faulkner's writing, so he said, just grew that way, the Choctaw way, made to endure so that matters of importance might not be lost with the next Chickasaw or Creek raiding party. With enough storytelling-listeners, identity can hang on through the Trail of Tears when the meteor shower of 1833 signified a world so broken that even the stars shook loose.

Before 1833, Faulkner's Northern Mississippi was Chickasaw territory. He rarely visited central or southern Mississippi, where it was generally held that he would never amount to much except a writer of dirty books who was giving the state a bad name. His opportunity to hear Choctaw stories must have been the year he lived in New Orleans's French Quarter. Faulkner walked the Quarter, interacted there, and listened to people's stories; the evidence exists in his short pieces published in *The Double Dealer* and in the Sunday feature section of *The New Orleans Times-Picayune* in 1925. Some of these sketches explore motifs that would be developed in *The Sound and the Fury*. His apartment in what is now Pirate's Alley was less than two blocks from the French Market, where in 1925 Choctaw basket sellers and storytellers set up among the vegetable stalls. Their descendants still live in the area off Canal just outside the Quarter where in 1925 the Choctaw would have frequented the little neighborhood club on Franklin (renamed Crozat) where Faulkner liked to listen to Georgia Boy Boyd play his jazz clarinet.

As a native Mississippian who reads and rereads Faulkner for the pleasure of falling under his spell, I willingly suspend analysis. But when Faulkner critic Malcolm Cowley places horsepower on a grocery scale, old memories stir. Rebecca Boyd's words roll in "like summer thunder," and I find that I am facing east in response to that familiar structure woven with only the cane's shiny sides showing. The teacher in me searches for direction to synthesize, to balance the whole, to integrate form with content, and I focus finally on that which is invisible in the teaching art. As a former fourteen-year resident of South Louisiana who still can taste the richness of the cultural mix and hear the easy interchange among the arts, I understand how ideas could work through Faulkner like the classics that he "swallowed whole" and found in his consciousness ten years later "in a series of delayed repercussions like summer thunder" (Faulkner, "An Introduction" 708–9). Working to codify the Choctaw storytelling structure and curious if Faulkner borrowed, appropriated, refashioned, dreamed, imagined, consciously adapted, or fell backward into his use of it, I research print, people, and my own memory. When I find that, like Faulkner's "delayed repercussions," I knew more than I knew, I can believe that Faulkner believed that he owned that pattern of listening-tellers and that he wrote *The Sound and the Fury* without a plan, the book that made him, the book that just grew into the shape of two doublewall Choctaw baskets.

NOTES

1. See, for example, Lewis M. Dabney or William Faulkner's *Faulkner in the University,* especially pages 8–9, 25, 43–4, 74. See also Elmo Howell, Jo LeCoeur.

2. See, for example, J.F.H. Claiborne, Angie Debo, Michael Boucher, H.S. Halbert, and Dorothy Milligan.

3. This tradition must predate Mrs. Boyd's childhood since the Gulf lies not only to the South but also to the east and to the southwest of Manchac, Louisiana. It is unlikely that she adapted the formula to our location, which is too far inland to smell the salty Gulf air.

4. Symbolic use of the North Star for direction may hint at an early sea voyage or contact with seagoing people. In the migration legend, direction came from a walking stick, not a star. I was unable to get Mr. Boyd to clarify the pairing of synthesis and prophecy, or how an archetypal navigational symbol came to be the source of direction for taking a look first at the total picture and then into the future.

REFERENCES

Boucher, Michael. Home page. 1 Jan. 2000. 18 Feb. 1999 <http://www.isd.net/mboucher/framhme2.htm>.

Boyd, Andrew. Personal Interviews. May–August 1996.

Boyd, Rebecca. Personal Interviews. 1946–1956.

Claiborne, J. F. H. *Mississippi as a Province, Territory and State*. Jackson: Mississippi Department of Archives and History, 1880.

Cowley, Malcolm. *The Portable Faulkner*. New York: Penguin, 1977.

Dabney, Lewis M. *The Indians of Yoknapatawpha*. Baton Rouge: Louisiana State UP, 1974.

Debo, Angie. *The Rise and Fall of the Choctaw Republic*. Norman: U of Oklahoma P, 1972.

Faulkner, William. *Absalom, Absalom!* New York: Vintage, 1990.

—. *Faulkner in the University*. Ed. Frederick L. Gwynn and Joseph Blotner. Charlottesville: UP of Virginia, 1959.

—. "Interviews in Japan." *Lion in the Garden: Interviews with William Faulkner 1926–1962*. Ed. James B. Meriwether and Michael Millgate. New York: Random House, 1968.

—. "An Introduction for *The Sound and the Fury*." Ed. James B. Meriwether. *The Southern Review* 8. 3 (1972): 705–10.

—. *The Sound and the Fury*. Ed. David Minter. New York: Norton, 1944.

Galloway, Patricia. *Choctaw Genesis 1500 –1700*. Lincoln: U of Nebraska P, 1995.

Gwynn, Fredrick, L. and Joseph L. Blotner, eds. *Faulkner in the University*. 1959. Charlottesville: UP of Virginia, 1995.

Halbert, H. S. "The Choctaw Creation Legend." *Publications of the Mississippi Historical Society* 4 (1901): 267–270.

Howell, Elmo. "William Faulkner and the Mississippi Indians." *Georgia Review* 21 (1967): 386–396.

LeCoeur, Jo. "Knit One, Purl Two: Fiction, Storytelling, History." *Myth and Cultural Identity*. Ed. Stuart Sillars and Amalia Mondríguez. San Antonio: U of the Incarnate Word, 1996. 98–108.

Milligan, Dorothy. *The Indian Way: Choctaws*. Byng School Class Interviews with Oklahoma Choctaws. n.p.: n.p, [c.1974].

Noley, Grayson. "The Early 1700s: Education, Economics, and Politics." *The Choctaw before Removal*. Jackson: UP of Mississippi, 1985.

"'The nigger that's going to sleep with your sister'": Charles Bon as Cultural Shibboleth in *Absalom, Absalom!*

Erin E. Campbell

William Faulkner's *Absalom, Absalom!* is a novel which confronts the gamut of Southern cultural controversies: miscegenation, plantation myths, primogeniture, Civil War, Reconstruction, and invented history. With its cacophony of narrative voices, the *truth* of the novel remains embedded in the thematic representations which the narrators embody. They refuse to offer absolute categorical definitions of their historical and social positions even while they represent and signify a culture which depends upon immutable distinctions between race, class, and gender for its ideological survival. Thus, the narrators provide us with characters like Clytie, who is both slave and sister to the master's children, who is an amalgamation of the white and black races, and who is, virtually and ironically, inheritor of Sutpen's plantation despite her female gender and Haitian ancestry. Clytie's counterpart and half-brother, Charles Bon, exhibits even further contradictions. In Charles Bon, Faulkner offers both an iconic representation of New Orleans and the conflicting ideologies of Southern culture as they culminate within a single character.

Bon's immigration from Haiti to New Orleans reflects an historical phenomenon. Haiti and New Orleans both existed under French rule and therefore maintain particular cultural similarities. The creation of the Republic of Haiti out of the rebellion against French hegemony coincides with the Louisiana Purchase of 1803 by the United States. The Haitian revolution caused many light-skinned free people of color to flee Haiti for the Gulf ports of the United States, especially New Orleans with its previously established society of light-skinned West Indian immigrants (Berlin 114, 116). The Haitian slave revolt that Thomas Sutpen helped to quash won him his first wife, Eulalia Bon.[1] This union establishes the paradigm of "Sutpen's 'history,' as it is given (and regiven), [as] fatally enmeshed with mulattoes and mulattas" (Roberts 92). Shortly after the birth of his son, Sutpen learns of Eulalia's supposed taint of black blood which renders both the marriage and the son illegitimate due to absolute rules about interracial marriage and patrilineal inheritance in the South. We might assume that once Sutpen repudiates Eulalia and Bon and thus relinquishes his protection of them in the event of subsequent slave revolts, Eulalia chooses to escape Haiti for the freedom and anonymity of New Orleans. Assuming that Bon's mother knows of her own mixed blood and her son's, she chooses the one urban American location where free people of color maintain a relatively high social status compared to the British-influenced seaboard cities. In New Orleans, also, it would be "easier for light-skinned freemen to pass for white . . ., [and] once they were accepted as 'white,' few questions would be asked" (Berlin 196). Thus, Bon passes for white and invokes the sexual and social privileges of an ideal wealthy, white, New Orleans gentleman.

Bon becomes an amalgamation not just of races but also of cultures and heritages, which contribute to his identification as a gentleman. As Joseph Conrad asserts in *Heart of Darkness* that "All of Europe contributed to the making of Kurtz" (65), we might claim that Faulkner allows all of historical New Orleans to contribute to the creation of Charles Bon. Bon represents the multicultural flavor of New Orleans in his heritage and breeding. Like the city, he is simultaneously black, white, and cosmopolitan. He is seductive and sybaritic, "lounging in one of the silk robes the like of which the youth had never seen before and believed only women wore" (Faulkner, *Absalom* 253), a feminization reflecting his city's architecture, which is "a little femininely flamboyant and therefore to Henry opulent, sensuous, sinful" (Faulkner, *Absalom* 87). He is wealthy, privileged, and yet ultimately, illegitimate because of his black blood. Trained in the codes of honor and dueling, he potentially wields a deadly rapier and wears a saber with a silk tassel at his side, uniting the feminized sensuality of the silk decoration with the masculine, phallic force of the saber. Raised within the tradition of French Catholicism, Bon is encoded with the highly ritualized culture of New Orleans, signifying his cultural difference and establishing him as an exotic other in Anglo-Saxon, Protestant Mississippi.

For Faulkner, New Orleans represents the ideological construct of all that contrasts with his provincial Mississippi, a contrast that is revisited in the deliberate social differentiation between Bon and Henry Sutpen. Violet Harrington Bryan argues that Faulkner's experience with New Orleans allowed him to "project a space that was not Puritanical, or ordered to some stern religious code. New Orleans . . . demanded an older order, from 'a bygone and more gracious age,' which rewarded pleasure, leisure, and experience, not the new and untried" (85). In "New Orleans," a series of sketches first published in *The Double Dealer* in 1925, Faulkner describes the city as "A courtesan, not old and no longer young . . . She does not talk much herself, yet she seems to dominate the conversation . . . a courtesan whose hold is strong upon the mature, to whose charm the young must respond" (*New Orleans Sketches* 49). This description concretizes Faulkner's poetic vision of the city and serves as a precursor to Bon, who mirrors the description of his adopted city as well as its function toward the characters he affects in the novel. Bon becomes the human manifestation of the city's metonymy as he seduces the novel's multiple generations first with his physical presence and subsequently with the theatrical power of his story.

Like his courtesan-city, Bon, the courtesan, talks little but dominates the novel. As Frederick Karl argues, "the physical presence of Bon is not so important as the textured shadow of the young man . . . His figure hovers over the entire novel, which while it doesn't seem to be about him is, in actuality, always about him" (211). Bon, at twenty-eight, is "actually a little old to be still in college," yet as "a young man of a worldly elegance and assurance beyond his years" (Faulkner, *Absalom* 58), he seduces Henry with the highly mannered differences of the not-old/not-young that his courtesan character reflects. Henry falls in love with Bon's careless and carefree style of dressing and his cosmopolitan manners. In a conversation that Quentin and Shreve invent between Henry and Bon, Henry expresses a fumbling (and ironic) desire to have Bon for his older brother, despite the implication that Henry would inherit none of his father's land or wealth if he was not the first–born son. In fact, Henry repudiates his birthright out of love for Bon and a desire to prove his father wrong about Bon's octoroon mistress. Bon's seduction of Judith actually occurs through Henry. Mr. Compson suggests that Bon and Judith could not have been alone long enough for Bon to seduce Judith himself, and thus Henry must have linked them together through his overpowering love for both of them. Henry and Judith share a relationship that borders upon incestuous in the way that Henry's relationship with Bon hints at homosexuality. Since the manifestation of neither incest nor homosexuality can earn acceptance in the rigidly provincial Southern culture of Henry's upbringing, one means of circumventing the impossible is for Henry to allow his two loves, his sister and his idol, to enter into the legitimate union of marriage, which Henry might vicariously join. As Mr. Compson suggests, "'this is the perfect and pure incest: the brother realising that . . . taking [the sister's] virginity in the person of the brother-in-law, the man whom he would be if he could . . . metamorphose into the lover, the husband; . . . whom he would . . . choose for the despoiler, if he could . . . metamorphose into the sister, the mistress, the bride'"(Faulkner, *Absalom* 77). For Henry, then, Bon garners Judith's affection by functioning as Henry's surrogate. Judith, in turn, accepts Bon's tacit proposal, which may have been concocted in Henry's imagination without impetus from Bon at all. Rosa, never seeing Bon alive or dead, vicariously joins the trend of devotion to Charles Bon by feeding upon Judith's desire. As Philip Weinstein argues, Bon is "the most compelling figure in *Absalom, Absalom!*—compelling in the sense that no one (not Rosa, Mr. Compson, Sutpen, Henry, Judith, Quentin, or Shreve—and not, therefore, the reader either) can take their eyes off him . . . Bon is genuinely —culturally—different. He is the erotic center of *Absalom, Absalom!* All who see him . . . run the risk of falling in love with him" (180). Bon's difference, which makes him so attractive to the characters in the novel, is exactly what causes his destruction once the potential truth of his race emerges.

One of Bon's many charms is his courtly manners. Bon reaps the benefits of being the son of a self-made man and conforms to the suggestion in *Correct Social Usage*, a conduct manual in its ninth revision in 1907, that "the old saying that it takes two generations to make a gentleman is being refuted every day, for Americans are remarked not only for their facility in amassing fortunes but in furnishing themselves with presentable manners on short notice" (29). Bon's manners and demeanor mark him as a man of honor and a genteel New Orleanian, yet like Sutpen, Bon enters northern Mississippi under a cloud of mystery. Bon is "handsome, apparently wealthy . . . with for background the shadowy figure of a legal guardian rather than any parents," according to Mr. Compson (Faulkner, *Absalom* 58). His curious ancestry echoes Sutpen's own, yet Bon has perfected the public attributes of gentility, internalized through his upbringing within the highly ritualized behavior codes of New Orleans's society: "a man with an ease of manner and a swaggering gallant air in comparison with which Sutpen's pompous arrogance was clumsy bluff and Henry actually a hobble-de-hoy" (Faulkner, *Absalom* 58). If Sutpen has read conduct manuals, Bon embodies them as the South's own Sir Philip Sidney, to whom deportment writers might look for exemplary behavior. As courtesy writer Florence Kingsland intimates of the young gentleman starting out in life, "his dress, his deportment, his behavior and his bearing toward his fellow-men are so many tests by which the world will judge him" (337). Ellen, Judith, and Henry of the world of Sutpen's Hundred judge Bon to be exactly what he claims to be; he seduces the three of them into "a fairy tale written for and acted by a fashionable ladies' club" (Faulkner, *Absalom* 60). Bon manifests "the outward and visible signs of aristocracy . . . shown in perfect breeding, charm of manner and unfailing courtesy of which the inward grace is an instinctive refinement that is not merely a decorative attribute" determined by the courtesy literature to be vital characteristics (Kingsland 1). Mr. Compson surmises of Bon that it was "Not just the outside, the way he walked and talked and wore his clothes and handed Ellen into the dining room or into the carriage and (perhaps, probably) kissed her hand and which Ellen envied for Henry, but the man himself" (Faulkner, *Absalom* 74). Thus, Ellen falls under Bon's spell like her children and appropriates the idea of him for "three concordant uses: a garment which Judith might wear as she would a riding habit or a ball gown, a piece of furniture which would complement and complete the furnishing of [Ellen's] house and position, and a mentor and example to correct Henry's provincial manners and speech and clothing" (Faulkner, *Absalom* 59). Ironically, Bon becomes the cosmopolitan polish necessary to refine the provincial crudities of Sutpen out of all of them.

In one of the most significant inversions of the novel, when Bon-the-courtesan takes a courtesan for himself, he unwittingly contracts a legal marriage bond because of his mixed-race heritage.[2] Bryan argues that "New Orleans' historical, virtually 'mythical,' tradition of interracial liaisons between white men and quadroon or octoroon women, all interact in Faulkner's image of New Orleans as courtesan" (86). Bon invokes the upper-class white male privilege, distinct to New Orleans's society, of keeping an octoroon mistress. Margaret Ripley Wolfe clarifies this practice as a

contractual concubinage [which] existed in an environment where free women of color outnumbered men of their own kind almost two to one. At 'quadroon' or 'fancy girl' balls, the *gens de couleur libres* paraded their young women. A well-to-do white man, promising the parents that he would protect their daughter and provide financially for any illegitimate offspring, negotiated for possession of her body and perhaps eventually earned her affection. (79)

As Roberts suggests, "The custom of keeping a quadroon or octoroon lover was well known, openly acknowledged in New Orleans while it was discreetly ignored in the rest of the South" (92). By the same token, "Miscegenation between a white male and black female posed almost no ethical problems for the antebellum Southern community, so long as the rules, which were fairly easy to follow, were discreetly observed" (Wyatt-Brown 307), rules which include relative silence about and among the white men who choose to engage in the practice among their slaves. While Henry doesn't blanch for an instant at his father's miscegenation with the slaves of Sutpen's Hundred, he reacts vehemently to Bon's octoroon mistress, whose relationship with Bon was contracted and solemnized through the ritual of the ball: "It would be the fact of the ceremony, regardless of what kind, that Henry would balk at: Bon knew this. . . . a ceremony entered into, to be sure, with a negro, yet still a ceremony" (Faulkner, *Absalom* 87).

The etiquette of the miscegenation differs between the plantation and New Orleans, but the results ultimately remain the same, and thus Bon goads Henry's provincial idealism and regional stereotypes by saying, "'Have you forgotten that this woman, this child, are niggers? You, Henry Sutpen of Sutpen's Hundred in Mississippi? You, talking of marriage, a wedding, here?'" (Faulkner, *Absalom* 94). The cultural and civil illegality of a union between a white man and a woman of color is an undisputed fact, stemming from Southern laws against interracial marriage as early as 1692 and as recently as 1930 in Mississippi (Roberts 71). Henry's puritanical upbringing and limited life experience prevent him from donning a cavalier attitude about the ceremony, which Bon has potentially been groomed not only to accept but to relish in the privilege of his class, "'a situation which was as much a part of a young New Orleansian's social and fashionable equipment as his dancing shoes'" (Faulkner, *Absalom* 80). In a conversation that Shreve invents between Bon and his mother, Bon glibly says, "'All the young men do it. The ceremony too'" (Faulkner, *Absalom* 246). His mother's reaction, "'But you. This is different'" (Faulkner, *Absalom* 247) implies Bon's racial heritage as it recalls Henry's resistance to the tradition, despite his infatuation with Bon: "'Not even you doing it makes it right'" (Faulkner, *Absalom* 94). Both Henry and Bon clearly represent the divergent ideological subtleties of their regions and thus become the physical manifestations of what Faulkner calls "cosmopolitan New Orleans or bucolic Mississippi" (*Absalom* 252).

Bon's proficiency with arms further reveals his adherence to the singularities of his culture. As a part of the expected training for one of his social class, Bon has practiced with his rapier and "'can recall at least one occasion in [his] life when [he] was glad he had'" (Faulkner, *Absalom* 249). Since duels exist to support a man's claim to both gentility and virility, Bon's exposure of Henry to his cosmopolitan world becomes a thinly veiled challenge to Henry's provincial perceptions. Bon's calculated introduction of Henry to his octoroon mistress reveals the divergence of experience and judgment between them. While Bon invokes the privilege of aristocratic white men of New Orleans to maintain such a mistress, he also reveals that a man "must usually risk his life or at least his blood for that privilege" (Faulkner, *Absalom* 93). In a bizarre paradox of the code of honor, these men must be willing to defend this practice on the dueling ground against those who suggest that the mistresses are whores or those who attempt to access the fiercely enclosed system. Dueling to redress a slight to a lady's honor represented a common practice across the South; these mixed-blood mistresses, however, curiously represent property, privilege, and prestige, and while they can never be proper ladies because of their black blood, the New Orleans man of honor defends his right of exclusive ownership of his mistress as fiercely as he would protect his home. Longstreet argues that "[New Orleans'] legend says a great many duels were fought by the gentlemen as the results of insults offered their mistresses" (111). Thus, the butler at Bon's octoroon mistress' home assumes that Bon must wish to redress a slight to his mistress' honor when Henry accompanies him to the courtyard. Bon disabuses the servant of this notion with a grin and an insult: "'With him? An American? He is a guest; I would have to let him choose weapons and I decline to fight with axes'" (Faulkner, *Absalom* 89). In bonding with the servant, Bon reveals his clear knowledge of dueling protocols as well as Henry's ignorance of both dueling etiquette and ideology, evoking an historically accurate experiential difference between them since very few novice duelists beyond the confines of Charleston or New Orleans would know anything about the ritualized protocols of the duel (Wyatt-Brown 355). Bon casually enlightens Henry about the marked social contrast between them as he explains the dueling process: "'The customary way is to stand back to back, the pistol in your right hand and the corner of the other cloak in your left. . . . Though there are some now and then, when the blood is especially hot or when it is still peasant blood, who prefer knives and the cloak, you see, each holding the other's wrist with the left hand. But that was never my way'" (Faulkner, *Absalom* 90). That peasant blood and fighting style recall the prejudice held by "civilized" French and Spanish New Orleanians over their "barbarian Anglo-American" counterparts (Kane 140). Bon implies as well that Henry's blood is still peasant and so must be Bon's social inferior, thus excusing Bon from a potential duel with him for his tacit insistence that Bon relinquish the octoroon mistress as well as Henry's affront to her honor by calling her a whore.

Bon's aborted duel with the lawyer reveals another level to his honor code and his role as a New Orleans gentleman. The lawyer which Quentin and Shreve construct as Bon's guardian keeps accounts against Sutpen as though he has a stake in the revenge that he presumes Bon will take once he learns that Sutpen is his father. Ironically, the lawyer as guardian reflects another historical precedent for the control of free people of color. Berlin reveals that "[t]o make every free Negro, no matter how light-skinned or wealthy, directly beholden to some white, most of the states of the Lower South required free Negroes to take guardians to supervise their legal affairs and to act as their agents" (215). Whether the lawyer knows about Bon's racial heritage or not depends upon the lengths to which he will go to seek revenge upon Sutpen. That Bon is yet ignorant of his blood is revealed by his vague assumption that all families, like his, necessarily consist of only mothers and lawyers to be manipulated and by his reaction to the lawyer's enactment of revenge. When the lawyer suggests that Judith might function as "lagniappe to the revenge . . . a nice little piece" (Faulkner, *Absalom* 270), Bon draws his own piece and strikes the lawyer's face with his hand. Such a blow constitutes one of the worst possible insults to a man of honor, and the lawyer has the right to challenge Bon for it, yet he backs down, nearly saving face and clearly saving his life. The exchange between the two men reveals the intricacies of rhetorical manipulation necessary to avoid a full-scale duel:

'If you feel that you require satisfaction, of course you know—'and the lawyer,. . . : 'I was wrong. I misunderstood your feeling . . . I ask your pardon' and Bon: 'Granted. . . . I will accept either an apology or a bullet, as you prefer' and the lawyer . . . 'I see you are going to collect full measure for my unfortunate misconception—even ridicule. Even if I felt that right was on my side (which I do not) I would still have to decline your offer. I would not be your equal with pistols.' (Faulkner, *Absalom* 270–1)

Bon appropriately volleys the decision about satisfaction to the lawyer, upon whose body the insult was written. Bon requires the lawyer to fully recant his position and his implication about Judith's honor, however, and the lawyer must not only admit that he was wrong but also that Bon is superior to him at arms. The lawyer publicly acknowledges his inferiority to Bon in both word and deed, thus averting the actual duel through verbal concession that both men accept as truth. Bon's victory over the lawyer remains Pyrrhic, however, as he realizes "*But only with knives or pistols or rapiers. So I cant beat him. I could shoot him. I would shoot him with no more compunction than I would a snake or a man who cuckolded me. But he would still beat me*" (Faulkner, *Absalom* 271). Here the lawyer wins, not on a matter of honor, but because he possesses the truth of Bon's parentage and Sutpen's refusal to acknowledge it. That truth and refusal ultimately result in Bon's death.

Quentin and Shreve invent a reason for Henry's murder of Bon that satisfies their sensibilities. The issue of Bon's octoroon mistress and his refusal to repudiate her, Mr. Compson's rationale for the murder, becomes evidence that "Quentin took . . . in stride . . . just as Shreve would have, since both he and Shreve believed—and were probably right in this too—that the octoroon and the child would have been to Henry only something else about Bon to be, not envied but aped if . . . possible" (Faulkner, *Absalom* 268–9). Henry's desire to remake himself in Bon's image can be checked only by the limits of race, allowing Quentin and Shreve to suggest that Bon is Sutpen's first–born son who was repudiated because of the taint of negro blood. Thus, Bon, the New Orleans gentleman fatalist whose honor disintegrates due to the blood taint, devolves into, for Henry, "*the nigger that's going to sleep with your sister*" (Faulkner, *Absalom* 286), which Roberts interprets as Bon's attempt "to define himself not only as black but as the black personification of rape" (94). Bon must construct this final and undesirable difference between himself and Henry in the most horrific manner possible to overcome Henry's sensibilities and to force his hand into shooting him. Bon gives Henry his personal pistol to settle the quarrel between them that the war failed to finalize, forcing Henry to "do the office of the outraged father's pistol hand when fornication threatened" (Faulkner, *Absalom* 146). Henry, initially the champion of marriage between Bon and Judith who becomes, antithetically, the inverse champion of preventing the marriage, is spurred to murder because "it's the miscegenation, not the incest, which [he] can't bear" (Faulkner, *Absalom* 285). Roberts intimates that "it was inevitable that someone tell that southern story about the black brother and white sister who wanted to become lovers: it was the unarticulated nightmare of the South" (95). Despite the bond between them and Henry's romantic desire to acquire the veneer of Bon's grace and style through emulation, Henry cannot deny his highly encoded Southern culture to allow the debauchery of his sister by a man with black blood.

Where Henry can discover historical precedent for incest among European royals, he cannot conceive of the possibility of historical precedent for a legitimate union between the races. As Richard King argues, "A socially sanctioned marriage between the two races threatened the purity of the white order" (127). The difference between them, which Henry thought merely an accident of the experience of divergent cultural codes, dissolves into the single ineradicable factor of race, enabling Henry to fulfill Bon's fatalist desire: "'Henry has done shot that durn French feller. Kilt him dead as a beef'"[3] (Faulkner, *Absalom* 105–6). To believe Mr. Compson's assessment of "Henry the romantic . . . and Bon the fatalist" (Faulkner, *Absalom* 97) requires a rejection of his assertion that "this man [was] miscast for the time and knowing it, accepting it for a reason obviously good enough to cause him to endure it" (Faulkner, *Absalom* 78). Bon plays his role as gentleman and fatalist perfectly according to the codes of his class, his New Orleans culture, and his presumed race: once Bon discovers his mulatto blood, the only gentlemanly reaction open to him is to force Henry's hand to murder him, thus freeing him from all of his quasi-spousal entanglements, as well as eliminating himself from a culture which refuses to allow him to continue his privileged existence. Even cosmopolitan New Orleans would not publicly acknowledge and sanction the marriage of a mulattto man to a white woman, clearly exposing the double standard of the *plaçage* system that Bon enjoyed while ignorant of his racial heritage and uniting the otherwise divergent beliefs held within New Orleans and Mississippi. Thus Henry, the romantic, saves his sister's honor, and Bon, the fatalist, exercises his last honorable option. Shreve's suggestion that "'the South is fine, isn't it. It's better than the theatre, isn't it'" (Faulkner, *Absalom* 176) implies the deliberate roles played by these aspirants and scions of honor and the stage effects which they use in order to assure that their face value remains unquestioned.

Henry responds viscerally to Bon's charms, considering himself lucky to bask in the glow of Bon's company, one of the elect that Bon-the-courtesan, as a symbol of Faulkner's New Orleans, invites to join his world. Henry fails to decipher Bon's mask, the theatricality of his self-construction that, perhaps, accounts for his attractiveness, "'that expression which was not smiling but just something not to be seen through'" (Faulkner, *Absalom* 249). Henry's horror at the possibility that Bon will unmask his ignorance and inexperience exacerbates his provincialism and allows Bon to manipulate him. Bon, conversely, like New Orleans, which he represents, is "foreign and paradoxical . . . at once fatal and languorous . . . at once feminine and steel-hard" (Faulkner, *Absalom* 86). With Bon as the principal actor in a drama outside his control, history becomes a play written on and through Bon's body as the site of unresolved historical conflict. In fact, "Charles Bon's body itself is part of the wandering 'reality' of the text" (Roberts 94). The marked contrasts between Bon and Henry, New Orleans and Mississippi, truth and history, suggest a culture at war with its own contradictions that the novel does well to foreground but is inevitably unable to resolve.

NOTES

1. "Eulalia" is the name given to Bon's mother by Faulkner in the chronology at the end of the novel, although her name is never actually mentioned in the novel proper. For ease of discussion, I refer to her as Eulalia.

2. At this point in the novel, Bon remains unaware of his own mixed blood. For him, the octoroon mistress is but the privilege of his class and presumed race. The ceremony actually becomes binding when we learn that Bon is part black like his mistress. One of the clues to Bon's racial mixture is that his son takes his surname; if Bon was "merely" white, he could not legally recognize his mixed-race son. Legitimate sons are not denied paternal recognition and privilege. Bon, who remains illegitimate, takes his mother's name.

3. Faulkner's word choice in calling Bon "beef" upon his death is reminiscent of the long-standing Southern attitude toward members of the African-American community during both the antebellum and post-bellum periods. African Americans were often considered by some in the white community to be on par, both intellectually and socially, with animals. Thus, Bon is further associated with this segment of society following his discovery of his mixed-racial heritage through Faulkner's description of him as beef.

REFERENCES

Berlin, Berlin. *Slaves Without Masters: The Free Negro in the Antebellum South*. New York: Pantheon, 1974.

Bryan, Violet Harrington. *The Myth of New Orleans in Literature: Dialogues of Race and Gender*. Knoxville: U of Tennessee P, 1993.

Conrad, Joseph. *Heart of Darkness*. Ed. Ross C. Murfin. New York: St. Martin's P, 1989.

Correct Social Usage: A Course of Instruction in Good Form, Style, and Deportment. 9th rev. ed. New York: New York Society of Self-Culture, 1907.

Faulkner, William. *Absalom, Absalom!: The Corrected Text*. New York: Vintage, 1990.

—. *New Orleans Sketches*. London: Sidgwick and Jackson, 1959.

Kane, Harnett C. *Gentlemen, Swords and Pistols*. New York: William Morrow, 1951.

Karl, Frederick. "Race, History, and Technique in *Absalom, Absalom!*." *Faulkner and Race: Faulkner and Yoknapatwapha 1986*. Ed. Doreen Fowler and Ann J. Abadie. Jackson: UP of Mississippi, 1987. 209-221.

King, Richard H. *A Southern Renaissance: The Cultural Awakening of the American South, 1930–1955*. New York: Oxford UP, 1980.

Kingsland, Florence. *The Book of Good Manners: "Etiquette for All Occasions."* Garden City, NY: Double, Page, 1912.

Longstreet, Stephen. *Sportin' House: A History of the New Orleans Sinners and the Birth of Jazz*. Los Angeles: Sherbourne P, 1965.

Roberts, Diane. *Faulkner and Southern Womanhood*. Athens: U of Georgia P, 1994.

Weinstein, Philip M. "Marginalia: Faulkner's Black Lives." *Faulkner and Race: Faulkner and Yoknapatwapha 1986*. Ed. Doreen Fowler and Ann J. Abadie. Jackson: UP of Mississippi, 1987. 170-191.

Wolfe, Margaret Ripley. *Daughters of Canaan: A Saga of Southern Women*. Lexington: UP of Kentucky, 1995.

Wyatt-Brown, Bertram. *Southern Honor: Ethics and Behavior in the Old South.* New York: Oxford UP, 1982.

"Huey Long" as Deep South Dictator:
A Lion Is in the Streets as Novel and Film

Philip Dubuisson Castille

Huey Pierce Long, the political strongman from Louisiana, was assassinated in 1935 at the age of forty-two. In death he attracted the attention of several prominent American novelists—including Sinclair Lewis, Mari Sandoz, John Dos Passos, and Hamilton Basso—but most notably Robert Penn Warren in *All the King's Men* (1946). Warren's novel proved most popular among critics and scholars and won the Pulitzer Prize for fiction in 1947. However, the readers' favorite and best-seller among the "Huey Long" historical novels (Rubin 423) was a book called *A Lion Is in the Streets*, written by Adria Locke Langley (1899–1983),[1] a journalist and social reformer. Her novel appeared in the spring of 1945, more than a year before *All the King's Men*. All but forgotten now, the book enjoyed enormous popular success and was translated into fifteen languages. In 1946, James Cagney's production company purchased the screen rights for $250,000, a record sum for the time. However, legal complications involving the Long estate held up the project for years. Meanwhile, the film adaptation of *All the King's Men*, starring Broderick Crawford in the role of Governor Willie Stark, appeared in 1949 and became the most honored American film of the year, receiving over thirty awards, including the Oscar for best picture. Not until 1953, after many delays and rewrites, did the Warner Brothers film version of *A Lion Is in the Streets* finally appear. By that time, Broderick Crawford's gruff, Oscar-winning performance as Willie Stark-Huey Long in *All the King's Men* had become ingrained in filmic memory, leaving little room in the popular imagination for Cagney's feisty and folksy version of the Kingfish. Most serious of all, however, the seven years that elapsed between the purchase of the film rights and the release of the movie had witnessed a sea change in American politics. Because of the second Red Scare and the Korean War, the rise of the Hollywood blacklist, and renewed cultural support for business and property rights, the movie adaptation *A Lion Is in the Streets* fell into ideological confusion, stressing the political dangers caused by economic protest movements rather than the root causes of social discontent.

Adria Locke Langley's fictional politician, Hank "Big Lion" Martin, owes a great deal to the Huey Long legend. In the novel he rises from impoverished origins in a Deep South state modeled upon Louisiana. He claws his way through stints as a farmhand and itinerant peddler, becomes a militant advocate for poor farmers, and wins the governorship. On the positive side, Martin accurately perceives the abuses perpetrated against small farmers and sharecroppers by the state's ruling aristocracy, which exploits the poor and keeps them in virtual serfdom. He advances the cause of democracy by galvanizing the rural poor into economic resistance and political self-awareness, registering many poor (white) farmers to vote, transforming muddy lanes into modern highways, and vastly improving public education. But the Big Lion's early high-mindedness gives way to public and personal corruption during his relentless drive for power, which includes designs on Congress and even the White House. His moral deterioration leads one of the forgotten "little people" (Langley 479) to shoot him to death in front of his grandiose state capitol building. All of these plot details closely resemble the facts of Huey Long's life, career, and assassination.

Beyond writing an engaging historical novel based upon the Long era in Louisiana, Langley means to raise serious questions about the vulnerability of American democracy to takeover by a home-grown dictator. However clownish they may seem at first, firebrands in the mold of Huey Long or Hank Martin can take power and destroy the freedoms that allowed them to rise. Such charismatic figures can inspire powerful insurgencies drawn from the impoverished masses and challenge the established political order. But after taking office, they exploit the political system that elevated them. Forgetting their campaign promises, they pursue unchecked personal power and material gain. Thugs from the underworld as well as corporate magnates from the owning class collude with them to smash the democratic center and dismantle constitutional rule—this much actually happens in a single Gulf South state in *A Lion Is in the Streets*. However, in Langley's projected future, such a leader could spread his base far beyond the borders of a small, rural state, impose a dictatorship upon the entire nation, and make tyranny a reality in America. She warns that state control of mass media combined with the use of paramilitary force can create a climate of crisis in which all sense of social order is lost. Soon the ruler and the ruled are plunged into a vortex in which nothing seems real, and the republic is carried down in ruins.

To one degree or another, Langley shares with the male authors of Huey Long-based fictions the theme that liberal democracy is fragile and contains many openings through which totalitarianism can arise. However, *A Lion Is in the Streets* is unique among the Huey Long novels in that it centers on the particular vulnerability of women. In writing her only novel, Langley attempts to influence political events by encouraging female activism to prevent the rise of an American dictatorship and to preserve the protections owed to women in a liberal democracy. To dramatize the woman's role in *A Lion Is in the Streets*, Langley makes the novel's central intelligence not the demagogue himself (or one of his henchmen, as in *All the King's Men*) but his wife, Verity Wade Martin, who provides the "most prominent female perspective" (Perry 234) in all of the Huey Long novels of the 1930s and 1940s. By casting Hank's widow as the point-of-view character, Langley portrays women and democracy alike as victims of a violent, proto-fascist society, symbolized by the Big Lion of male authoritarianism.

Langley signals her political intent in the novel's biblical epigraph, drawn from the Book of Proverbs: "The slothful man saith, there is a lion in the way; A Lion Is in the Streets. As the door turneth upon its hinges, so does the slothful [man] upon his bed." In keeping with this biblical admonition, the novel is a warning against the dangers of political complacency: decent citizens are like the slothful man of the proverb when they allow demagogues to rise through democratic means to seize dictatorial power. It is important to note, however, that the underlying sources of poverty, inequality, and resentment are genuine, even if the messenger ultimately betrays the message.[2]

The novel version of *A Lion Is in the Streets* is told in flashback. After Hank's assassination, Verity listens to a national radio eulogy and recalls the Big Lion's rise and fall. Now in her mid–thirties, she remembers how she had moved south in 1922 from her native Pennsylvania as a nineteen-year-old Quaker schoolteacher. From the outset, Verity is established for the reader as a high-minded and principled woman. By contrast Hank is presented as a consummate con man, a barely literate but handsome twenty–three–year–old house–to–house salesman. Much of the opening section of the novel deals with Verity's deep-seated fear of men, yet Langley also makes it clear that Verity is physically attracted to Hank from the first. Her description of him gives her away, couched as it is in the language of desire: "Silhouetted against the setting sun . . . she saw him as a magnet with warm radiance. His thick, dark, wavy hair glistened in the strong light, giving him a copper and purple crown. . . .his beaming eyes spanned the distance between them, embracing her" (6). With this god-like description of the young Lion, Langley captures Verity's girlish admiration. Hank senses her need and plays upon it, leading her on with kisses and caresses. While such episodes are common for a coming-of-age novel, they also bear upon the novel's political theme. Langley makes Verity, a non-Southerner, a symbol for the whole American body politic, represented here in the form of a principled but inexperienced and gullible girl, first led on, then later betrayed, by male lust for flesh and power.

As Hank's young wife, Verity sees the beginnings of Hank's political activism and listens to his ringing call to "Divide the Earth's Riches"—Langley's thinly–veiled version of Huey Long's "Share Our Wealth" pitch. During his rounds as an itinerant salesman, Hank begins to win a following among the state's sharecroppers. As she travels with her husband, Verity is appalled by the poverty that she encounters in the Magnolia State, a condition for which the plantation aristocracy is largely to blame. Primitive transportation systems, steep poll taxes, and widespread illiteracy keep the poor at the mercy of the owning class. With genuine outrage at the abuses of the rich and the state legislature that they control, Hank rouses small farmers throughout a five-parish area to militant opposition against corrupt gin owners, who short weight the cotton. Hank makes the highly astute point that the owners deliberately block improvement of the state's rutted backroads so that farmers cannot take their cotton to competing gins for better prices.

For dramatic purposes Langley compresses the state's ruling class into a single character, Robert J. Castleberry IV, whom Hank nicknames "the black skimmer"—a swamp bird that in a swoop drops its beak into the water and gorges itself on countless tiny creatures. Castleberry runs a fiefdom of gins, banks, law enforcement officers, and compliant legislators, and Hank makes him his personal adversary. Surrounded by armed followers, Hank leads a march on Castleberry's gins and proves that the scales are rigged. Hank's militant protest exposes the corruption of Castleberry and upper-class predators like him, but it also leads to four deaths by gunfire (151) and the jailing of one of Hank's followers. While awaiting trial, the prisoner is shot to death through the window of his cell to prevent his testimony. Even though the defendant is dead, Hank orchestrates a bizarre "trial" to clear the prisoner's name. These courtroom theatrics ensure that the evidence of short-weighting at the Castleberry gins goes into the public record and that the daily newspapers give wide coverage to Hank. This statewide publicity solidifies Hank's following among the rural poor and wins new recognition from urban voters. Desperate to protect his name, Castleberry falsely blames his managers for the short-weighting scandal, ruins their reputations, and fires them (224). While Hank's crusading puts Castleberry and the owning class on the defensive, his idealism already is mixed with personal ambition. Verity's worries—and the reader's—are awakened by Hank's apparent willingness to use the common people for political gain (166). Verity wonders if Hank is a hollow man, lacking genuine conviction about economic injustice and using "it only as a way to get a following that will take him to power?" (226). However, the brutality of his enemies in the owning class seems far worse, so she looks the other way, but she remains concerned by Hank's tendency to silence her with his booming rhetoric. In her voicelessness Verity feels "imprisoned, in a strange role of inactive onlooker, impotent" (230). When she tries to speak up, Hank infantilizes her, holding her on his lap and teasing her with kisses and caresses. Despite her efforts to resist, Verity repeatedly gives in to Hank's use of sex to smother her concerns. This pattern of attraction and betrayal is repeated on numerous occasions, causing Verity to cry bitterly that she hates herself (301) for submitting to Hank's physical appeal.

Much as Huey Long had done, Hank schools himself in the law and passes the bar examination. Against long odds, he enters the race for State Commissioner of Public Works and Highways. He makes campaign promises to build farm-to-market roads, bring electric power to rural areas, distribute free schoolbooks, and provide homestead exemptions—all worthwhile goals in the backward Magnolia State. From the state archives he digs up what he calls "'Hank Martin's Grandpappy Law'" (274), an obscure 1898 statute which he invokes to circumvent literacy tests and property requirements and thus secure the farm vote. But to win a statewide election, he needs urban support. To her dismay, Verity sees him cutting deals with big-city crimelords to secure block votes in Crescent City and pad his personal wealth. Verity feels "like a dull automaton, or like a ventriloquist's dummy" (282), powerless to prevent Hank's moral erosion and political takeover. Also, her anxieties about Hank's need for female attention are incited when at a campaign stop she catches Hank embracing Sunny Lou (Flamingo) McMenimee, an eighteen-year-old admirer. She overhears as Hank huskily recites a passage from Song of Solomon (297), a seductive strategy that he once had used on Verity when Verity was a teenager. To make matters worse, Hank is interrupted by another young woman, who hisses that he has been reciting the same seductive lines to her. As usual Hank tries to placate Verity with "the great narcotic, the universal drug" of sex, which numbs the moral sense with "a longing for love and forgetting" (220).

Determined to win the commissioner election at any cost, Hank recruits armed thugs, and political killings swirl around his campaign. To Verity's horror, her husband casually admits involvement in a mobland murder. Hank dismisses her indignation and advances his ruthless belief in what he calls "'nictitating,'" a self-serving rationale for looking the other way—much as, he says, an eagle on high ignores what happens to little creatures below. Such high-flying birds of prey draw a membrane like a third eyelid across their sharp eyes "'so's they can shut out what ain't worth the seein'" (320). This callousness in the face of homicide causes Verity to drop out of her husband's campaign. Even so, she cannot resist her desire to mother Hank. On election day she steps between Hank and a hit squad, risking her life but preventing his murder. In this dramatic way Langley shows that it is easier for Verity to face death than it is for her to confront Hank with his worsening corruption.

Because she cannot talk to him, Verity sinks into depression, becoming alienated and sexually unavailable. She perceives that Hank's winning the commissionership is merely a means to higher office. Verity reflects "that in the beginning he had wanted to help people, maybe truly help them; but even then his eye was on the power and the pinnacle" (373). She withdraws to their country cabin, where she turns to books on economics and sociology, trying to forge her own opinions. In the newspapers she studies pictures of Mussolini with "his strutty, bull-like posture, his jutted chin, his menacing fists, his bemedaled chest" (396) and draws negative comparisons to her husband. All the while Hank never stops campaigning for higher office. As road commissioner, he stuffs his war chest with kickbacks from contractors and names yes-men to appointive offices. No longer stumping for votes along the backroads, he starts his own radio station in the state capital and broadcasts throughout the state. He salts his radio addresses with soak-the-rich promises and claims biblical authority for his political ambitions. Langley assigns a special and ominous role to the media for fueling Hank's rise from backwoods obscurity to statewide political legitimacy. She suggests that once the media become tools of power politics, individual citizens have little chance to learn the truth or to halt the rise of authoritarianism. The public is overwhelmed by the false reality that Hank projects and fails to perceive or respond correctly to the ugly reality of Hank's political machine.

In a mere two years, Hank wins the governor's office. He adopts what he calls his "'sheep's-clothin' tactics'" (427) to lull the opposition into complacency until he can devour it. He sets about abolishing party politics, co-opting political opponents into his machine, appointing rubber-stamp bureaucrats to carry out his orders, and abolishing constitutional separation of powers. From now on, only the Big Lion rules, and he swells the public payroll with countless new state jobs, all stemming directly from him to foster his cult of personality. He starts his own newspaper and uses state vehicles to spread his propaganda. He turns the state militia into a private army to intimidate political opponents. Dirty tricks, frame-ups, blackmail, and hush-money become routine means of enforcing compliance. He resorts to unconstitutional measures to subdue the judiciary and control the legislature. He expands his media outreach, now broadcasting fiery speeches across the country on national radio networks. No longer is state office enough for the Big Lion. Hank's ambitions extend "'to that round glitterin' dome in Washington'" (442–43). Langley presses the parallels between Hank's regime and the rise of European fascism when she has Jules Bolduc, a high-minded intellectual, lecture Hank about the menace posed abroad by Nazi Germany. Explicitly comparing the Big Lion with the Führer, Bolduc speaks of false leaders who capitalize on the people's legitimate longings for a better life, catch "'the pulse of the people—sense their hopes and deliberately misguide them'" (438). Langley's point is that fanatics can come to power by democratic means, as Adolf Hitler did in 1933—a point which is lost on Hank, but not on Verity, as the end of the novel makes clear.

During Hank's tough campaign for reelection as governor, Verity faces up at last to the truth of his long-running affair with Flamingo, an infidelity which substantiates his many other betrayals, private and public. She denounces her husband for the harm he has inflicted upon the women in his life and, in the novel's pattern of imagery, upon the people: "'I see that everyone pays too high a price for loving you. I, your wife, have paid too much; Flamingo, your mate, has paid too much; Hancy, your [daughter], has paid too much'" (458). Verity recognizes that in Hank she has nurtured a vicious male predator. Over fifteen years of marriage, she has "watched him turned by the black magic of power and more power into the Big Lion" (461). Now Hank is a rogue beyond control, threatening to take away all civil liberties and destroy the electoral process. His hunger for power cannot be separated from his gender. Women's rights and the survival of democracy are alike imperiled: "'you, and men like you all over the world have pillaged this generation! You've pillaged our faith and struck at our freedom,'" Verity cries (461). She concludes that Hank has failed as a husband and father, failed even as a philanderer, and failed as a political reformer who once vowed to put the needs of his supporters ahead of personal gain. Verity at last sees her husband as a totalitarian threat to women and the nation, and her effort to protect her daughter from him expresses her new-found sense of social responsibility.

On the day after his reelection as governor Hank is shot by an anonymous gunman. The assassin, who belongs to a statewide conspiracy to stop the Big Lion, is merely the one who drew the short straw—in this case a slip of paper marked with a hand-drawn image of a fallen lion "with many little people dismounting from the lion's back" (479). The straight-arrow journalist Saber Milady defends the assassination and marvels that there are thousands like the gunman, decent "'men who do not hold with killing'"(479) but who will resort to murder when democracy is at peril. Langley implies that the preservation of egalitarian government requires that the rank–and–file members of society, who have little power individually, must band together to overthrow a despot, by violence if necessary. Dry-eyed, Verity accepts this rationale and expresses relief and even satisfaction at her husband's death, thinking to herself "that Hank had been tried for years—tried by more than twelve good men and true—tried by the people and found guilty" (480). In the novel's last scene Verity looks down from the governor's mansion and apostrophizes the entire nation. She calls upon the citizenry to arise from torpor and return to the armed patriotism of the Boston Tea Party and Valley Forge: "'You're my kinsmen–you're the people! Only the people can blow the trumpet–the incorruptible trumpet of faith and justice, of equality and truth'" (482). In this conclusion, Langley makes plain her conviction that the people are not to blame for the rise of a totalitarian state. The American body politic is fundamentally good and just. However, if the people are lulled into political complacency and misled by distortions of the truth by the media, they can fail to react in time to prevent the emergence of an authoritarian regime which destroys democracy.

At the most basic level, *A Lion in the Streets* is a topical work growing out of the Depression, drawn from a set of historical circumstances centering on the rise and fall of Huey Long, and written to dramatize a stirring anti-fascist message. As such the novel gains significance as a left-wing political novel of the 1940s, published shortly before the second Red Scare and the onset of the arms race and the Cold War. In *A Lion Is in the Streets* Langley means to alert the American public to what she sees as an inherent American tendency toward fascism, as long as economic opportunity remains maldistributed, and poverty is widespread. What Langley advocates through her spokesman Jules Bolduc is "'a more equalized distribution of money'" (229) in the United States, to be brought about democratically and non–violently by reforming laissez-faire capitalism. There must be "'a change in the rules of the money game,'" Jules argues, enough to open markets and promote fair competition. Bolduc's call for change amounts to a denunciation of the American status quo as an unjust economic system which places control of the nation's vast money supply in the hands of a core elite. If economic reform does not occur in America, Jules predicts, social unrest will give rise to new "'leaders thinking of power and place,'" even worse men than Hank Martin. Langley warns her readers that, although the Great Depression is over, history could repeat the circumstances of the 1930s and create conditions that might lead to a future fascist takeover of the United States. A decade after Long's death in 1935, she retrospectively justifies his assassination as a patriotic act done for the good of the nation. But she ominously suggests that another dictator who would rule America could emerge and not be stopped in time.

Thus, unlike the ambivalent portrayal of the protean Willie Stark in *All the King's Men*, Hank Martin is roundly condemned in *A Lion Is in the Streets*. From the novel's feminist perspective, Langley ties Hank's private crimes against his wife to his betrayal of the people of the Magnolia State, so that sexual and political degeneracy go hand in hand. Seducing, manipulating, neglecting, and abandoning women are not only morally reprehensible acts in themselves, in Langley's view, but also parallel Hank's exploitation of his political supporters. At the end Verity listens as male intellectuals like Bolduc make the abstract case against Hank for transgressions against democracy, and she agrees with their analysis of Hank's political evil. But Verity also personalizes and feminizes this point by adding that Hank's misuse of the electorate was anticipated by his mistreatment of her, their daughter, and other women, including his mistresses. Thus, Langley gives women a central role as guardians of democracy, a role that she proclaims on the dust jacket of *A Lion Is in the Streets*: "I can never say enough for the fighting spirit of women. They will risk today's bread and a boycott if it will do anything for the next generation." This declaration implies Langley's belief that women uphold higher moral and political standards than men and will work harder for social justice and governmental reform. However, as *A Lion Is in the Streets* effectively dramatizes, women also will suffer first and worst under an American authoritarianism of the future—a claim pressed vigorously forty years later by Margaret Atwood in *The Handmaid's Tale* (1986).

From the outset, the project to film *A Lion Is in the Streets* was plagued with problems. The rights to the novel were purchased by Cagney Productions, which had come into being in 1942 as a partnership of James and his brother William to produce movies for United Artists (Hagopian 24–25). While the script was in development, the Cagneys switched to Warner Brothers studios, which would eventually shoot the film. The Huey Long estate objected to perceived defamatory parallels between the Hank Martin character and the late Senator from Louisiana and threatened to sue if the film adaptation of Langley's novel did not distance itself from Long's life and career. Negotiations delayed the project, and the script sanitized the novel—notably, Martin's abusive womanizing—in order to appease the Long family. Even so, the screenplay as developed by the young scriptwriter, Luther Davis, maintained much of the political span of Langley's novel. The script followed Martin's rise from itinerant peddler to agrarian organizer, political climber, and governor. His public rise was mirrored by a personal descent into deceit, adultery, and power-mania, leading to his assassination in office. However, the veteran director Raoul Walsh, with whom Cagney had worked on such Warner Brothers' hits as *The Strawberry Blonde* (1941) and *White Heat* (1949), complained that the shooting script was too long and ordered cuts. Rewrites resulted in an eighty–eight–minute piecework plot with a watered-down ending in which Hank Martin is shot to death not by an anti-fascist political conspirator but by a disillusioned early admirer. Martin is a much scaled-down character, not a dictatorial governor like Huey Long at all, merely an unsuccessful candidate for governor.

The film adaptation of *A Lion Is in the Streets* has received little critical attention, even though James Cagney regarded it as a major production. In a brief, but highly perceptive analysis, film historian Robert Sklar argues (260–262) that the softened movie adaptation was forced upon Cagney as a response to the rightward shift in American politics that occurred between the novel's publication in 1945 and the movie's release in 1953. This eight-year span witnessed vast changes in American society and politics. Beginning in 1947, the House Un-American Activities

Committee (HUAC) hearings on alleged Communist infiltration of the film industry intimidated and smeared many Hollywood figures on the Left. These hearings, in turn, lifted to prominence right-wing elements in the film colony and led to studio blacklistings of many Hollywood liberals. In 1950 the Korean War broke out, and Senator Joseph McCarthy stunned the nation by claiming that 205 Communists had infiltrated the State Department. Then the second round of HUAC hearings in 1951–1953 made headlines because of a parade of witnesses "naming names"—that is, confessing to past Communist activities and accusing others of taking part—which led to more purges in the film industry. Cagney's name, along with those of prominent actors such as John Garfield and Edward G. Robinson, was linked to Communist front organizations and placed on Federal Bureau of Investigation (FBI) lists of potential subversives.

Although Cagney was never called to testify before Congress, production of *A Lion Is in the Streets* in 1952 coincided with the second wave of House hearings and with the height of Senator McCarthy's power. In this Cold War climate of political repression, the progressive politics of Langley's novel seemed out of date, even dangerous. As conservative, even reactionary values rose to the fore in American popular entertainment, it was "courting subversiveness to suggest that an unprincipled man could gain high office in the United States" (Sklar 260). Thus, it became unthinkable to suggest that a proto-fascist such as Hank Martin was electable to high office. So it is not surprising that Cagney Productions toned down the left-wing sensibilities of the novel. Filming in Technicolor and overlaying a bouncy Hollywood musical score further thinned the film's seriousness and all but obliterated the reformist intent of Langley's book. The movie as released was too folksy and too heavy on Hollywood "production values" to capture the novel's harsh atmosphere of injustice, rage, insurgency, and betrayal.

A top acting performance from Cagney might have offset these severe shortcomings. Instead, Cagney's role is ill-conceived and confused. At fifty-three, he seems too old and paunchy to carry off a part in which he must portray a charismatic young charmer in his twenties and thirties. Matters are not helped by the script's heavy reliance upon dialect. Langley's original text suffers badly from long stretches of poor dialect writing, which betray the author's uncertain command of Southern accents. In stereotypical Hollywood fashion, the screenplay attempts to preserve this artificial aural Southern flavor, to great disadvantage. Many passages of dialect seem more a caricature of Southern speech than a depiction of it, particularly in the strained romantic scenes involving Cagney and the much younger actresses playing his wife Verity (Barbara Hale) and his mistress Flamingo (Anne Francis). One memorable howler comes when Flamingo whispers to Hank, "I've been your wife ever since I knowed what the word meant." Other infelicities abound. Cagney does little to help matters, as his enunciation strays far from the movie's Deep South setting toward the tough Irish neighborhoods on New York's East Side, where he grew up. In sum, Cagney's biographer John McCabe concludes that it was an ill-conceived role from the start to portray James Cagney as "a lovable, old, gal-kissin' cracker slob" (McCabe 276).

Furthermore, the actor was obviously uncomfortable with the role of the would-be Southern political boss that he was playing. Cagney had built a celebrated career by portraying fast-talking, edgy, even violent men, but his signature roles were portraits of twentieth-century urban figures—from the deadly gangster in *The Public Enemy* (1931) to the song-and-dance man in *Yankee Doodle Dandy* (1942)—but not country boys. Cagney seemed wholly uncertain about playing a pol in brogans and overalls. Further, Hank Martin's demagoguery was poles apart from Cagney's own political sympathies. Since rising to stardom in the early Depression years, Cagney often had been publicly associated with radical causes. He financially supported unions and strikers, Hispanic farm workers, the Scottsboro defense, and the Loyalist side during the Spanish Civil War. According to Cagney's brother Bill, Jim's liberal politics and past support for left-wing causes would not let him empathize with the Southern proto-dictator whom he was playing: "'I think he was so out of tune with Huey Long, who [sic] he was playing— he hated him so—that he did not get the audience to go along with him like he could when he was playing the worst killer'" (McCabe 277).

Bill Cagney's observation calls attention to what is perhaps the central contradiction of the movie. From the opening of the film, with its controlling image of a huge lion attempting to maul the statue of President Lincoln in the Lincoln Memorial, the audience is instructed to see Hank Martin as a danger to American government. However, the movie's early episodes work against this predetermined meaning. As if he were in another movie, perhaps a social-problem film from the 1930s or the early 1940s, Cagney plays the young Hank Martin as a pugnacious, reform-minded organizer whose message of economic and social protest rings true. Hank witnesses first-hand the desperate need of country people, even though the film's insistently upbeat production values put a bright and shiny face on rural poverty. However, when Hank tells oppressed sharecroppers that they stay poor because the rich exploit them and because the state neglects the educational and health needs of their children, they are willing to fight for him to be heard.

As in the novel, Hank bravely exposes corruption at the cotton gins, where small farmers are short-weighted by the owners and paid far less for their cotton than they are owed. In Langley's novel, this episode demonstrates Hank's early idealism and sets a moral benchmark against which his decline into despotism is measured. But the film quickly delegitimizes Hank's protest by undermining his character, showing him to be a cheating husband and, by extension, a cheating politician. These character attacks seem at cross purposes with Cagney's crowd-pleasing performance in the dramatic showdown at the cotton scales. This stirring episode is not dramatized at all in the novel because the book's point-of-view character, Hank's wife, Verity, is not there to see it; she only hears about it afterward, but to the credit of Davis's very uneven screenplay, it is the best scene in the movie. Full of defiance and determination, Cagney faces down a posse of armed deputies to test the accuracy of the scales. His acting is tough and taut, worthy of comparison with some of his most compelling screen roles, but the film's insistent anti-populist message denies Cagney's character any credit for bravely exposing criminal fraudulence at the gins and laying responsibility on the owners. Just the opposite, the movie teaches that Hank Martin is dangerously wrong when he blames the owning class for the sufferings of the poor. In the short-weighting scandal, the screenplay contradicts Langley's novel by vindicating the aristocratic owner, Robert Castleberry, of malfeasance. According to the film, the sharecroppers have been cheated not by the honest gin owner but by his conniving working-class employees, who line their pockets with what should be the farmers' earnings and the owner's profits. Such filmic distortions obscure Langley's presentation of Castleberry as a totally depraved character. In the novel, when he is publicly exposed as a thief, Castleberry shifts the blame from himself, falsely blames his managers, and fires them. In other words, the novel's false cover story—the desperate and cruel invention of a rich man to protect his aristocratic reputation—becomes the film's confirmed truth. In this way the film adaptation reinforces the reactionary message of 1950s Hollywood that the rich are not to blame for the troubles of the poor. Any economic injustice suffered by the downtrodden sharecroppers results from their own fecklessness or the venality of corrupt employees, not from any basic problems in the economic class structure. Thus, Cagney's vibrant performance is undercut by the script's ideological stance against the legitimacy of any form of organized protest, much less any militant action against the status quo. The American economic system, audiences are assured by the film, is at basis just and should not be challenged.

Following the encounter at the gin, in a choppy sequence of events the film turns against Hank and shows him to be a hypocrite and villain. He exploits the judicial system as well as his impoverished followers solely to gain a political base to run for governor. He makes under-the-table deals with big city political bosses who can deliver urban precincts. However, his political machine bogs down when heavy rains on election day cause flash floods and a light rural turnout. Refusing to concede the election, Hank calls upon his supporters to arm themselves, march on the capital, and stage a coup. In their desperation to gain political power and redress their economic wrongs, they are willing to follow him into attempting to overthrow the government. Thus, the film pounds home the point that political protest movements, however well intentioned, are at basis subversive and lead only to anarchy. What had begun months earlier as a seemingly justified grass-roots effort to get fair cotton prices has now degenerated into a wild lynch mob, hell-bent on dismantling the democratic system itself. On the brink of fomenting mob rule, Hank finally is stopped, shot down by a widow whose husband has given his life in Hank's cause. Hank's lies, adultery, and under-the-table deals at last are brought to light with the help of his wife and first supporters, who now turn against him. They quell the mob by killing and discrediting its leader. At the same time the film discredits the political message along with its disgraced messenger. The violent ending papers over the film's initial critique of undemocratic government, controlled by the propertied classes for their own economic and social self-interests. Instead, the movie punishes the leader of the protest movement, condemning him and his ideas. His assassination is justified as a civic good, and his insurgency is portrayed as a failure that rightly falls with him.

Although the reviews were generally kind when the movie appeared in late September 1953, many critics noted that *A Lion Is in the Streets* compared poorly to Columbia Pictures's film adaptation of Warren's *All the King's Men,* made four years earlier on much the same theme. But more was involved in the failure of the film version of *A Lion Is in the Streets* than unflattering comparisons to a better and more honored movie released a few years earlier. Perhaps by the early 1950s making a political film had become too difficult or even impossible, with the shadow of the blacklist hanging over old-line liberals like James Cagney. The movie adaptation of *A Lion Is in the Streets* tried to fall into step with times by reversing the leftist politics of the original novel and extolling the sanctity of property rights and economic privilege. Reflecting the reactionary politics of the early Cold War era, the film shied away from any suggestion that there were any class-based economic inequities in 1950s America. Nor did the film propose any political remedies to social ills, presuming instead that the reasons for protest fell with the leader. No matter how committed James Cagney might have been at one time to encouraging poor people to organize and take action against injustice, his bizarre characterization of Hank Martin is at best confused and at worst a sellout to McCarthy-era politics. Despite rousing early scenes of populist protest and activism, Cagney's performance turns upon itself and reinforces the film's determination to portray Hank Martin as the evil leader of a misguided cause. In all likelihood, the overlay of many bright and bouncy production touches, including a big song-and-dance-number, was an effort to mask the film's ideological contradictions. At any rate the movie fizzled at the box office. *A Lion Is in the Streets* turned out to be the last movie made by Cagney Productions. Lacking the resources of a major studio and without a hit movie to bring in new money, Cagney Productions folded under financial stress.

It may come as a surprise that more serious literature has been based on the life and career of Louisiana's Huey Long than on any other politician of the American twentieth century. To a number of novelists and scriptwriters who lived through the Long Era in the United States and witnessed the contemporaneous spread of fascism in Europe, the Kingfish's rise to prominence during the Depression demonstrated that fascism could become an American domestic threat. This anti-fascist position was passionately held by Adria Locke Langley in her story of the rise and fall of Hank Martin, the Big Lion from the Deep South. Her novel exhorts all good citizens to shake off political lethargy, and if necessary, take violent countermeasures, including assassination, to prevent the rise of a dictator, such as she believed Huey Long had been in Louisiana in the late 1920s and 1930s. However, Langley recognizes that overthrowing the would-be dictator does not do away with the root causes of poverty and inequality that led to his rise, and she warns that class struggle and social unrest will continue until economic justice is achieved in America. The film adaptation of *A Lion Is in the Streets* conveys quite a different message. At the close of the movie, Hank Martin's defeat at the polls reassuringly teaches movie audiences that American democracy is too resilient and fair for a demagogue to lead a successful takeover here. However consoling Hank's political downfall might be to Cold War movie audiences, troubling questions about class privilege and economic inequity in twentieth-century America nevertheless go unanswered—questions which are raised directly in Langley's novel but which are suppressed in the James Cagney motion picture. In other words, the movie promotes precisely the same political complacency against which the novel preaches.

NOTES

1. In 1889 Langley was born in Iowa and reared by her Quaker family in Stanton, Nebraska. She attended Northwestern University, married in her teens, and divorced in 1929, the mother of an infant daughter. While living in New York City, she became a leading member of the Women's Organization for National Prohibition Reform, which sought the repeal of Prohibition. For her pains, in the early 1930s she was denounced as a Communist, shot at, and jailed in Cooperstown. By 1933 she was publicity director for the New York State Democratic Committee. During the Depression she wrote articles for the *New York Post* calling attention to the poverty of groups as diverse as upstate dairy farmers and urban slum dwellers. During World War II she lived in California and worked as a riveter at a plant in Santa Monica. *A Lion Is in the Streets* was her only novel, and its Southern setting drew partly upon her early life experiences as a traveling saleswoman. With the novel's stunning popular success, in 1946 she sold the movie rights for $250,000, a record for the time. In her later years she taught writing classes in California. She died in Los Angeles in 1983. Keith R. Perry offers the only substantial critical reading of the novel, *A Lion Is in the Streets*. His thorough 1997 dissertation, "The Kingfish in Fiction: Huey P. Long and the Disguised Historical Novel," focuses on ways in which Langley and other novelists of the 1930s and 1940s drew upon the facts of Long's career and translated them into fiction. In general, my interpretation of *A Lion Is in the Streets* differs from Perry's in that his holds that the novel's rejection of Hank Martin is more moralistic than political.

2. Langley denied that Hank Martin was a fictionalized version of Huey Long. She said that the Big Lion stood for the universal demagogue. See *Current Biography, 1945* (New York: Wilson, 1946).

REFERENCES

Hagopian, Kevin. "Declarations of Independence: A History of Cagney Productions." *The Velvet Light Trap* 22 Nov. 1986: 16–32.

Langley, Adria Locke. *A Lion Is in the Streets.* New York: McGraw–Hill, 1945.

McCabe, John. *Cagney.* New York: Knopf, 1997.

Perry, Keith Ronald. "The Kingfish in Fiction: Huey P. Long and the DisguisedHistorical Novel." Diss. U of South Carolina, 1997.

Rubin, Louis. "Huey Long in Fiction." *Georgia Review* 8 (1954): 422–34.

Sklar, Robert. *City Boys: Cagney, Bogart, Garfield.* Princeton: Princeton UP, 1992.

Mr. Pontellier's Cigar, Robert's Cigarettes: Opening the Closet of Homosexuality and Phallic Power in *The Awakening*

Suzanne Disheroon-Green

> *Sometimes a cigar is just a cigar.*
> —*Sigmund Freud*

Modernist writers of the late nineteenth century ranging from Henry James and Tennessee Williams to Edith Wharton and Kate Chopin grappled with the emergence of an increased social awareness of sexuality, an awareness which included the recognition of alternative lifestyles and sexualities. The moral code of the Victorian era, which many Modernist writers rebelled against in their creative works, demanded that sexual impulses of any variety be tightly constrained, deeming them indecent for public display or discussion. Behind the scenes, however, the Victorian era in both Great Britain and the United States was an era typified by the practice of homosexuality, autoeroticism, and pornography, which was distributed through such underground publications as *The Pearl*. In short, Victorian society was affronted with "the magnetism of desire" at every turn (Cotkin 130). Not surprisingly, American writers presented fictional characters who were reminiscent of the types individuals whom they encountered in their daily lives. Accordingly, writers such as Kate Chopin drew for her readers a wide assortment of characters: traditional men like Léonce Pontellier and David Hosmer; effeminate boy-men such as Robert Lebrun; mother-women in the character of Adèle Ratignolle; neglectful mothers who were sexually experimental such as the dissatisfied Edna Pontellier; and single women who were considered "disagreeable" and "imperious" (Chopin 905), such as Mademoiselle Reisz, whom critics such as Kathryn Seidel and Elizabeth LeBlanc have argued are considered so because of their lesbian tendencies[1]. Chopin's cast of characters is wide-ranging, touching on nearly every level of race, social class, gender expectations, and sexual identity, yet in Chopin's most famous novel, *The Awakening*, the issue of male homosexuality has yet to be thoroughly examined. A close examination of Chopin's representation of male sexuality in *The Awakening* reveals two opposing characterizations: that of the overbearing, yet emotionally absent, traditional husband and that of the homosexual male, who is figuratively emasculated by his heterosexual acquaintances. Chopin underscores these characterizations through her manipulation of phallic images throughout the text, effectively designating Léonce Pontellier as heterosexual and Robert Lebrun as homosexual[2].

Chopin relies on phallic imagery as a code which suggests the sexual identities of her male characters to her readers. Critics occasionally point out that not all cigars in literature—or in life—are phallic symbols, but as Harriet Kramer Linkin has aptly observed, although "Freud may have cautioned 'sometimes a cigar is just a cigar,' practitioners of feminist criticism know that cigars always represent . . . smoke; a cigar need not signify the phallus directly to demonstrate the masculinist power" (130). Léonce Pontellier often exerts his masculine supremacy over his wife, Edna, while smoking a cigar. His cigar smoking serves as a phallic symbol, illuminating his patriarchal attitudes toward his wife. The phallic nature of his cigar acts as an emasculation image when associated with Robert Lebrun, the single male figure in the novel who does not expect to be treated as a superior creature simply because of his masculinity. Robert serves as a foil to Mr. Pontellier, who is overpowering and demanding, modeling the type of behavior that was accepted from—and even expected of—husbands in late nineteenth century America. Conversely, Robert is conciliatory and kind, effeminate and more comfortable in the beautiful world of women than in the smoke-filled clubs of men, a characterization with which Chopin suggests that he has homosexual tendencies. He is the antithesis of Mr. Pontellier and prompts readers to question the prevalent nineteenth-century male role, and to seek a more sensitive role that may converge with the newly-defined femininity of women like Edna Pontellier. In the end, however, Robert cannot fulfill the role that Edna desires and instead fearfully retreats in the face of Edna's emerging sexuality, claiming the cloak of propriety as his motivation. Robert retreats from Edna not because he fears society's condemnation for carrying on an illicit affair with a married woman, but because he is unable to respond to Edna's sexual advances. Robert's homosexual nature precludes a physical relationship with Edna, and Chopin's depiction of his behavior clearly places him in a homosexual role.

Victorian society defined the stratified roles that men and women were expected to fulfill, and to a large extent, literary authors were bound by these conventions if they wanted their works to be popularly accepted. Women were expected to function as the angel of the house, protective and pure, placing the needs of husband and children above their own. As Anne Goodwyn Jones has demonstrated, "womanhood specifically denies the self" (4) and is "within the family sacrificial and submissive" (*xi*). Women of this era, particularly Southern women, were charged with directing the day-to-day domestic events associated with a smoothly running household, and because they were trained to pamper their men, they could in return expect such leeway as finances would allow to run their homes without male intervention. Chopin herself spent the years of her marriage in the South during the Victorian era, becoming well acquainted with the expectations placed upon women. Even after returning to her native St. Louis following the death of her husband, Chopin repeatedly illustrates Victorian and Southern attitudes toward gender roles, demonstrating in her fiction that she neither accepts societal conventions which treat women as "the property of others" (Stange 23) nor those which utterly disregard individuals who engage in alternative lifestyles. Indeed, in order to tell Robert's story alongside of Edna's, Chopin abandoned "the nineteenth-century literary conventions she had learned" in her attempts to "imagine the healthy eroticism of a culture" (Gubar and Gilbert 95).

Not surprisingly, writers of the late nineteenth century found the manner in which they could discuss alternate lifestyles quite limited, yet many authors, including Herman Melville and Henry James, examined these lifestyles despite the restrictions of contemporary culture. Given the untrodden nature of the literary path, readers should not find it surprising that Chopin provides clues to Robert's sexual identity without specifically giving voice to that identity. In order to represent Robert as possessing an alternate sexual identity, Chopin was forced to exercise her "resourcefulness," so that homosexual themes could be "codifi[ed] in 'polite' terms" (Adams 11). Contemporary readers found the "very idea of sex between men in love . . . demonic, the most hideous of all taboo subjects, [and] the act itself was never talked about directly" (Spencer 263). Such subject matter was encoded to allow deniability under most circumstances, yet the subtexts of some literary works of this era offered examinations of taboo subjects to those who cared to discern such an interpretation. For example, Eve Kosofsky Sedgwick argues that homosexual themes are addressed by Herman Melville in *Billy Budd, Sailor* and by Oscar Wilde in *Dorian Gray*, and that in fact, novels such as these "set the terms for a modern homosexual identity" in literature (49). Sedgwick asserts that "it has been notable that foundational texts of modern gay culture . . . have often been the identical texts that mobilized and promulgated the most potent images and categories" (49); many texts which have come to be considered important in gay culture were canonical works long before it was deemed acceptable to write about alternative sexualities. Part of the need for deniability stemmed not only from Victorian mores, but from the historical fact that "it was only close to the end of the nineteenth century that a cross-class homosexual role and a consistent, ideologically full thematic discourse of male homosexuality became entirely visible" (Sedgwick 201). Homosexuality as a literary theme did not become socially acceptable until well into the twentieth century, and prior to this time, writers carefully codified their references to the topic.

As *The Awakening* opens, Léonce Pontellier is introduced as the prototypical heterosexual husband of his era. He is an overbearing, self-centered man who is primarily interested in his own comfort and the external images of himself and his family which reflect his success. His wife is an expected accoutrement whom he expects to be a credit to his lifestyle and good taste. In this vein, the reader is rapidly confronted with Mr. Pontellier's superior attitude as he assumes that his needs are of paramount importance to everyone around him. For example, the first time he is introduced, he is grumbling to himself about the noisy birds that demonstrate the audacity to disturb his peaceful enjoyment of the daily paper

(Chopin 881). He is further distracted from his task by his children at play and the "bustling" of his hostess (Chopin 881). Despite his marginal position as a guest of Madame Lebrun's *pension*, since he is male and the breadwinner for his family, Léonce expects quiet when he wants to read and is more than a little disgruntled when confronted with noise instead. After a lengthy discourse on his myriad of petty disruptions—which further include two young girls practicing the piano, an old woman praying and clicking her rosary beads, and his hostess giving cheerful directions to her servants—he "finally lit a cigar and began to smoke" (Chopin 882). Lit at the conclusion of his catalogue of irritants, Mr. Pontellier's cigar symbolizes what his behavior has already indicated—that he is a man who is convinced of his own importance. He does not smoke until he has delineated all of his disturbances, arrogantly rising above and then dismissing these intrusions as so many small gnats.

Mr. Pontellier's cigar smoking also commences just as he sees his wife returning from the beach in the company of Robert Lebrun. Directly after lighting his cigar, "he fixed his gaze upon a white sunshade that was advancing at a snail's pace from the beach...beneath its pink-lined shelter were his wife, Mrs. Pontellier, and young Robert Lebrun" (Chopin 882). Mr. Pontellier sees Robert approaching, and he lights the cigar that he will shortly use to pointedly emasculate the man whom he perceives as less masculine. He illustrates his ownership of his wife in front of Robert Lebrun, illustrating both to whom Edna belongs and that Robert is not enough of a man to look after her properly. He then models his idea of the appropriate treatment of a wayward wife, scolding Edna for swimming during the heat of the day and for allowing herself to get sunburned (Chopin 882), all in the presence of the man who was complicit in her actions. Léonce's reason for chastising Edna is clear: he "looked at his wife as one looks at a valuable piece of personal property which has suffered some damage" (Chopin 882). The proof of his ownership is further underscored when Edna holds out her hand to reclaim her wedding rings—the golden bonds that tie her to her exacting husband, which she removes when she goes to the beach in Robert's company. Edna's rings symbolize her supposedly irrevocable union with Léonce Pontellier, yet Chopin uses them to demonstrate Edna's growing willingness to forsake this union in order to cure her dissatisfaction with her life. When she accompanies Robert, the young man for whom she will develop the only deep, sexual feelings that she experiences in her life, she removes her rings and returns them to Léonce. Symbolically, Edna rejects Léonce and her ties to him in favor of the possibility of a more fulfilling relationship with Robert.

When Edna places the rings back on her fingers, she looks at Robert and laughs: "she slipped the rings upon her fingers; then clasping her knees, she looked across at Robert and began to laugh. The rings sparked upon her fingers. He sent back an answering smile" (Chopin 882). The interplay between Robert and Edna, while innocent at this juncture, suggests a developing bond. Edna and Robert's smiles are conspiratorial, reminiscent of those shared by mischievous children or young lovers. Léonce does not appear to see anything symbolic in Edna's removal of her rings, though. He unconcernedly holds them in his pocket while his wife is away and hands them back to her when she returns to his sphere of influence, serenely smoking his cigar while his wife puts the rings back on her fingers.

In the same scene in which he demonstrates his control over and disregard for his wife, Mr. Pontellier illustrates his opinion of Robert Lebrun. Throughout the novel, Robert amply demonstrates that he prefers the company of women to that of men, "but in a Platonic sense only" (Rowe 32). He devotes himself to the ladies on a regular basis: "Robert each summer at Grand Isle had constituted himself the devoted attendant of some fair dame or damsel" (Chopin 890). Further, he poses as "inconsolable" after the death of the previous year's love–interest—a girl not yet of marriageable age and far outside of his social class in any event—all the while flirting with yet another married woman, Madame Ratignolle (Chopin 890). Mme. Ratignolle is indicative the type of women Robert chooses as friends: married women, older widows, or girls too young to be considering marriage, but never young women of the age to be seeking a husband. Robert consistently gives the appearance of emotional intimacy with safe women—women who are unattainable—yet, wasting days at a time dallying with unavailable women is hardly behavior that Mr. Pontellier would find acceptable in a man. A man should go to the club for billiards and return to the city to work during the week (Chopin 884, 887) while the women vacationed. A real man also would not waste his time with married women; he would set about the business of getting married in the same way that he should conduct his professional affairs—with dispatch—so that he could refocus his attention on appropriately masculine goals.

Even if Mr. Pontellier senses a hidden agenda between his wife and young Robert—which appears unlikely, given that Robert is a man who is willing to stroll along the beach with an unavailable woman under the shade of a pink parasol—he finds no threat in the relationship. He finds their laughter "utter nonsense...not...half so amusing when told" (Chopin 882). His reaction to their silliness is to get up from his chair and prepare to leave—hardly the reaction of a husband who feels threatened by the presence of another man. Clearly, Léonce Pontellier does not find it disturbing for Robert to spend time with his wife.

Chopin further encodes the characterization of Robert as a non–threatening presence for the perceptive reader, referring to Edna's husband as Mr. Pontellier in scenes which include Robert or scenes in which he is chastising his wife. We know, however, that in private moments, such as the occasion on which Léonce gives Edna money following his billiard game, she addresses her husband by his first name. Robert, however, is always called Robert and never Mr. Lebrun. The one exception to this trend occurs when Mr. Pontellier invites Robert to the club for a game of billiards. In this single instance Mr. Pontellier addresses Robert as Lebrun and resumes calling him by his first name when his invitation is refused. Robert is never accorded the respect of being addressed by a title combined with his surname, but is instead referred to only by his given name, indicating Mr. Pontellier's superiority. Chopin's subtle use of hierarchical names for her male characters serves to heighten the masculinity associated with Léonce Pontellier and the more effeminate nature of Robert Lebrun.

Robert further proves his worthlessness as a man by refusing Mr. Pontellier's invitation to play billiards, a refusal which leads Mr. Pontellier to look down on him. The result of Robert's refusal is that Mr. Pontellier effortlessly emasculates Robert, taking leave of him with the same attitude that one would have towards the non-threatening presence of a harem eunuch. He instructs his wife to "send [Robert] about his business when he bores you" (Chopin 883). Throughout this conversation, Mr. Pontellier puffs on his cigar—the phallic symbol representing his masculine sexuality. Robert's obvious preference for female company diminishes him in Mr. Pontellier's eyes, and the cigar hanging from Léonce's lips symbolizes the power of the phallus, which Robert unwittingly denigrates and rejects by seeking companionship from women who can never be more than friends to him.

In contrast to Mr. Pontellier, Robert smokes cigarettes, ostensibly because he cannot afford cigars; the effeminate male smokes the smaller, more frail counterpart of the cigar (Chopin 883). Robert's cigarettes seem to be another of Chopin's subtle ways of indicating Robert's sexual preference. While Mr. Pontellier, the model heterosexual male with two children, proudly smokes the cigar, Robert, the emasculated male who does not engage in sexual relationships with women, smokes the significantly smaller cigarette. Robert mentions that he has one cigar, which he is saving for after dinner (Chopin 883), showcasing the implement of greater size for a time when he is apt to be observed by a greater number of people. His intention to publicly exhibit the masculine symbol serves to highlight his closeted status. Robert's public persona is that of a straight male, and maintaining this persona requires him to behave in a prescribed way, a way which is supported by smoking a cigar. However, in private, Robert is perfectly happy with his cigarettes, an inferior phallic symbol at best. Appropriately, the cigar was given to him by Mr. Pontellier, perhaps in a weak effort to make Robert into more of a man, but more likely to emphasize Robert's lack of masculinity. By offering him the cigar, symbolizing a man's virility, Léonce ridicules Robert's effeminate qualities while also illustrating that he has masculinity to spare.

Mr. Pontellier's perception of Robert's feminized demeanor appears to be exactly the quality which attracts women to him. Robert communicates on an intimate level with the ladies, and his relationship with Edna is no exception. He deviates from societal norms, becoming engaged in women's conversations and pastimes. For example, he tells stories to Madame Ratignolle as she sews, sits with Edna as she draws or cuts out a pattern, and brings tea to Madame Ratignolle in an effort to mollify her after they disagree. Chopin's other male characters only interact with women for two reasons: to initiate or maintain a marriage or to lure them into a sexual relationship, as in the case of Alcée Arobin's relationship with Edna. Beyond relationships based upon marriage or sex, the only male-female interactions that Chopin shows take place between a pair of young lovers who spend all of their time together and are essentially one character[3]. Robert and his lady friends give us the only insight into any male-female relationships in *The Awakening* that fall outside of the sphere characterized by Mr. Pontellier.

The symbolism of Mr. Pontellier's cigar is further illustrated by his late night tirade about their sons. Arriving at home late after an evening at his club, Léonce rudely awakens his wife with inane chatter about his evening, then is offended by her lack of interest in "things which concerned him" (Chopin 885). Ironically, Léonce's ineffectiveness in awakening Edna from sleep mirrors his inability to awaken her sexually or emotionally. He is oblivious to her needs, and, in fact, has no idea that she has needs that he is not meeting. Léonce stays very much in character, blustering and gossiping, but when his remarks elicit no response from Edna, he tries a different approach. He reproaches her for her neglect of her children, berating her until she gets out of bed to check on their son's non-existent fever.

As Léonce drones on the topic of Edna's failings as a parent, he is again smoking a cigar (Chopin 885). When he finishes smoking, he goes directly to bed and "in half a minute he was fast asleep" (Chopin 886). The scene serves as a verbal enactment of an assault by the conquering male. Once Léonce has fulfilled his needs—in this case, gaining Edna's attentive submission—he is overcome by the need for a refractory period and goes to sleep. His cigar, once again, symbolizes his masculine prowess. His needs are temporarily satisfied, and the cigar is extinguished. Edna receives no pleasure, either physical or emotional, from this encounter with her husband; instead, she is the unwilling recipient of his attentions. His conquest is complete. Edna, meanwhile, is "thoroughly awake. She began to cry a little...the tears came so fast to Mrs. Pontellier's eyes that the damp sleeve of her *peignoir* no longer served to dry them...she could not have told why she was crying. Such experiences as the foregoing were not uncommon in her married life" (Chopin 886). Edna feels violated by Léonce's tirade, just as surely as if he had forced her to submit to unwanted sex. This scene serves as a critical step in her growing need for a relationship with Robert, as Léonce's behavior not only highlights the elements missing from the marriage, but at the same time places the more sensitive Robert in a very favorable light.

In direct contrast to the master-subordinate relationship shared by Edna and Mr. Pontellier, is the burgeoning relationship between Edna and Robert. They often sit idly together "exchanging occasional words, glances or smiles which indicated a certain advanced stage of intimacy and *camaraderie*" (Chopin 890). *Camaraderie* is the key in this situation, as the term does not imply any kind of sexual tension or romantic intention. Rather, it implies a warm, friendly relationship that could just as easily exist between people of the same or the opposite sex. In her newly awakening state, however, Edna confuses Robert's feelings of affection with passion, attributing to him a passion that he will never return to her.

Before Robert leaves Grand Isle, he consistently attempts to present himself as a heterosexual male, perhaps because he is trying to deny his sexual identity. He becomes offended by Madame Ratignolle's suggestion that he leave Edna alone because she might mistakenly take his attentions seriously. Their encounter quickly becomes confrontational:

His face flushed with annoyance . . . "Why shouldn't she take me seriously?" he demanded sharply. "Am I a comedian, a clown, a jack-in-the-box? Why shouldn't she? You Creoles! I have no patience with you! Am I always to be regarded as a feature of an amusing programme? I hope Mrs Pontellier does take me seriously. I hope she has discernment enough to find in me something besides the *blagueur*." (Chopin 900)

Robert becomes irritable when he is questioned about his relationship with Edna. He is nervous, blushing and taking off his hat to play with it, despite the fact that since he and Edna have not engaged in any behavior that would have been considered morally questionable, he has no reason to become defensive when questioned. He feels insecure about having his relationship questioned because it could reveal his alternative sexual identity. Despite all the time he spends with Edna and her increasingly obvious attraction to him, he does not return her interest because he is not interested in women romantically or sexually, and his reaction demonstrates his fear of discovery.

The tenor of Robert's argument with Adèle gives further evidence of homosexual tendencies, for he protests his wish to be taken seriously too vehemently, questioning why he, of all men, should not be considered a threat. His protests of suitability as a candidate for women's attentions are excessive, and Robert ends up appearing as if he is trying to hide something. Adèle adeptly puts Robert back in his place, interpreting his overreaction as the cross complaints of a disgruntled boy. Robert suddenly realizes that he is close to creating suspicion about his motives, and he clearly has no desire to reveal his inclinations to the other vacationers. He quickly drops the argument with Adèle, saying simply "Oh! Well! That isn't it" (Chopin 900). His reaction provides additional evidence to support the suspicion that he is gay. He does not protest when Mme. Ratignolle suggests that he is talking like a womanizer, as he probably would have if womanizing were the only accusation he feared. Instead, he diverts the subject to men who are womanizers, such as a tenor in the French Opera and Alcée Arobin, and effectively drops the subject of his own motivations, as if what could be discovered about him must not be discussed.

As the story progresses and Edna becomes more enamored with Robert, the masculine power symbolized by Mr. Pontellier's cigar is altered. Léonce returns at midnight one evening to find Edna in the hammock outside of their cottage (Chopin 911). He alternately commands, cajoles and insists that Edna come into the house immediately. Robert's considerate behavior is again contrasted with Léonce's as Edna lies in the hammock. Robert asks Edna if she would like him to stay with her, fetches her shawl for her, and sits silently beside her (910). When Léonce finds Edna outside in the middle of the night, he merely tries to force her to go in the house and go to bed, expressing his dismay at finding her outside to begin with. He gives all kinds of reasons why she should enter the house immediately: "It is past one o'clock" he says. "You will take cold out there...the mosquitoes will devour you" (Chopin 911). When he realizes that Edna is not going to do his bidding and come into the house, Léonce becomes kinder in his requests: "Edna, dear, are you not coming in soon?" (Chopin 912). When kindness fails, he orders his wife into the house; again, his strategy fails. Finally, he plants himself next to the hammock, uninvited, and begins to drink and smoke, at which point Edna eventually rises to enter the house. His presence "awakens [her] gradually out of a dream...to feel again the realities pressing into her soul" (Chopin 912), and his cigar smoking symbolically wins. Again, Léonce attempts to assert his masculinity yet fails to reach Edna in any way. When Edna goes inside, he does not accompany her. Instead, we see him metaphorically flex his muscles, telling Edna that he will come in "just as soon as I have finished my cigar" (Chopin 913). Mr. Pontellier's phallic power does not have the same effect on Edna at this point, however. She does not cry or become miserable. Having tired of Léonce's posturing, Edna simply goes into the house and goes to bed. She finally succumbs to her husband's demands, returning to the house while Mr. Pontellier remains outside to finish smoking, but only after he has ceased ordering her about and demanding that she enter the house. His victory, in this case, comes more slowly than in previous interviews with his wife. Edna begins to assert herself in small ways and Mr. Pontellier has to smoke more cigars before he forces his wife to submit to his will.

Meanwhile, Robert continues to gain Mrs. Pontellier's affections through his warmth and friendship, albeit without fully realizing the effect he is having on her. Robert considerately places Edna's hat on her head after convincing her to go swimming with him, making her feel that he would miss her company greatly were she to decline his invitation (Chopin 892). He places his head on her arm often, despite Edna's early discomfort with his closeness and the social impropriety of his actions (Chopin 891). He sits with her beside the hammock late at night until a crowd returns from the beach, and unlike Mr. Pontellier in the same situation, Robert is a welcome guest (911). Throughout the series of scenes between Robert and Edna, he offers no apology for his behavior. He merely continues to listen to her—a welcome experience for Edna.

In the hammock scene, Robert again smokes a cigarette. In this very private and intimate scene with a woman who quite obviously, by now, has feelings for him, "no multitude of words could have been more significant than those moments of silence, or more pregnant with the first-felt throbbings of desire" (Chopin 911). Despite the setting and Edna's mood, Robert shows no romantic interest in her at all. He attempts no conversation and does not try to touch her. Although desire plainly throbs in this scene, Chopin does not attribute the desire to Robert, but to Edna. Robert rolls a cigarette, symbolic of his status as a feminized man, while Edna watches him in silence. When Robert assumes that Edna is asleep and leaves her, he does not seem reluctant to so. It is Edna who watches "his figure pass in and out of the strips of moonlight as he walked away"—quite a romantic description (Chopin 911). Robert and Edna's differing expectations are well delineated in this scene. Robert sits smoking and calmly leaves what could have been a very romantic, intense moment. Edna, on the other hand, is pointedly watching Robert, and the description implies that she is feeling more than simple *camaraderie*.

Edna develops stronger feelings for Robert than he does for her although Robert perceives Edna's growing affection. Robert responds to Edna's attraction by leaving town, intending to not see Edna again until her feelings become more controlled. Robert's abrupt departure is commonly read as an escape from his illicit feelings for a married woman, but I argue that he is masking his homosexuality. He likes Edna and enjoys her company but is not physically attracted to her. Since homosexuality was not an acceptable lifestyle choice in turn-of-the-century Louisiana, he solves the dilemma by departing from Grand Isle. During their separation, Robert expects Edna's growing passion to cool. However, on the chance that it does not, he avoids meeting her after they each return to New Orleans the next fall. Robert's choice of Veracruz, Mexico, as his destination upon leaving Grand Isle is also revealing. According to Juan Carlos Hernández, Veracruz has long been known because of the bisexuality of its male population, a fact that would most likely have been known to the well-read and cosmopolitan Kate Chopin. Before he leaves, Robert tells Edna that "he could only meet the gentleman whom he intended to join at Vera Cruz by taking such and such a steamer" (Chopin 923). He does not refer to the family friend, Montel, as a business associate or a mentor, but as "the gentleman whom he intended to join," leaving the nature of the relationship ambiguous. We learn later that despite of Montel's "doing everything toward his advancement," Robert's "financial situation was no improvement over the one he had left in New Orleans" (Chopin 943). Further, Robert is very matter-of-fact when he tells Edna of his impending departure, despite her obvious discomfiture with the news. His response to her inquiries as to the length of his absence is equally ambiguous, telling her that he may stay gone "forever . . . It depends upon a good many things" (Chopin 926). Edna presses Robert for answers, becoming emotional and "striving to detain him" (Chopin 926). Despite Edna's entreaties, however, Robert leaves, and although he admonishes her not to part from him "in an ill humor," he shows little regret at leaving her, telling her that he hopes that she "won't completely forget" him (Chopin 926). Edna's reaction would make it difficult for a man who returned her emotional feelings to part with her, but Robert extricates himself from Edna with relative dispatch, walking toward the beach to the boat that will take him to New Orleans without a backward glance. Robert departs for his new life in Veracruz, leaving Edna to grapple alone with the implications of her dissatisfying life.

Following Robert's abrupt departure, Mr. Pontellier and his cigar finally lose their influence over Edna. Upon returning to the city, Edna decides to move out of the family home and live alone (Chopin 965). She does not seek her husband's approval and is unconcerned when Léonce writes to her, remonstrating her for her "rash impulse; and he begged her to consider...what people would say" (Chopin 977). Disregarding her husband's demands that she stay in the family home, Edna moves out anyway. The lengths to which Mr. Pontellier goes to "save appearances" (Chopin 977) are described in great detail, yet the cigar is noticeably absent from the entire description. Symbolically, the phallic superiority that Mr. Pontellier wields throughout the novel gradually loses its stranglehold on Edna. She is not yet completely free from her husband's grasp, however. She realizes that the community accepts his explanation of her change of residence—he has let it be known that their house is being remodeled, therefore necessitating Edna's sudden move—and Edna "was apparently satisfied that it should be so" (Chopin 977). Edna is perfectly happy to allow people to think that she and her husband are still together, so long as he is not interfering with the awakening which she is experiencing on nearly a daily basis.

Ironically, Robert's homosexual nature, though stripped of masculinity by Mr. Pontellier, is the nature to which Edna's awakening sexuality responds. Robert ultimately bolts from Edna and her sexuality, however, retreating behind a cloak of propriety. He permanently disappears from her life with only a note because her openness and her newly–found sexuality terrify him, as his homosexuality precludes any physical response to Edna's advances. He states that he returned to town hoping that her husband would set her free (Chopin 992), yet it seems unlikely that he really had any such hopes, especially since he only began seeing Edna again by accident, and only continued to do so at her insistence. He speaks of having been "demented, dreaming of wild, impossible things," attributing his dreams to stories of other men setting their wives free. What Robert does not say, though, tells the rest of the story. He tells Edna that he came back to New Orleans "full of vague, mad intentions. And when I got here—" (Chopin 992). He avoids Edna because he cannot pursue a romantic relationship with her. Edna senses that something is amiss, responding to his claims by reminding him that "When you got here you never came near me!" (Chopin 992). Edna gently scorns the idea that either Robert or Mr. Pontellier could pass her back and forth like a possession: "if he were to say, 'Here, Robert, take her and be happy; she is yours,'" Edna says, "I should laugh at both of you. His face grew a little white. What do you mean? he asked" (Chopin 992). Edna's response to his avoidance of her, and to his excuses for doing so, convince Robert that she is sincere about pursuing a romantic relationship with him, and make him realize that he must take action before his true sexual identity is revealed.

Robert is frightened by Edna's sexual freedom, fearing that his homosexual nature will be revealed should Edna continue to pursue intimacy. She openly continues to describe how she loves him and how they will "love each other" (Chopin 993). Robert's discomfort increases with her professions of love, and he begs Edna to stay with him when Mme. Ratignolle summons her, seemingly in the hope that her presence will quell his fear, that he will be able to stay with her and fulfill her expectations. Even as he tries to convince her to stay, he kisses her warmly but not passionately, arguing that he has been in love with her since the summer in Grand Isle. He proclaims that he "forgot everything but a wild dream of your some way becoming my wife" (Chopin 992). Edna, however, has questions about his behavior: "Why have you been fighting against it?" (Chopin 992). Robert is ready with a response: "I realized what a cur I was to dream of such a thing, even if you had been willing" (Chopin 992). Robert seems to hope that Edna would rebuff him for his bold statements, removing him from an untenable situation and allowing him to remain honorable. In spite of Robert's hopes to the contrary, Edna rejects the conventional path that she has gradually rejected as her husband's control over her has lessened. Instead, she agrees that they should be together. Robert tries to respond to her advances; he kisses her, speaks of love, and even begs her not to leave (Chopin 992-93). Ultimately, though, when Robert realizes that he will have to become involved in a sexual relationship with Edna, he cannot go through with it. His homosexuality keeps him from consummating the relationship, so instead of having his preference revealed, he leaves Edna. His final words give no specific explanation for his abrupt departure, but they are not the words of a man who wishes for the end of a woman's marriage: "I love you. Good-by— because I love you" (Chopin 997). Rather than be humiliated by his inability to perform sexually with Edna, and rather than hurting Edna with his lack of sexual interest in her, Robert leaves. Edna assumes that he departs because he does not want to disgrace either of them by conducting an illicit relationship, but in actuality he leaves to hide his homosexuality. The simplicity of Robert's note implies all that it does not say. For all of his emotional identification with women, Robert ironically retreats to the man's world of phallic cigars where emotional commitment is not expected of him, and more importantly, where his sexual identity will not be revealed.

Despite her Modernist impulses, particularly with regard to representations of love, Chopin was not writing in an era when she could have portrayed Robert more openly as a homosexual. Because of the mores of Victorian society, she was presented with limited options through which to explore alternative sexualities beyond the coded references that she offers in her text. Given the critical response that *The Awakening* received, it is not hard to imagine the outcry which would have ensued had Robert's sexual identity been more clearly articulated. Chopin's use of the coded references to Robert's sexuality described in this discussion should not be mistaken for lack of a clear characterization of this man whose identity would not have been readily accepted had it become common knowledge.

Finally, through suicide, Edna permanently removes herself from both Robert's fearful retreat and Mr. Pontellier's overbearing objectification. She alone has fully experienced the results of her newly awakened sexuality and the reactions that it has brought from the men in her life. Suicide is perhaps the only avenue left to Edna, and by liberating herself from her husband, she emasculates Mr. Pontellier in the same manner that he feminized Robert. Edna's decision to take her own life represents a choice that Léonce could not control. She no longer allows herself to be an object in his collection of materials, and she retains control of the sexuality that Robert rejects. Edna, then, through her suicide, effectively puts out the fire of Mr. Pontellier's cigar and unwittingly allows Robert to maintain the secrecy of his sexual preference.

NOTES

1. Kathryn Seidel, in her article titled "Art is an Unnatural Act: Mademoiselle Reisz in *The Awakening*" has argued that Mademoiselle Reisz is a lesbian and that her sexuality effects Edna's own developing sexuality. Elizabeth LeBlanc, in "The Metaphorical Lesbian: Edna Pontellier in *The Awakening*," argues that Edna herself is a lesbian who can only find fulfillment in the company of women, rather than in the arms of men.

2. This discussion of Robert as a homosexual figure originated with a paper titled "Mr. Pontellier's Cigar: Emasculation and Effeminacy in Kate Chopin's *The Awakening*," which I presented at the South-Central Modern Language Association in New Orleans, Louisiana in November, 1994.

3. For a discussion of the role of the pair of young lovers in *The Awakening*, see my article titled "Whither Thou Goest, We Shall Go: Lovers and Ladies in *The Awakening*" which is forthcoming in *Southern Quarterly*.

REFERENCES

Adams, Stephen. *The Homosexual as Hero in Contemporary Fiction*. London: Vision P, 1980.

Chopin, Kate. *The Awakening*. *The Complete Works of Kate Chopin*. Ed. Per Seyersted. Baton Rouge: Louisiana State UP, 1969.

Cotkin, George. *Reluctant Modernism: American Thought and Culture, 1880-1900*. New York: Twayne, 1992.

Gilbert, Sandra M. and Susan Gubar. *No Man's Land: Sexchanges*. New Haven: Yale, 1989.

Hernández, Juan Carlos. "Bisexuality in Veracruz State: the Case of Tecolutla." *Reconceiving Sexuality: International Perspectives on Gender, Sexuality and Sexual Health*. Rio de Janeiro. 14 - 17 April 1996.

LeBlanc, Elizabeth. "The Metaphorical Lesbian: Edna Pontellier in *The Awakening*." *Tulsa Studies in Women's Literature* 15 (1996): 269-88.

Linkin, Harriet Kramer. "'Call the Roller of Big Cigars': Smoking Out the Patriarchy in *The Awakening*." *Legacy* 11.2 (1994): 130-142.

The Pearl: A Journal of Facetive and Voluptuous Reading. 1879. New York: Grove, 1968.

Rowe, Anne. "New Orleans as Metaphor: Kate Chopin." *Literary New Orleans: Essays and Meditations*. Ed. Richard S. Kennedy. Baton Rouge: Louisiana State UP, 1992.

Sedgwick, Eve Kosofsky. *Epistemology of the Closet*. Berkeley: U of California P, 1990.

Spencer, Colin. *Homosexuality in History*. New York: Harcourt Brace, 1995.

Stange, Margit. *Personal Property: Wives, White Slaves, and the Market in Women*. Baltimore: Johns Hopkins, 1998.

Toth, Emily. *Kate Chopin*. New York: Morrow, 1990.

c

Selected Bibliography

LOUISIANA HISTORY, CULTURE, AND FOLKLIFE

Ancelet, Barry Jean, ed. *Cajun and Creole Folktales: The French Oral Tradition of South Louisiana*. Jackson: UP of Mississippi, 1994.

—. "Research on Louisiana French Folklore and Folklife." *French and Creole in Louisiana*. Ed. Albert Valdman. New York: Plenum, 1997. 351–59.

Baker, Vaughan Burdin, ed. *Visions and Revisions: Perspectives on Louisiana Society and Culture*. Lafayette, LA: Center for Louisiana Studies, 2000.

Bardaglio, Peter W. *Reconstruction the Household: Families, Sex, and the Law in the Nineteenth–Century South*. Chapel Hill: U of North Carolina P, 1995.

Bergeron, Maida, Nancy K. Bernstein, Janice Dee Gilbert, Joyce Jackson, and Susan Garrett Davis. "People of the Florida Parishes: Their Arts, Their Crafts, and Their Traditions." *Folklife in the Florida Parishes*. Baton Rouge: Louisiana Folklife Program and Center for Regional Studies, 1989. 116–36.

Brasseaux, Carl A., Keith P. Fontenot, Claude F. Oubre, and Clifton Carmon. *Creoles of Color in the Bayou Country*. Jackson: UP of Mississippi, 1994.

Bryan, Violet Harrington. *The Myth of New Orleans in Literature: Dialogues of Race and Gender*. Knoxville: U of Tennessee P, 1993.

Cash, W. J. *The Mind of the South*. 1941. New York: Vintage, 1991.

Castillo, Susan. "Stones in the Quarry: George Cable's Strange True Stories of Louisiana." *Southern Literary Journal* 31.2 (1999): 19–34.

Daigle, Ellen M. "Traiteurs and Their Power of Healing: The Story of Doris Bergeron." *Louisiana Folklore Miscellany* 6.4 (1991): 43–48.

DeCaro, Frank. "New Orleans, Folk Ideas, and the Lore of Place." *Louisiana Folklore Miscellany* 7 (1992): 68–80.

Donlon, Jon. "Three-to-Five on the Red, Three-to-Five on the Red! Fighting Cocks, Ritual Betting, and Wagering Skill in South Louisiana." *Mississippi Folklife* 28.2 (1995): 33–38.

Dorman, James H. *Creoles of Color of the Gulf South*. Knoxville: U of Tennessee P, 1996.

Edwards, Jay D. "The Origins of Creole Architecture." *Portfolio: A Journal of American Material Culture* 29.2–3 (1994): 155–89.

Fagaly, William A. "The Christmas Bonfires of St. James Parish." *Folk Art* 20.4 (1995–96): 54–61.

Frantom, Mercy. "Gravehouses of North Louisiana: Culture, History, and Typology." *Material Culture: Journal of the Pioneer American Society* 27.2 (1995): 21-48.

Gaudet, Marcia. "The Cajuns and Their Culture." *Documenting Cultural Diversity in the Resurgent American South: Collectors, Collecting, and Collections.* Ed. Margaret R. Dittemore and Fred J. Hay. Chicago: Association of College and Research Libraries, 1997. 77–89.

Gaudet, Marcia. *Louisiana Folklore Miscellany.* Special Issue on Louisiana Folklore and Literature. 10 (1995).

Gray, Richard. *Southern Abberations: Writers of the American South and the Problems of Regionalism.* Baton Rouge: Louisiana State UP, 2000.

Green, Suzanne Disheroon and Lisa Abney. *Songs of the New South: Writing Contemporary Louisiana.* Westport, CT: Greenwood P, 2001.

Hobson, Fred. *The Southern Writer in the Postmodern World.* Athens: U of Georgia P, 1991.

Holman, David Marion. *A Certain Slant of Light: Regionalism and the Form of Southern and Midwestern Fiction.* Baton Rouge: Louisiana State UP, 1995.

Hyde, Samuel C., Jr., ed. *Plain Folk of the South Revisted.* Baton Rouge: Louisiana State UP, 1997. 228–49.

Jackson, Joyce. "Music of the Black Churches." *Folklife in the Florida Parishes.* Baton Rouge: Louisiana Folklife Program and Center for Regional Studies, 1989. 97–102.

Kein, Sybil, ed. *Creole: The History and Legacy of Louisiana's Free People of Color.* Baton Rouge: Louisiana State UP, 2000.

Kennedy, Richard S., ed. *Literary New Orleans: Essays and Meditations.* Baton Rouge: Louisiana State UP, 1992.

—, ed. *Literary New Orleans in the Modern World.* Baton Rouge: Louisiana State UP, 1998.

Lindahl, Carl. "The Presence of the Past in the Cajun Country Mardi Gras." *Journal of Folklore Research* 33.2 (1996): 125–53.

—, Maida Owens, and C. Renee Harvison, eds. *Swapping Stories: Folktales from Louisiana.* Jackson, MS: Louisiana Division of the Arts–UP of Mississippi, 1997.

— and Carolyn Ware. *Cajun Mardi Gras Masks.* Jackson: UP of Mississippi, 1997.

McDonald, Roderick A. *The Economy and Material Culture of Slaves: Goods and Chattels on the Sugar Plantations of Jamaica and Louisiana.* Baton Rouge: Louisiana State UP, 1993.

Nakagawa, Tadashi. "Louisiana Cemeteries: Manifestations of Regional and Denominational Identity." *Markers: Annual Journal of the Association for Gravestone Studies* 11 (1994): 28–51.

Oliver, Paul. "That Certain Feeling: Blues and Jazz . . . in 1890?" *Popular Music* 10.1 (1991): 11–19.

Orso, Ethelyn G. "Louisiana Live Oak Legends." *Louisiana Folklore Miscellany* 7 (1992): 59–67.

Spitzer, Nicholas R. "The Creole State: An Introduction to Louisiana Traditional Culture." *Festival of American Folklife* (1985): 8–12.

Valdman, Albert. "The Place of Louisiana Creole Among New World French Creoles." *Creoles of Color of the Gulf South.* Ed. James H. Dorman. Knoxville: U of Tennessee P, 1996. 144–65.

Ware, Carolyn. "Croations in Southeastern Louisiana: Overview." *Louisiana Folklore Miscellany* 11 (1996): 67–85.

Wyatt, Brown, Bertram. *Southern Honor: Ethics and Behavior in the Old South.* Oxford: Oxford UP, 1982.

RACE, GENDER, AND CLASS

Brasseaux, Carl A. *A Refuge for All Ages: Imigration in Louisiana History*. Lafayette, LA: Center for Louisiana Studies, 1996.

Brown, Dorothy H., and Barbara C. Ewell. *Louisiana Women Writers: New Essays and a Comprehensive Bibliography*. Baton Rouge: Louisiana State UP, 1992.

Cable, George W. *The Creoles of Louisiana*. Gretna, LA: Pelican Pouch, 2000.

Cole, Karen. "A Message from the Pine Woods of Central Louisiana: The Garden in Northrup, Chopin, and Dormon." *Louisiana Literature* 14.1 (1997): 64–74.

Dauphine, James G. *A Question of Inheritance: Religion, Education, and Louisiana's Cultural Boundary, 1880-1940*. Lafayette, LA: Center for Louisiana Studies, 1993.

Domínguez, Virginia R. *White By Definition: Social Classification in Creole Louisiana*. New Brunswick, NH: Rutgers UP, 1997.

Dunbar-Nelson, Alice. "People of Color in Louisiana." *Journal of Negro History* 1 (1916): 361–76.

—. "People of Color in Louisiana." *Journal of Negro History* 2 (1917): 51–78.

Edwards, Laura F. *Scarlett Doesn't Live Here Anymore: Southern Women in the Civil War Era*. Urbana: U of Illinois P, 2000.

Fairclough, Adam. *Race & Democracy: The Civil Rights Struggle in Louisiana, 1915-1972*. Athens: U of Georgia P, 1995.

Gehman, Mary. *The Free People of Color of New Orleans: An Introduction*. New Orleans: Margaret Media, 1994.

Guillory, Monique. "Under One Roof: The Sins and Sanctity of the New Orleans Quadroon Balls." *Race Consciousness: African-American Studies for the New Century*. Ed. Judith Jackson Fossett and Jeffrey A. Tucker. New York: New York UP, 1997. 68–92.

Hall, Gwendolyn Midlo. *Africans in Colonial Louisiana: The Development of Afro-Creole Culture in the Eighteenth Century*. Baton Rouge: Louisiana State UP, 1992.

Hanger, Kimberly S. *Bounded Lives, Bounded Places: Free Black Society in Colonial New Orleans, 1769-1803*. Durham, NC: Duke UP, 1997.

Hirsch, Arnold R. and Joseph Logsdon, eds. *Creole New Orleans: Race and Americanization*. Baton Rouge: Louisiana State UP, 1992.

Jones, Anne Goodwyn and Susan V. Donaldson, eds. *Haunted Bodies: Gender and Southern Texts*. Charlottesville: UP of Virginia, 1997.

Jones, Anne Goodwyn. *Tomorrow is Another Day: The Woman Writer in the South, 1859-1936*. Baton Rouge: Louisiana State UP, 1981.

Jordan, Rosan Augusta, and Frank de Caro. "'In This Folk-lore Land': Race, Class, Identity, and Folklore Studies in Louisiana." *Journal of American Folklore* 109.431 (1996): 31–59.

Lindig, Carmen. *The Path from the Parlor: Louisiana Women 1879-1920*. Lafayette, LA: Center for Louisiana Studies, 1986.

Manning, Carol S., ed. *The Female Tradition in Southern Literature*. Urbana: U of Illinois P, 1993.

Mills, Gary B. *The Forgotten People: Cane River's Creoles of Color*. Baton Rouge: Louisiana State UP, 1977.

—. "Shades of Ambiguity: Comparing Antebellum Free People of Color in 'Anglo' Alabama and 'Latin' Louisiana." *Plain Folk of the South Revisted*. Ed. Samuel C. Hyde, Jr. Baton Rouge: Louisiana State UP, 1997. 161–86.

Schafer, Judith Kelleher. *Slavery, the Civil Law, and the Supreme Court of Louisiana*. Baton Rouge: Louisiana State UP, 1994.

Seidel, Kathryn Lee. *The Southern Belle in the American Novel*. Tampa: U of South Florida P, 1985.

Tunnell, Ted. *Crucible of Reconstruction: War, Radicalism, and Race in Louisiana, 1862-1877*. Baton Rouge: Louisiana State UP, 1984.

Warren, Nagueyalti and Sally Wolff. *Southern Mothers: Fact and Fictions in Southern Women's Writing*. Baton Rouge: Louisiana State UP, 1999.

Yaeger, Patricia. *Dirt and Desire: Reconstructing Southern Women's Writing, 1930-1990*. Chicago: U of Chicago P, 2000.

RELIGION

Burkart, Julia. "Plantation Christianity." *Mid-America Folklore* 13.2 (1985): 12–17.

Hicks, William. *History of Louisiana Negro Baptists and Early American Beginnings from 1804-1914*. Lafayette: Center for Louisiana Studies, 1998.

Jacobs, Claude F. and Andrew J. Kaslow. *The Spiritual Churches of New Orleans: Origins, Beliefs, and Rituals of an African-American Religion*. Knoxville: U of Tennessee P, 1991.

Sexton, Rocky. "Cajun and Creole Treaters: Magico-Religious Folk Healing in French Louisiana." *Western Folklore* 51:3–4 (1992): 237–48.

Tallant, Robert. *Voodoo in New Orleans*. Gretna: Pelican Pouch, 1998.

INDIVIDUAL AUTHORS

Alvarez, Joseph A. "The Lonesome Boy Theme as Emblem for Arna Bontemp's Children's Literature." *African American Review* 32.1 (1998): 23–31.

Bauer, Margaret D. "When a Convent Seems the Only Viable Choice: Questionable Callings in Stories by Alice Dunbar-Nelson, Alice Walker, and Louise Erdrich." *Critical Essays on Alice Walker*. Ed. Ikenna Dieke. Westport, CT: Greenwood, 1999. 45–54.

Bendixen, Alfred. "George W. Cable and the Garden." *Louisiana Studies* 15 (1976): 310–15.

Benfey, Christopher. *Degas in New Orleans: Encounters in the Creole World of Kate Chopin and George Washington Cable*. New York: Knopf, 1997.

Bongie, Chris. "Resisting Memories: The Creole Identities of Lafcadio Hearn and Eduoard Glissant." *Substance: A Review of Theory and Literary Criticism* 26.3 (1997): 153–78.

Brown, Dorothy H. "Ruth McEnery Stuart: A Reassessment." *Xavier Review* 7.2 (1987): 23–36.

Bryan, Violet Harrington. "Creating and Re-creating the Myth of New Orleans: Grace King and Alice Dunbar–Nelson." *Publications of the Mississippi Philological Association* (1987): 185–96.

—. "Race and Gender in the Early Works of Alice Dunbar-Nelson." *Louisiana Women Writers: New Essays and a Comprehensive Bibliography*. Ed. Dorothy H. Brown and Barbara C. Ewell. Baton Rouge: Louisiana State UP, 1992. 122–38.

Butcher, Philip. "George W. Cable and George W. Williams: An Abortive Collaboration." *Journal of Negro History* 53 (1968): 334-44.

Cleman, John. "College Girl Wilderness: Nature in the Work of George W. Cable." *Markham Review* 5 (1976): 24–30.

Dixon, Nancy. *Fortune and Misery: Sally Rhett Roman of New Orleans: A Bibliographical Portrait and Selected Fiction*. Baton Rouge: Louisiana State UP, 1999.

—. "An Introduction to 'Mrs. Grundy, an Etching' by Sallie Rhett Roman." *Louisiana Literature* 13.2 (1996): 75–88.

Dresner, Zita Z. "Irony and Ambiguity in Grace King's 'Monsieur Motte.'" *New Perspectives on Women and Comedy*. Ed. Regina Barreca. Philadelphia: Gordon and Breach, 1992. 168-83.

Eaton, Richard Bozman. "George W. Cable and the Historical Romance." *Southern Literary Journal* 8 (1975): 84–94.

Elfenbein, Anna Shannon. *Women on the Color Line: Evolving Stereotypes and the Writings of George Washington Cable, Grace King, Kate Chopin.* Charlottesville: UP of Virginia, 1994.

Farrah, David. "The Liberation of Spirit and the Story in Zora Neale Hurston's *Their Eyes Were Watching God.*" *Shoin Literary Review* 26 (1993): 45–54.

Ford, Sarah. "Necessary Chaos in Hurston's *Their Eyes Were Watching God.*" *College Language Association Journal* 43.4 (2000): 407–19.

Gaudet, Marcia. "Images of Old Age in Three Louisiana Short Stories." *Louisiana English Journal* 1.1 (1993): 62–4.

Goebel, Rolf J. "Japanese Urban Space and the Citation of Western Signs." *Comparative Literature Studies* 35.2 (1998): 93–106.

Green, Suzanne Disheroon. "Fear, Freedom, and the Perils of Ethnicity: Otherness in Kate Chopin's 'Beyond the Bayou' and Zora Neale Hurston's 'Sweat.'" *Southern Studies* 5 (1994): 105-118.

Green, Suzanne Disheroon and David J. Caudle. *At Fault by Kate Chopin: A Scholarly Edition with Background Readings.* Knoxville: U of Tennessee P, 2001.

—. *Kate Chopin: An Annotated Bibliography of Critical Works.* Westport, CT: Greenwood P, 1999.

Grimwood, Michael. "Lyle Saxon's Father Mississippi as a Source for Faulkner's 'Old Man' and 'Mississippi.'" *Notes on Mississippi Writers* 17.2 (1985): 53–62.

Hair, William Ivy. *The Kingfish and His Realm.* Baton Rouge: Louisiana State UP, 1991.

Hall, Joan Wylie. "Ruth McEnery Stuart." *Legacy* 10.1 (1993): 47–56.

Harvey, Cathy Chance. "Dear Lyle/Sherwood Anderson." *Southern Studies* 18 (1979): 320–38.

Hatley, Donald W. "A Preliminary Guide to Folklore in the Louisiana Federal Writers' Project." *Louisiana Folklore Miscellany* 6.2 (1986-1987): 8–14.

Hull, Gloria T. "Shaping Contradictions: Alice Dunbar-Nelson and the Black Creole Experience." *New Orleans Review* 15.1 (1988): 34–37.

—. "'Two-Facing Life': The Duality of Alice Dunbar–Nelson." *Collections* 4 (1989): 19–35.

James, Charles L. "Arna Bontemps's Creole Heritage." *Syracuse University Library Associates Courier* 30 (1995): 91–115.

—. "Arna Bontemps: Reflections on Flyleaves." *The Langston Hughes Review* 13.1 (1994–1995): 45–49.

Kadlec, David. "Zora Neale Hurston and the Federal Folk." *Modernism-Modernity* 7.3 (2000): 471–85.

Keely, Karen A. "Marriage Plots and National Reunion: The Trope of Romantic Reconciliation in Postbellum Literature." *Mississippi Quarterly* 51 (1998): 621–48.

Kinney, Arthur F. "Faulkner and Problematics of Procreation." *Connotations: A Journal for Critical Debate* 8.3 (1998–1999): 325–37.

Ladd, Barbara. *Nationalism and the Color Line in George W. Cable, Mark Twain, and William Faulkner.* Baton Rouge: Louisiana State UP, 1996.

Lund, Michael. "Kate Chopin and Magazine Publication: Human Birth and Periodical Issue at the End of the Nineteenth Century." *Nineteenth Century Feminisms* 1 (1999): 95–117.

Montesi, Albert J. "Huey Long and *The Southern Review.*" *Journal of Modern Literature* 3 (1973): 63–74.

Murray, Paul. *A Fantastic Journey: The Life and Literature of Lafcadio Hearn.* Folkestone: Japan Library, 1993.

Nimeiri, Ahmed. "'Reconstruction, which was also war. . .' Realism and Allegory in Grace King's *The Pleasant Way of St. Medard.*" *Mississippi Quarterly* 41 (1988): 39–54.

Olson, Kirby. "Surrealism, Haiti, and Zora Neale Hurston's *Their Eyes Were Watching God.*" *Real: The Journal of Liberal Arts* 25.2 (2000): 80–93.

Payne, Ladell. "Willie Stark and Huey Long: Atmosphere, Myth, or Suggestion?" *American Quarterly* 20 (1968): 580–595.

Reagan, Daniel. "Achieving Perspective: Arna Bontemps and the Shaping Force of Harlem Culture." *Essays in Arts and Science* 25 (1996): 69–78.

Roskelly, Hephzibah. "Cultural Translator: Lafcadio Hearn." *Literary New Orleans: Essays and Meditations*. Ed. Richard S. Kennedy. Baton Rouge: Louisiana State UP, 1992.

Rubin, Louis D., Jr. "Politics and the Novel: George W. Cable and the General Tradition." *William Elliott Shoots a Bear: Essays on the Southern Literary Imagination*. Baton Rouge: Louisiana State UP, 1975. 61–81.

Seidel, Kathryn Lee. "Art is an Unnatural Act: Mademoiselle Reisz in *The Awakening.*" *Mississippi Quarterly* 46 (1993): 199–214.

Simpson, Ethel C. "Ruth McEnery Stuart: The Innocent Grotesque." *Louisiana Literature* 4.1 (1987): 57–65.

Smith, Katherine Capshaw. "Conflicting Visions of the South in Grace King's *Memories of a Southern Woman of Letters.*" *Southern Quarterly* 36.3 (1998): 133–45.

—. *George W. Cable: The Life and Times of a Southern Heretic.* New York: Pegasus, 1969.

Sneller, Judy. "Old Maids and Wily 'Widders': The Humor of Ruth McEnery Stuart." *New Directions in American Humor*. Ed. David E. E. Sloane. Tuscaloosa: U of Alabama P, 1998. 118–28.

Snyder, Robert E. "The Concept of Demagoguery: Huey Long and His Literary Critics." *Louisiana Studies* 15 (1976): 61–83.

Stevenson, Elizabeth. *The Glass Lark: A Study of Lafcadio Hearn*. New Brunswick: Transaction, 1999.

Tapley, Philip A. "Negro Superstitions in *Children of Strangers.*" *Louisiana Folklore Miscellany* 4 (1976-1980): 61–72.

Taylor, Helen. *Gender, Race, and Region in the Writings of Grace King, Ruth McEnery Stuart, and Kate Chopin*. Baton Rouge: Louisiana State UP, 1989.

Toth, Emily. *Kate Chopin*. New York: Morrow, 1990.

—. *Unveiling Kate Chopin*. Jackson: UP of Mississippi, 1999.

— and Per Seyersted. *Kate Chopin's Private Papers*. Bloomington: Indiana UP, 1998.

Treu, Robert. "Surviving Edna: A Reading of the Ending of *The Awakening.*" *College Literature* 27.2 (2000): 21-36.

Trotman, C. James. "George W. Cable and Tradition." *Texas Quarterly* 19.3 (1976): 51–58.

Turner, Arlin. *Critical Essays on George W. Cable*. Boston: Hall, 1980.

Umemoto, Junko. "The Liberation of Women in Works Retold by Lafcadio Hearn." *Comparative Literature Studies* 35.2 (1998): 132–28.

Warren, Robin O. "The Physical and Cultural Geography of Kate Chopin's Cane River Fiction." *Southern Studies* 7 (1996): 91–110.

Watson, James G. *William Faulkner: Self-Preservation and Performance*. Austin: U of Texas P, 2000.

Watson, Reginald. "Mulatto as Object in Zora Neale Hurston's *Their Eyes Were Watching God* and John O. Killens's *The Cotillion.*" *College Language Association Journal* 43.4 (2000): 383–406.

Whitlow, Roger. "Alice Dunbar-Nelson: New Orleans Writer." *Regionalism and the Female Imagination: A Collection of Essays*. Ed. Emily Toth. New York: Human Sciences, 1985. 109–25.

Yu, Beongcheon. *An Ape of the Gods: The Art and Thought of Lafcadio Hearn*. Detroit: Wayne State UP, 1964.

RELEVANT JOURNALS

Journal of American Folklore. Publication of the American Folklore Society. Arlington, Virginia.

Journal of Southern History. Publication of the Southern Historical Association. Baton Rouge, Louisiana.

Louisiana Folklife. Publication of the Folklore Society of Louisiana. Northwestern State University, Natchitoches.

Louisiana Folklore Miscellany. Publication of the Louisiana Folklore Society.

Louisiana History. Publication of the Louisiana Historical Society. Lafayette, Louisiana.

Louisiana Literature. Publication of the Southeastern Louisiana University. Hammond, Louisiana.

Mississippi Quarterly. Publication of Mississippi State University.

Southern Literary Journal. Publication of the Department of English, University of North Carolina at Chapel Hill.

Southern Quarterly. Publication of the University of Southern Mississippi.

Southern Studies. Publication of Northwestern State University.

Index

About the Editors and Contributors

LISA ABNEY is the director of the Louisiana Folklife Center and is an assistant professor of English at Northwestern State University. She holds a Ph.D. from the University of Houston and an M.A. and B.A. from Texas A&M University. Dr. Abney's research interests include sociolinguistics, dialectology, folklore, southern literature, and American and British modernist literature. Dr. Abney's recent publications include articles about contemporary novelists Clyde Edgerton and Michael Lee West will appear in *The Regional Literary Atlas of the United States* (forthcoming Fall 2001). She has also published "The Milieu of the Louisiana Timber Industry and Kate Chopin's *At Fault*" in a new edition of that novel. Her other articles include "Textual Suppression in George Sessions Perry's *Hold Autumn in Your Hand* and Alice Walker's *The Third Life of Grange Copeland*," which appears in *Humanities in the South,* and "Foodways and Folk Traditions in Michael Lee West's *She Flew the Coop*" in *Songs of the New South: Writing Contemporary Louisiana.* "Business and Technical Writing: Importance, Accessibility, and Contextualization in the Liberal Arts Curriculum," recently appeared in the *Louisiana English Journal* (1999). In 1999, Dr. Abney completed a multimedia project, which includes written text, audio, photographs, and video, entitled "The Natchitoches/NSU Folk Festival" for the Local Legacies Program of the American Folklife Center, Library of Congress. Recently, she has completed, with Dr. Suzanne Disheroon Green, a compilation of works about Louisiana writers called *Songs of the New South: Writing Contemporary Louisiana.* Dr. Abney, again with Dr. Green, is editing *The Dictionary of Literary Biography: 21ˢᵗ Century American Novelists*. She has served as guest editor for *Southern Studies* and is the general editor of *Louisiana Folklife.*

ROBERT ALLEN ALEXANDER, JR., is an assistant professor in the Department of Languages and Literature of Nicholls State University in

Thibodaux, Louisiana, where he teaches courses in early American literature, southern literature, Louisiana literature, and the American novel. He earned his doctorate from Florida State University (1997), his M.A. from the University of North Carolina (1987), and his B.A. from Middle Tennessee State University (1984).

ERIN E. CAMPBELL has recently completed her doctorate at the University of Mississippi where she wrote her dissertation entitled "Remembering Who We Are and What We Represent: The Social Construction of Identity in Shakespeare and Faulkner." She currently teaches English and Writing at Abraham Baldwin College in Tifton, Georgia. She is the author of essays on Robert Olen Butler, Faulkner, and Shakespeare and a regular poetry contributor to a variety of small presses.

PHILIP DUBUISSON CASTILLE is professor of English and dean of the College of Arts and Letters at Eastern Washington University. He graduated Phi Beta Kappa in Philosophy and English from Tulane University and received advanced degrees from Tulane and the University of North Carolina at Chapel Hill. He has published studies of works by William Faulkner, F. Scott Fitzgerald, Robert Penn Warren, James M. Cain, Raymond Chandler, William Alexander Percy, and Huey Long. He is co-editor of *Southern Literature in Transition: Heritage and Promise* (Memphis State UP, 1983) and a member of the St. George Tucker Society. His entry on Huey Long will appear in *The Companion to Southern Literature: Themes, Genres, Places, People, Movements, and Motifs,* forthcoming from the LSU Press.

RICHARD COLLINS, associate editor of the *Xavier Review*, has published essays on Wilkie Collins, George Gissing, Alfred Lord Tennyson, Joseph Conrad, Oscar Wilde, and Andrei Codrescu. A Fulbright lecturer in Romania (1992-94), he has also taught at the American University in Bulgaria. His book *John Fante: A Literary Portrait* was published by Guernica Editions in 2000. His entry on Lafcadio Hearn will appear in *The Literature of Travel and Exploration: An Encyclopedia.*

SUZANNE DISHEROON-GREEN serves as assistant professor of American literature at Northwestern State University in Natchitoches, Louisiana. She received her Ph.D. in English from the University of North Texas in 1997. She is co-author of *Kate Chopin: An Annotated Bibliography of Critical Works* (Greenwood Press, 1999) and *At Fault by Kate Chopin: A Scholarly Edition with Background Readings* (U of Tennessee Press, 2001) with David J. Caudle and of *Songs of the New South: Writing Contemporary Louisiana* with Lisa Abney (Greenwood Press, 2001). She has published and presented numerous articles on Kate Chopin and other Southern writers, including "How Edna Escaped: The LIFE IS A JOURNEY Conceptual Metaphor in *The Awakening*" in *The Poetics of Cognition* from Cambridge University Press and "Southern Gentility Meets Modern Morality: The Case of James Aswell" in *Southern Studies.* She is presently editing an anthology of Southern literature, titled *Voices of the American South,* which will by published by Longman Publishers. She is also presently editing a volume of *The*

Dictionary of Literary Biography: 21ˢᵗ Century American Novelists with Lisa Abney. She has served as guest editor for *Southern Studies.*

NANCY DIXON is the author of *Fortune and Misery: Sallie Rhett Roman of New Orleans, a Biographical Portrait and Selected Fiction* (LSU Press, 1999), winner of the Louisiana Endowment for the Humanities *Book of the Year* award, 2000. She lives in New Orleans, where she teaches English at the University of New Orleans

TIFFANY DUET teaches in the Department of Languages and Literature at Nicholls State University in her hometown of Thibodaux, Louisiana. She draws this essay from a chapter of her master's thesis, which she completed at North Carolina State University. Currently, she is a doctoral candidate at the University of Southern Mississippi researching the domestic in American literature.

LARRY D. GRIFFIN serves as professor of English and dean of Arts and Sciences at Dyersburg State Community College, Dyersburg, Tennessee. More than fifty of his essays have been published. His short stories appear in *A Gathering of Samphire and Other Stories* (Poetry Around, 1990). His poetry books include *Larry D. Griffin: Greatest Hits: 1968-2000* (Pudding House, 2000), *New Fires* (Full Count, 1982), *The Blue Water Tower* (Poetry Around, 1984), and *Airspace* (Slough Press, 1989). Griffin exhibits his paintings and photographs throughout the United States.

JOAN WYLIE HALL teaches American literature at the University of Mississippi. Author of *Shirley Jackson: A Study of the Short Fiction*, she has published essays on Willa Cather, William Faulkner, Lee Smith, Carolyn Wells, Eudora Welty, Tennessee Williams, and other writers. She is working on a book about Ruth McEnery Stuart and 1890s southern regionalism.

SUSIE SCIFRES KUILAN is a Ph.D. candidate at Louisiana State University. She has published articles on military Jody calls and Pat Conroy. She has also guest-co-edited a volume of *Southern Studies*, which collected essays from the Kate Chopin conference. She has presented papers at several conferences primarily on Southern literature, which will be the focus of her dissertation.

JO LECOEUR grew up in a small Mississippi town in the Bienville National Forest. She went to Louisiana State University in Baton Rouge for a Ph.D. and taught at Loyola University in New Orleans before moving to San Antonio. She is a professor of English at the University of the Incarnate Word.

PAMELA GLENN MENKE, professor and chair of English at Regis College (Weston, MA), is former director of the Division of Education for the National Endowment for the Humanities. After twenty-two years as a senior academic administrator at several colleges, she returned to full-time teaching. With Barbara Ewell of Loyola University, New Orleans, she is co-editing an anthology of late nineteenth-century local color (*Southern Local Color: Stories of Race and Gender, 1873-1899*) to be published by the University of Georgia, Fall 2001. Her research interests include late nineteenth-century women writers, literature of the American

South, and contemporary women writers of color and has published on Kate Chopin, George W. Cable, Zora Neale Hurston, and Toni Morrison.

ROBIN MILLER has been a journalist for fifteen years, working for newspapers in Louisiana and Mississippi. She has written extensively on the Cane River area in Louisiana, which includes Melrose Plantation near Natchitoches, to which the "Artful and Crafty Ones of the French Quarter" often traveled and participated in an artists colony. Her articles have won her numerous state and regional Associated Press awards. She lives in Alexandria, Louisiana.